Shards of Glass
Children Reading and Writing Beyond Gendered Identities

Revised Edition

Bronwyn Davies

Language and Social Processes
Judith Green, editor

Shards of Glass
Children Reading and Writing Beyond Gendered Identities

Revised Edition

Bronwyn Davies
James Cook University

Printed in the United States of America

Library of Congress Cataloging-in-Publication Data

Davies, Bronwyn, 1945
    Shards of glass : children reading and writing beyond gendered
    identities / Bronwyn Davies. -- Rev. ed.
        pm. c. -- (Language and social processes)
    Includes bibliographical references and index.
    ISBN 1-57273-365-9 (pbk: alk. paper)
        1. Sex differences in education--Australia. 2. Gender identity in
    education--Australia. 3. Language arts (Elementary)--Social
    aspects--Australia. 4. Sexism in education--Australia. 5. Sex roles in
    children--Australia. 6. Educational equalization--Australia.
    I. Title. II. Language & social processes.

    LC212.93.A8 D38 2002
    306.43.--dc21
                                                                2002017120

Hampton Press, Inc.
23 Broadway
Cresskill, NJ 07626

Contents

Acknowledgments

I am indebted to the Australian Research Council for providing me with a two year grant to conduct a study called 'A poststructuralist analysis of gender and of primary school children's discourse with a particular focus on narrative structures'. With this grant I was able to employ Chas Banks during 1990 and 1991 to collect the major part of the primary school data and to transcribe the bulk of the tapes. During those two years Chas and I worked on some of the data together, and wrote two major papers. Some of the insights included in this book come from that joint writing and from the many discussions we had during those two years. Each reader will no doubt come to appreciate the extent and value of her contribution as they read the many excerpts from the conversations that she had with the children that appear throughout the book.

I am also indebted to those friends and colleagues who have read various drafts of the manuscript and given me the benefit of their reactions to what I have written. Margaret Somerville, Chas Banks and Johanna Wyn read early drafts of each chapter as it was written, their comments and reactions giving me the insights I needed to make clear the ideas I was struggling with. Carolyn Baker, Linda Christian-Smith, John Davies, Judith Green, Joseph Schneider and Valerie Walkerdine each read the (almost) completed manuscript and gave me invaluable insights from their varying perspectives. The enthusiasm and support of each of these people for what sometimes seemed like a too daunting task was wonderful. I would also like to thank my students, in particular Jill Golden, Mary Bastable, Laura Hartley and Simon Swinson, who have read parts of this work, and whose energy and enthusiasm for the ideas we have shared is a constant source of inspiration. I would like to thank all the primary school students who talked to me and talked to and worked with Chas. Finally I would like to thank my son Daniel for his stories, my son Jacob for the drawing on the cover, and my son Paul who, like the other two, has provided me with many invaluable insights into the experience of masculinity. And of course the three of them have provided me with a major part of my knowledge of what it means to be a woman. I dedicate this book to all of these people, with love.

Transcript Notation

(( ))	author or observer's comment or observation
( )	unclear talk
don't	raised voice
/	interruption
-	self interruption or break in flow of sentence
?	interrogative or upward intonation
...	material deleted
slo:ow	sound extended
UPPER	reading from text
T	teacher
S(s)	unidentified student(s)
(was)	best guess for words spoken

Note: most of the pseudonyms of the children in the study groups were chosen by them. In those cases where they did not get around to choosing a name, I chose names, in consultation with Chas. Names were agreed on when we both felt the name 'suited' the particular child.

Prologue *or* How I Came to Write This Book in the Way That I Have

The hope that I expressed at the end of my study on preschool children and gender (*Frogs and Snails and Feminist Tales*) was that we might find ways of interacting with children and ways of speaking and writing that disrupted the apparent inevitability of the male–female binary. I wanted to open up the possibility of multiple genders, of fluidity between gender categories, of movement in and out of a range of ways of being which were not limited by the binary categories of maleness and femaleness. I thus began the primary school study that gave rise to this book. I wanted to know how feminist stories could be made not only hearable but also livable in the worlds of primary school children. But obviously this could not be something that was imposed on children. Since I had abandoned socialisation theory as a useful way to make sense of how children become gendered I could hardly set about 're-socialising' them. Neither my respect for children nor my understanding of the ways in which gender is actually taken up make any sense of an attempt at re-socialisation. The plan I conceived, then, was to share with them some of my developing understandings of the way in which we become gendered. I wanted to explore *with them* the possibility of speaking into existence different ways of being at the same time as we explored the constitutive force of the discursive practices through which gender relations are done. In choosing the children to work with it was imperative to choose children from a range of social and ethnic backgrounds since, as *Frogs and Snails* and much of the other work on gender were making increasingly clear, there is not one masculinity or one femininity, but many versions of each both within and across class and cultural boundaries. That recognition of multiplicity is itself fundamental to dislocating the press of the binary thinking that almost inevitably comes into play when talking and thinking about gender. It also seemed imperative to include boys in the study. Many gender equity programmes and much research into gender only makes girls relevant. This is partly a hang-over from liberal feminism where the issue is to recognise the underprivileged position of girls and women and to ensure them access to whatever it is that the privileged males have access to. It is also partly a result of radical feminist thinking in which the downgrading of the feminine is addressed by a counterbalancing celebration of femininity accompanied by a questioning of the celebration of masculinity that goes on all around us. Poststructuralist feminism, while recognising the validity, even necessity, of each of these strategies, also recognises that masculinities and femininities are constituted *in relation* to each other. They cannot be understood independently of each other, nor does it make sense to make the possibility of change available to girls if it is not also being made available to boys. The burden of change cannot and should not lie entirely with girls.

With these ideas in mind I sought an Australian Research Council Grant with which I was able to employ Chas Banks for two years to plan and carry out the study with the primary school children. We worked together in planning the study, to locate the ways in which poststructuralist theory might be made available to primary school children such that they could develop the deconstructive/reconstructive skills we envisaged for them. The work carried out by Chas with the three study groups gave me both material through which I could analyse the observable work that children are caught up in when constituting themselves in terms of the malefemale binary, and some insights into the processes through which they might begin to re-speak/re-write gender.

At the same time as this primary school study was being planned and carried out I had begun working with Haug et al.'s (1989) notion of collective biography or 'memory work'. This involves groups of adults working together on their remembered stories of some aspects of childhood. Haug et al. had worked in particular on the sexualisation of the female body. I ran work shops where we recounted our first awareness of being male or female. The purpose of such story-telling was not to reveal our private idiosyncratic selves, but to explore the very cultural/discursive threads revealed in our stories out of which we had become the gendered beings that we each were. That collective biography work has been of critical importance in enabling me to rethink what it means to be a specific person at the same time as that specificity becomes visibly woven out of the materials available in the contexts in which we find ourselves. It is thus a fascinating way to collect data but also a very effective means of working with the fabric of one's own life to find and perhaps unpick and restitch the invisible cultural/discursive threads.

When I first sat down to write this book I found myself strangely distant from the data that Chas had collected—'strange' because I had previously always collected my own data and knew it intimately, in a way that I realised I could never come to know this work. There in the transcripts, Chas was interacting with the children in ways necessarily different from the ways I would have done. The intimate first-hand observations that had brought the preschool study to life were not available to me. This created a serious dilemma for me and there were a number of false starts before I could make my way into this book. Chas and I discussed the possibility of joint authorship as a way of acknowledging the extent to which she would appear in the book in the conversations with the children and also of bringing her knowledge of the children more readily into the writing. Our initial agreement had been that she would write a Masters and that I would write a book out of different aspects of the data and that we would jointly write some papers on aspects of shared interest. Although she was reading each chapter as I wrote it in order to ensure that I hadn't misinterpreted or missed aspects of the conversations that only she could know about, she finally decided that to be joint author would too seriously interfere with her thesis writing. This was so even if I took full responsibility for the writing.

At the same time, my father's death only a few months earlier had thrown up many memories of and questions about my own childhood. Poststructuralist theory calls into question the authority of the author and breaks down the division between the one who knows (and tells) and the ones who are written about. It seemed obvious therefore, once I had thought of it, to include some of my own stories here, as a way of getting inside the experience of being gendered as a primary school child. The collective biography workshops had already given me a way of thinking about and writing stories of my own. My own stories are not included in order to reveal my private life as something special and different, but to assert 'a communicational bond between the teller and the told within a context that is historical, social and political, as well as intertextual' (Hutcheon, 1989, p. 51). I also decided to include what other writers writing of their childhoods had to say. Of course there are multiple possible tellings of any one life, even of any particular event in anyone's life. The story of my brother with which I begin Chapter 4, for example, has led us to a radical re-visioning of our childhoods in a startling and unexpected way.

With the addition of these autobiographical stories and the collective biography stories, this book has become more than the reporting of the research conducted with the study groups. The first part of the book uses the data from all of these sources to examine the process of becoming gendered from a poststructuralist perspective. It looks at the process of subjectification, at the usual ways in which knowledge is constructed in classrooms and at the nature of femininities and masculinities as they are experienced by primary school children. It also looks at sexuality as it is experienced in the lives of children of this age. In the last two chapters the focus is centrally on the work with the three study groups and the reading and writing skills that they were learning. But here too, I draw on the lives of others and the writing of others to broaden the base from which this story is told.

So I am present in this book in many ways. I am here as writer, but also as child, as researcher, as mother and as daughter. My approach to childhood and to gender, my ways of making sense of what I see and hear and feel are also currently profoundly affected by my current immersion in poststructuralist theory. But my history as a researcher of children and classrooms is also relevant to what I see and what I understand as worth telling. Before going forward then into the world of poststructuralist theory and the world of primary school children and gender, I want to go back and look at that research history.

I first undertook research with primary school children in the mid-1970s. I had just completed my training as a primary school teacher. I felt uneasy about what I regarded as the serious limitations in what I had learned. None of the research on children that was available at that time gave me any clue about how children viewed what went on in classrooms (or how they viewed what went on in any other aspects of their lives for that matter). I wanted to know how the social world looked to them—how my own or others' actions and words might be interpreted, made sense of, from their positions as children and as pupils. At that time there were no research methodologies that I could discover in terms of which my question could be either asked or answered. After planning and abandoning a number of structured, measurement-oriented research projects, I finally abandoned them all. I decided that what I needed to do, quite simply, was to ask the children to tell me what the world looked like to them. I gained entree to a primary school. The Principal agreed that the children in one particular classroom could come and talk to me whenever they wished. I set myself up with my tape recorder and waited. My major anxiety revolved around the question of whether the children would want to talk to me, but I discovered that the children had an apparently boundless wish to talk. The idea of having free access to a setting where their talk was listened to carefully, where their understanding of the world was taken seriously, where they could use the setting to explore their own perceptions of whatever was currently happening in the classroom or playground, was so attractive to them that they literally had fights at the door about whose turn it was to come and talk. They were fascinated by the idea that I recorded their talk, transcribed it and was planning to write a book on it. If I didn't understand the point they were making at any one point in time they were at endless pains to make it clear to me. They would even volunteer to recreate conversations and events when the tape recorder stopped and I didn't notice, having become too absorbed in their talk. I have since come to believe that the greatest gift one person can give another is such careful listening. It is in hearing with care the detailed specificity of the other that the specificity of each of us is made possible.

Only at the time of writing up my conversations with those children did I discover that I was part of a research community that was growing up elsewhere. The qualitative, interpretive research going on with adolescents in the USA and UK that was just beginning to be published had much in common with the work I was doing. Having found no such community in Australia, I made my way to the UK to talk to the researchers using symbolic interactionist, ethnomethodological and ethogenic frameworks.

My research did not fit instantly into any of these frameworks. Symbolic interactionism insisted on the researcher's immersion in the scenes the participants were making accounts of. While I had spent some time observing these scenes I could not pretend I had immersed myself in them. Ethnomethodology insisted on the study of 'naturally occurring scenes' rather than talk about those scenes. I did not see my conversations with the children as 'naturally occurring', though of course they were just as 'natural' as any other social scene. Analysis of the conversations through which the children and I constituted the research event itself was central to my interests, but I also wanted to analyse the scenes they were *talking about*, in the playground and the classroom. This seemed to rule out using the language of ethnomethodology to frame my analysis. Ethogeny, on the other hand, was much more free-wheeling in its discussion of how researchers might go about discovering the life worlds of the people they were interested to study. Indeed they began with the same question of youth as I had of children: 'why not ask them?' (Harré and Secord, 1972).

There was a lively debate at that time between the symbolic interactionists and the ethnomethodologists. The symbolic interactionists, much like anthropologists, but studying people in their own everyday world rather than other cultural groups, listened to informants' accounts and participated in their worlds. Their aim was to make those specific worlds or cultures reportable, describable. Particular sub-cultures were the objects of interest and participants' talk was useful and interesting to the extent that it gave the researcher a genuine understanding of that culture. But they were inclined to proceed as if the culture they were examining had a life independent of the participants. In contrast, the ethnomethodologists did not assume that the culture or group existed independent of the talk itself. That which might be perceived as a particular group or sub-culture with a recognisable set of rules for proceeding within any particular setting, was studied as an achievement, as something collaboratively constituted by the members of the group through the observable activity and talk within the setting itself. It was that constitutive work in which ethnomethodologists were interested. I was interested in both these interpretive approaches. Ethogeny seemed to straddle the interests of both these perspectives, wanting to observe and participate in social worlds and to listen to participants' talk about those social worlds, but also seeing the ways in which talk within settings and talk about those settings is constitutive of those settings.

I decided to use the language of ethogeny to frame what I had done with the children, though drawing on the other conceptual frameworks whenever that seemed appropriate. My research was published in an ethogenic series called *The Social Worlds of Childhood* (Davies, 1982).

From my current perspective there are two serious flaws I can now see in that early study of primary school children. One is that I heard and interpreted the children speaking *as children*, and could not then hear the gendered nature of their talk. When the boys talked about their outrage with the school Principal, for example, when he got them into trouble for something he had not previously defined as wrong, I did not see it as relevant to my analysis that the girls were doing quite different talk about the same event. The boys saw the Principal's own rule being broken. It was defined as such through his prior practice. The rule as they had observed it was that any misdemeanour is defined as such before it becomes punishable. They felt that their own outrage was entirely justifiable. They therefore experienced no guilt about the activity in question. The girls, on the other hand, were deeply shaken by the Principal's wrath (see p. 52). Although I heard what the girls said, I did not hear it as gender difference. I interpreted the boys' account as unproblematically the account of the whole group—as what *children* thought about such events. Gender was, in a fundamental sense, not yet visible to me at that time. It was transparent. Since that time, of course, I have become so attuned to gender that I see it everywhere. In texts it literally leaps out of the page at me. It has become highly visible and reportable as both this book and my previous book on preschool children and gender show.

The other major flaw that I find in retrospect in that early research was methodological. Because of the ways of understanding what it meant to be a person that were available to me then, I believed that each person would be giving me consistent non-contradictory accounts of the world as they perceived it. If they appeared to be contradicting themselves, I assumed that I was not yet understanding what they had to say. I worked my way into the detail of what each child had to say until I could see it as smooth, linear and non-contradictory. The symbolic interactionists made a different assumption in order to maintain the same illusion of the unitary non-contradictory person. They assumed that informants were likely to attempt to deceive them and so could dismiss accounts that did not fit their own observations or the observations of 'good informants'. I did not feel comfortable with this approach and could find no valid basis for interacting with the children either if I continually assumed they were setting out to deceive me or if I regarded their words as dismissable. We nevertheless both managed to achieve, with these radically different attitudes to the people we talked to, the reporting of seamless, non-contradictory versions of the world as it was seen by them.

With the advent of poststructuralist theory into the study of social worlds and social relations, contradictions both within each person's experience of the world, and within each group's methods of making sense of the world, are understood as inevitable and even fundamental to the human condition (Davies and Harré, 1992). But in the 1970s and early 1980s the primacy of the rational mind over body and emotion, and the capacity of the rational mind to take up one non-contradictory position had not yet been called into question. Far from seeing contradictions as fascinating points of tension between different ways of speaking the world into existence, as I do now, I saw the confirmation of my interpretive skills and my interviewing skills as lying in my ability to see and understand the rational, non-contradictory accounts that I believed the children were giving me.

In the early 1980s and after completing *Life in the Classroom and Playground*, I undertook a number of studies of primary school classrooms, making videotapes of various lessons. Such a study was imaginable because this new technology had just become available.

Having listened to the children talk for so long about their different teachers and being very much influenced by the ethnomethodological imperative to study lived experience rather than the accounts of that experience, I wanted to know how different teachers went about creating the order of their classrooms. When I began to view and analyse the various tapes I had made, I was startled to see the extent of the collaborative work the children were doing to create the particular order of any classroom (Davies, 1983). My adultist assumption that teachers created classroom order was fairly rapidly dispelled. What became of particular interest to me then, was how and why particular children disrupted the collaborative enterprise that they seemed, for the most part, so willing to engage in (Davies and Munro, 1987).

At the same time, gender was becoming readily visible to me in my own everyday life. I had been born into a conservative, relatively well-to-do family where I had come to understand that girls could have careers, that hard work and ability would be both recognised and rewarded and that the men who controlled the world were both benevolent and just. I understood that the *individual* was the relevant variable in any social situation: individuals who strove would succeed. But I was beginning to see that this might not be the case. I discovered that the term 'individual' did not always include women as I had assumed it did. Moreover, the isolation of women, their marginality in the institutions they worked in, meant they had little or no bargaining power and the individual men who had power in those institutions were anything but benevolent or just when it came to the restricted careers of individual women. I discovered the importance of collectivities such as the union for the achievement of justice and for having my individual voice heard. The relevance of social structures as they made possible or precluded certain forms of action became starkly evident to me. The feminist women who had created the anti-discrimination legislation made it possible for individuals and collectivities to see the gendered nature of the structures they lived and worked in and to begin to challenge and shift them. They were thus instrumental in creating a new discourse, that is, a new way of making meaning of the events of any one life. The observable failure of women to make their way forward in the public world need no longer be explained in terms of their own individual shortcomings.

Gender had become something intriguing that I wanted to examine. But where to begin? Two events set me on the path of carrying out the study of preschool children and gender. One was a picnic with some friends where a rough tough little kid that I had not met before was mistaken by me and several others as a boy. When someone addressed her as Penny I was quite startled. One of the children asked her mother, with tears in her eyes, 'Mummy, why are they calling that boy Penny?'. Over the ensuing weeks I kept wondering why did it matter so much. What was it about getting one's own gender and others' gender 'right' that involved such strong emotions? The other event occurred in relation to the story, *The Paper Bag Princess*. I had read this several times with great enthusiasm to the five-year-old daughter of a friend, before I realised that although she found the story amusing, she did not share my enthusiasm, nor hear the feminist story that I thought I was reading. This seemed to warrant investigation.

And so I began the study in which I read feminist stories to children and asked them questions as we went along about their hearing of each story. I also observed them at play, talked to them about that play and became, on occasion, involved in that play. My participation and involvement with the preschoolers was correct by symbolic interactionist standards. My attention to the fine detail of how gender was being done was strongly influenced by my reading of ethnomethodology. But my involvement in the reading of stories did not fit any sociological frameworks that I had access to at that time.

Further, I found when I set out to analyse that data that none of the familiar understandings about how people become gendered were adequate to explain my data. These children were not being pressed into masculinity and femininity as sex role socialisation theory suggested. Rather, in learning to be coherent members of their social worlds they were actively taking up their assigned gender as their own in ways not necessarily compatible with the ways teachers and parents were telling them gender should be done. In learning the discourses through which maleness and femaleness are spoken into existence, they learned to locate themselves within and through the category systems through which gender is constituted. They learned to make sense of the world and of themselves through the bipolar categories of male and female, recognising the obligatory nature of being identifiably one and not the other, of being one that is also *opposite* to the other. Any discourse about equity that adults might introduce them to could only affect the minor detail of this difference, and then only if that detail had not become a key signifier of masculinity or femininity. It was possible to see and articulate this, again, because of work going on elsewhere that gave me a different language, a new set of conceptual tools with which to see the detail of my data in a way that I would not otherwise have been able to see it. Valerie Walkerdine's work, in particular, using poststructuralist theory to look at classroom interaction and young girls' readings of comic books, introduced me to the possibility of seeing the constitutive force of discourse. This was similar to ethnomethodology and yet significantly different in that it made the words, the discourses being used by any speaker, visible in a new way. If words were tools with which to constitute a world, *the nature of the tools* dictated the kinds of worlds which might be constituted in ways of which the speakers themselves might not be conscious.

Poststructuralist theory undoes the boundaries between the disciplines of sociology, psychology, history and studies of literature. It demonstrates that we need to look not just at the work that collectivities collaboratively do to construct gendered worlds but also to look at the work the language does to limit, shape, make possible, one kind of world or another. At the same time, it makes relevant the emotional, psychic and physical embeddedness of individuals in the discursively constituted categories to which they are subjected. Unlike any previous theoretical or conceptual framework I had come across, poststructuralist theory looks at the constitutive force of social structures and of language as well as at the individual person (or subject) and sees each of these in their social and historical contexts. The individual subject is understood at one and the same time to be constituted through social structures and through language, and becomes a speaking subject, one who can continue to speak/write into existence those same structures through those same discourses. But, as a speaking subject, they can also invent, invert and break old structures and patterns and discourses and thus speak/write into existence other ways of being.

1 Postructuralist Theory and the Study of Gendered Childhoods

> *'Words and things' is the . . . ironic title of a work that modifies its own form, displaces its own data, and reveals at the end of the day, a quite different task. A task that consists not—of no longer—treating discourses as groups of signs (signifying elements referring to contents or representations) but as practices that systematically form the objects of which they speak.*
>
> —Foucault (1972, p. 49)

HOW DO we become gendered beings? How are 'male' and 'female' constituted as opposite categories of being, with 'male' superior to and more powerful than 'female'? What part do schools play in this? Is it possible to deconstruct and move beyond the binary categories of 'male' and 'female'? Can this be done in the school context? What part does poststructuralist theory play in enabling us to examine such questions?

This book on primary school children and gender follows on from my earlier work on preschool children and gender, published as *Frogs and Snails and Feminist Tales: Preschool Children and Gender* (Davies, 1989a, rev. ed. 2003). That earlier study involves a feminist post-structuralist analysis of the ways in which gender is constituted through the discourses with which we speak and write ourselves into existence. It looks in particular at storylines or narratives and at the ways in which gender is implicated in preschool children's understandings of the dominant cultural storylines that they encounter both in text and talk.

This book is an extension of that earlier study in that it explores further the processes through which our maleness and our femaleness are established and maintained during childhood. But it also explores the radical possibility of giving children the capacity to disrupt the dominant storylines through which their gender is held in place.

Unlike strategies for change based on sex role socialisation theory, this book does not seek to explore how we might act upon girls to shape them differently, to make them more autonomous, to give them self-esteem, or to make them want to do maths and science. Kenway and Willis (1990) have shown how such programmes rest the burden of change on girls, as if it were somehow the inadequacy of girls that needed to be mended rather than the gender order itself which needed to be called into question. Poststructuralist theory opens up the possibility of a quite different set of strategies for working with both boys and girls based on a radically different conceptualisation of the process of becoming a (gendered) person. Within the frame of this different understanding it makes more sense to introduce children to a discourse which enables them to see for themselves the discourses and storylines through which gendered persons are constituted, to see the cultural and historical production of gendered persons that they are each caught up in. In this different approach, children can be introduced to the possibility, not of learning the culture, or new aspects of it, as passive recipients, but as producers of culture, as writers and readers who make themselves and are made within the discourses available to them. It allows them to see the intersection between themselves as fictions (albeit intensely experienced fictions) and the fictions of their culture—which are constantly being (re)spoken, (re)written and (re)lived.

THE DATA

There are a number of resources drawn on in this book. The first is a series of follow-up interviews with seven of the children in the preschool study and of Penny, a 'tomboy' who appeared briefly at the beginning of *Frogs and Snails*. The children are eight or nine at the time of these interviews and Penny is fourteen. Some of these interviews were conducted by me and some by Chas Banks. The purpose in extending the earlier data with some of the same children was to gain access to the continuities and discontinuities in the subjectivities of the children, particularly as they are manifested in their reading/hearing of text. These have been reported in some detail in Davies and Banks (1991a).

One reason for conducting the longitudinal aspect of the study was to examine the stability of children's positioning within the discourses through which they speak themselves, and are spoken, into existence. Through access to new discourses or through shifts in positioning within the old, I was interested to find changes in interpretation of their genderedness and of the possibilities they saw being open to them as males or females. We found considerable continuity between their interpretations of themselves as preschool children and themselves as primary school children. We interpreted this in terms of the commitments or investments they had made to specific positionings in specific discourses. At the same time, because there are inevitably contradictions in the discourses in which any of us have invested ourselves, and because we are each exposed to new positionings and new discursive practices in the various settings in which we find ourselves, the children displayed interesting shifts and developments in their interpretations of their own and others' genderedness.

A second and major source of data was gathered with three study groups of fifth and sixth grade primary school children who met with Chas over a period of twelve months. Each of the groups was made up of six or seven children who met with her each week for approximately one-and-a-half hours. Two groups of both boys and girls were from State schools, one in a predominantly low socio-economic area and including Aboriginal children (Karobran Public), and one from a relatively well-to-do area (Eastern Public). The third group was from a private girls' school (St Clement's) with well-to-do parents coming from Italy, Germany and Colombia as well as Australia.[1]

The children in each of the three schools were invited to participate in the study groups to explore their experiences of being gendered and to gain access to a variety of concepts with which they might open up those experiences to analytic scrutiny. Their parents' permission was sought by letter. Only one parent refused, claiming that he would only let his daughter participate if she was to be taught to know her place as woman, that is, as 'servant of man and God'. Chas managed to persuade him to let his daughter participate on the grounds that the intention of the study was not to impose a particular version of gender on her, but rather to give her an opportunity to examine and extend her own understanding of being gendered.

Chas began the study groups by inviting the children to talk about their ideas and beliefs about gender and by making visible the centrality of gender to their subjectivity. They talked about the ways in

---

[1]These three groups are not analysed separately in a comparative way, as if they were separate cultures to be compared. The point of the range of different backgrounds was to ensure that the analysis was not 'one-eyed', that it did not fall into the familiar trap of assuming that ways in which masculinities and femininities are achieved in any one social or cultural group are the same as in any other group.

which their ideas and beliefs were encoded in their own bodies and in the textual images they found in popular magazines and in photographs such as those found in Wex (1979). In order to enable them to grasp the concept of discourse and, in particular, its constitutive force, they examined the cultural and historical locatedness of categories which are generally understood as 'natural' and inevitable. This was done in the first instance through an examination of the child–adult binary. Looking at pictures of children in different cultures and at different times and sharing information about childhood in different cultures and times they explored the way in which the concept of 'goodness' and of 'child' is specific to time and place and embedded in particular understandings of adult–child relations. The concepts of power and powerlessness were made relevant in these discussions as was discourse, using the phrase 'discourse of the good child' and 'discourses of resistance'. These concepts were explored in terms of the children's own experiences of being powerless or powerful and of the power of adult discourses to position them in powerless ways. The children were particularly conscious in these conversations of the shift away from the old maxim 'children should be seen and not heard'. They linked the recent television and school programmes emphasising the right of children to refuse sexual molestation at the hands of any adult with the idea of discourses of resistance.

Throughout the year of the study they looked at a wide variety of texts to see the detail of the ways in which gender is constituted through text. In the first instance they looked at visual representations of male and female children, seeing how body language and placement of people in particular physical positionings in relation to each other and to objects within the picture were constitutive of the idea of male and female as opposite. These observations were linked to discussions about their own experience of themselves as embodied males and females and to the ways they experience that embodiment and also to the ways they signal their locatedness in one category or the other. Central to this discussion was the idea of positioning, which was used as a way of making problematic the taken-for-granted concepts of the individual as architect of their own subjectivity.

The children brought photos of themselves as small children to the study groups so that they could read those photos as gendered texts, finding the ways in which they were being culturally located as male or female. These photos were discussed and stories were told and written about them. Photocopies of the photos were used to make a collage of photos and stories about themselves as gendered beings. Following a discussion of Chappell's photography workshops with adolescent girls (Chappell, 1984) they then discussed the idea of telling their own lives in the present through photos they might take themselves and stories that could be told about these. They were given disposable cameras and instructed on some aspects of photography, including the idea of looking for 'naturally occurring scenes' rather than asking people to pose for them. The aim of this project was to create images and to tell stories in relation to those images, about their relationships with the people that mattered to them.

They were also introduced to written text and to the idea of reading those texts in the way they had read the photographs—looking at the text itself to see the way in which character, emotion and desire are created. Central to this aspect of the project was the concept of positioning the reader within the text. They examined the ways in which they entered into the text, positioning themselves with particular characters and reading the story from that character's own position within the story. They talked about films they had seen and books they had read where they had been aware of where they positioned themselves in the story. They talked about how that positioning influenced their patterns of desire in relation to both lived and fictional stories. They read stories together using the concepts of storyline and desire as central to the analysis of story. In reading *Snow White*, for example, they were shown how to discard, for the moment, the detail of the story and to see that the storyline is made up of specific well-known images or patterns within the culture. The storyline of a vulnerable young woman falling victim to a powerful adult, being cast adrift from the domestic scene and only able to be returned to the safety of a new domestic scene through the agency of a heroic male was thus made both visible and analysable in terms of its constitutive force. It becomes evident, for example, that the attraction of the heroic male to the heroine, his desire to save her, depends entirely on her absolute virtue and on her passivity. And, in Snow White's case, this is a passivity approximating death. The relevant desire for any reader positioning herself as Snow White would therefore be to be sufficiently virtuous and passive that she might be saved by a prince who would give her security in an otherwise dangerous world.

They discussed these stories in terms of their own readings of it and their own bodily and emotional responses to the story as they had listened to it. They also looked more closely at the detail in the text to see how these interactions between reader and text are created. They looked for the silences in the text, the cultural givens, the things that the author thought did not need to be said. Their own relations with each other and the experience of being gendered were made relevant to these discussions. The political implications of the boys' positioning of themselves with the powerful male in the text were discussed along with the emotions and patterns of desire made relevant by that powerful positioning. They examined the ways in which stories become their own lived stories through a process in which they take up as their own the obviousnesses, the patterns of interpretation and the patterns of desire. Central to these discussions was the recognition that there is no one story to be heard in any one text, and that there is not even any one set of obviousnesses to be assumed in any specific text. Their different readings and the relation of these to their own lived experiences and to the gendered struggles they engaged in with each other around these readings were fundamental to the discussion.

These readings of traditional stories were followed by readings of feminist stories. The ways in which the female hero in these stories resists the dominant discourse were explored in detail as were the implications in their own lives of such possibilities. The conversations around these texts included the boys' anger at being cast out of the heroic role and the girls' pleasure in the new possibilities that were being opened up. It also included the boys' open attacks on the girls (as well as their attacks on the heroic female characters in the text) which usually took the form of sexualising them, making them vulnerable to sexual attack, presumably in an attempt to re-position them in the traditional romantic storyline where they not only know their place but also desire that place.

In relation to the discussions of both feminist and traditional stories, the study groups also talked about their own futures and the ways they imagined these futures falling out. The apparent inevitabilities of marriage, heterosexuality, powerful work for men and child care for women were examined in detail, both in terms of the ways in which the children already felt bound by traditional expectations and desires and in terms of the ways these traditional patterns were already changing in the world around them.

Following on from these discussions the study groups took on the task of writing their own group story that resisted the dominant discourses. This, they discovered, was extraordinarily difficult to do. They repeatedly drew on traditional patterns and images, not knowing how to abandon them or how to find alternatives. Their embeddedness in binary forms of thought, particularly in relation to women (if they are not pretty and desirable they must be ugly) had to be constantly struggled with. Resisting the dominant discourse seemed to them to involve simple reversals, the use of whatever is opposite. The meaning of what a discourse of resistance might be had therefore to be established as something much more subtle and complex than this. As well, the boys' wish to maintain the ascendancy in the stories was a tension needing constantly to be dealt with. The main task in this group story writing was not so much to create a perfect finished product but to give the children an opportunity to examine the process, to experience the task itself and to make that experience observable, analysable and thus something that could be changed.

Two final tasks were undertaken by the study groups. One was the creation of the collages of themselves in the photos that they had taken. They brought whatever skills they had for reading text to tell stories and talk about these images from their everyday lives. The other was that each of the children was asked to write their own stories in their own time. They were asked to take up some of the challenges that the group had explored during the year. They were not given any direction about what these stories should be about other than that they should resist dominant discourses.

Fundamental to the success of these strategies was the shift in authority relations between student and teacher, student and text, and the *mutual* exploration of the constitutive power of text and talk in teacher and student lives. Although the students and Chas often fell into the traps of traditional adult–child relations, the most productive work occurred when they managed to abandon these and to work together, each making their lives, emotions and experiences relevant to the task at hand.

The follow-up study and the data from the three study groups are supplemented by some interviews and readings of stories that I undertook with children in fifth grade in a progressive primary school in the United States. As well, I draw on the collective biographies on the process of becoming gendered that I have carried out in the United States and in Australia. I also draw on stories from my own childhood, and on the stories of others' childhoods as these have been told to me or written about in autobiographies and other texts. These are from a number of different countries, including Australia, Britain, the United States, New Zealand and Italy.

POSTSTRUCTURALIST THEORY AND THE CONCEPTS OF IDENTITY AND SUBJECTIVITY[2]

The division of people into males and females is so fundamental to our talk as usual and to our understanding of identity, that it is generally understood as a natural fact of the real world rather than something that we have *learned to see* as natural. Indeed, a world not so divided is

---

[2]The remainder of this chapter is something that newcomers to poststructuralist theory might want to skip now and come back to after having read the rest of the book. Once these concepts have been encountered in use they will be easier to understand in the more abstract form that follows.

almost unimaginable because there is no discourse through which it can be articulated, no way of speaking or writing it into existence. But poststructuralist theory has enabled us to see that what we had defined as 'nature' is as much 'metaphysical' as natural:

> Derrida labels as 'metaphysical' any thought-system which depends on an unassailable foundation, a first principle or unimpeachable ground upon which a whole hierarchy of meanings may be constructed. If you examine such principles closely, you can see that they may always be constructed. First principles of this kind are commonly defined by what they exclude, by a sort of 'binary opposition'. Deconstruction is the name given to a critical operation by which such oppositions can be partially undermined. (Sarup, 1988, p. 40)

The male–female binary is one of the most basic metaphysical constructions. It is an unquestionable base or first principle on which so much else rests. Feminist poststructuralists in particular have begun the work of deconstructing the male–female binary. This book is an examination of the ways in which that binary is held in place through discourse. It is also an exploration of the ways in which it might be deconstructed. Deconstruction, or putting a concept or word under erasure, is a political act. It reveals the generally invisible but repressive politics of any particular form of representation.

Central to any feminist deconstruction is an excitement about discovering the very mainsprings of power that have held women and other marginalised groups in place. It may also be depressing to discover how subtle, how invisible, how pervasive, and how *much our own* are the discursive mechanisms and structures through which we have learned to know our place and to remain within it. But to know how oppression is achieved is the essential first step to knowing how to change it.

Being a child and being a person as we now understand these terms are quite recent inventions (Aries, 1962). Identity, for example, only appeared as a word during the Enlightenment, around the sixteenth century. The concept of *identity* is central to modern(ist) thinking and is a concept necessarily *under erasure* in poststructuralist writing. That is, it is a term we still need and use, but which needs deconstructing and moving beyond. The cross through the word, leaving the word still visible, is Derrida's idea for signalling precisely this—that the concept is *sous rature*. The concepts of subjectivity, subject position and subjectification and speaking subject are the conceptual tools developed in poststructuralist writing to elaborate a different understanding of the processes through which being a (gendered) person is achieved.

Sarup points out that the poststructuralist term for the person, 'subject', signals important shifts away from humanist conceptions of identity:

> The term 'subject' helps us to conceive of human reality as a construction, as a product of signifying activities which are both culturally specific and generally unconscious. The category of the subject calls into question the notion of the self synonymous with consciousness; it 'decentres' consciousness. (1988, p. 2)

Two attributes 'essential' to identity in the way this is currently understood in modern(ist) Western culture are autonomy and agency (Harré, 1989). To achieve full human status, children must therefore achieve a sense of themselves as beings with *agency*, that is, as individuals who make choices about what they do, and who accept responsibility for those choices. At the same time those choices must be recognisable as 'rational', that is, as following the principles of decision making acceptable to the group and inside the range of possibilities understood by the group as possibilities. In modern(ist) thinking about persons, it is the agency and autonomy that are most visible, that are foregrounded. Individual identity is made central to any story that is told, with the discursively constituted nature of the range of choices and the desirability of any particular choice being the unfocused upon background. The shock value of poststructuralist theorising, such as that of Walkerdine and Lucey in *Democracy in the Kitchen*, comes from the switching of foreground and background. Through the analysis of the interactions between middle class mothers and their daughters they reveal the work that those mothers do to create the belief in their daughters that they have freedom to choose, at the same time subjecting them to the set of values that will shape their 'choices'.

While full subject status requires being constrained by the rules and structures of the social world, and at the same time acting as if one is an autonomous agent who is responsible for one's own actions and the outcomes of those actions, children, like women and other marginalised groups, are constantly deprived of agency. Their subject status is never fully guaranteed. It is always partial and conditional. They can be positioned as beings without agency and autonomy at any moment, usually when they are read by adults as not knowing how they *should* behave. When children appear obsessed with what one ought to do, this need not necessarily be interpreted as something 'natural' to children (that they like rules and categories) but rather as stemming from the fact that effective claims to identity require a knowledge of how to 'get it right'. At the same time, 'getting it right' does not mean behaving exactly as everyone else behaves, but rather it means practising the culture in an identifiably individual way. This means knowing the ways in which cultural practices can be varied. Radical or even disruptive variations are generally only accepted by others if one's capacity to know what ought to be is not likely to be called into question (Davies, 1982).

The processes through which subjectivities are constituted are imbricated, not only in ways of speaking and ways of making meaning, but also in the contexts and relations in which particular acts of speaking take place.[3] Unlike identity, subjectivity is not a semi-fixed essence (as the concept of socialisation within humanist theory suggests) but is constantly achieved through relations with others (both real and imagined) which are themselves made possible through discourse:

> One Lacanian tenet is that subjectivity is entirely relational; it only comes into play through the principle of difference, by the opposition of the 'other' or the 'you' to the 'I'. In other words, subjectivity is not an essence but a set of relationships. It can only be induced by the activation of a signifying system which exists before the individual and which determines his or her cultural identity. Discourse, then, is the agency whereby the subject is produced and the existing order sustained. (Sarup, 1988, p. 29)

One of the observations made in *Frogs and Snails* was that there were many different ways of being male and female and that in an ideal world, we would each have access to many or all of these possible ways of being. In the current social order, it was observed, there are limitations not only in terms of gender and on what is thought proper to each sex/gender,[4] but also limitations inherent in humanist/ modern(ist) versions of identity. The assumptions made within humanist discourses about identity were liberatory in their original intention and in many of their effects. Yet humanism also constrains each person to constitute themselves as rational, unitary and non-contradictory, and as if they were distinct and fundamentally separate from the social world. This prevents them from seeing the multifaceted

---

[3]Imbrication is a metaphor for overlapping elements of a larger whole such as tiles of a roof or cut skin where the new cells on each side become part of the same skin as they grow together.

[4]Sex and gender were originally terms used to distinguish the biological from the social. Recent biological research as well as analyses being undertaken from a poststructuralist perspective show that this boundary is now so blurry that the distinction is no longer a meaningful one. One way of signalling the collapse of these terms into one another is to slash the terms as I have done here. Another is to abandon one of the terms altogether and use the remaining term to gather together the previously separated meanings. Until now I have used gender in such a way. It is useful however, to occasionally use the combined terms slashed to remind us of their indivisibility.

and fluid nature of their own experience, drawing tight boundaries around the self and its possibilities.[5]

Humanist discourse pervades school texts and talk. The preschool children's understanding of being male or female and of the possibilities of liberation from traditional binary understandings of these and other related terms was severely limited by the available discourses through which both they and their social worlds were constituted. These were not interpretations they had been explicitly taught. Rather, they were embedded in the ways of seeing, knowing and being that were made available to them through text and talk.

The connection between agency and desire in the primary school children's talk is of particular interest. Their interpretations of themselves as people who can make choices and act upon the world—their beliefs about agency—are based, to a large extent, on a humanist definition of themselves as having desires or 'wants' that stem from and signal who they 'really' are. The fulfillment of their wants or desires is seen as a confirmation of this self. That those desires might be discursively constituted or might result from the influences of others is apparently not thinkable within children's interpretive frameworks. In this book I will explore some attempts to make the unthinkable thinkable to the primary school children in the three study groups.

Within humanist conceptions of the person, desire signals the 'real', stable identity of any person. Because desire is understood as being constituted through discourse within poststructuralist theory it is possible to see human subjects as not fixed but constantly in process, being constituted and reconstituted through the discursive practices they have access to in their daily lives.

The tensions and instabilities in each person's subjectivity become visible in a poststructuralist analysis through an examination of the discourses and practices through which our subjectivities are constituted. Discourses shift in meaning according to context and to the positioning of the subjects within them (Davies and Harré, 1990). Further, the discourses and practices through which we are constituted are also often in tension, one with another, providing the human subject with multiple layers of contradictory meanings which are inscribed in their bodies and in their conscious and unconscious minds.

A metaphor for capturing this multiple layering of discourse in our minds and bodies is *palimpsest*. This is a term to describe the way in which new writings on a parchment were written over or around old

---

[5]Since this claim is almost opposite to the intention of most humanist thought it is one that needs careful and detailed study in order to see how this contradiction comes about. Further reading on this point can be found in Davies and Harré, 1992; Henriques et al., 1984; Walkerdine, 1981; Weedon, 1987.

writings that were not fully erased. One writing interrupts the other, momentarily overriding, intermingling with the other; the old writing influences the interpretation of the imposed new writing and the new influences the interpretation of the old. But both still stand, albeit partially erased and interrupted. New discourses do not simply replace the old as on a clean sheet. They generally interrupt one another, though they may also exist in parallel, remaining separate, undermining each other perhaps, but in an unexamined way.

Another idea central to poststructuralist theory is that the person is not simply the rational person invented through seventeenth century Enlightenment thought. In the Enlightenment version of the person, it was thought that as rational beings we should be able to *choose* to give up those aspects of ourselves and our desires that we wish to discard after recognising their oppressive weight or after encountering new and more desirable discourses.[6] But the person is much more than this rational mind in control of action and of desire. Desire may stem from rational argument, but it also stems from the inscribed bodies and emotions of each person, from images and storylines, from the imbrication of ways of knowing in the metaphors and patterns of the discourses through which we come to know. These ways of knowing are not necessarily able to be consciously articulated. Nor is desire constituted outside social structures. Social structures condone, support, approve or make viable certain patterns of desire and outlaw or marginalise others.

My examples will only span the twentieth century and thus only spin the thread of a relatively short timespan. It is useful, nonetheless, to see this analysis of being a child and being a (gendered) person as located in a wider frame in which gender and personhood have been conceived quite differently, and in which agency and individuality have not always been so fundamental to the construction of human existence.

POSTSTRUCTURALIST THEORY COMPARED
WITH OTHER CONCEPTUAL FRAMEWORKS

A poststructuralist analysis, while having its roots in structuralism (e.g., Saussure, 1974; Marx, 1976) differs fundamentally from it. Structuralism recognises the constitutive force of discourse and of the social structures that are constituted through those discourses. Poststructuralism opens up the possibility of agency to the subject through the very act of making visible the discursive threads through which their experience of

---

[6]'Desirable' because either they make possible ways of being that are more in keeping with a new set of ideas or values, or because they are less constricting—less limiting—than old familiar discourses.

themselves as specific beings is woven. It also defines discourse and structure as something which can be acted upon and changed. Although some poststructuralist writers do not see any revolutionary potential in poststructuralist theory, finding themselves lost in an anomic relativism, some feminist writers do see that potential (Weedon, 1987; Hutcheon, 1989; Davies, 1991). In seeing how it is that power and maleness are constituted in relation to each other, in understanding how it is that apparently intractable and debilitating patterns of desire are put in place and maintained in place, in discovering the possibility for disrupting old discourses, paths open up for speaking into existence other ways of being which are not organised in terms of the binary opposition between male and female. Central to that re-speaking are:

- the recognition of the *psychic and bodily implications of discourses* and specific positionings within them, such that the individual can recognise the need for, and develop strategies to begin to extract themselves from, the psychic and bodily patterns of desire that restrict them;
- the development of educational strategies which enable students to undertake *critical readings of text* such that they understand the constitutive force of discourse, the political implications of particular discourses and the positionings made available through them (Davies, 1991); and
- the development of deconstructive strategies that reveal the ways in which language holds certain meanings in place along with the development of *new ways of writing and speaking* that reconstitute the world in significant ways.

A poststructuralist analysis also differs fundamentally from a constructionist perspective (Davies, 1982). Constructionism focuses on subjects' accounts primarily as a resource to find out about the social world and the detail of that constructed world as it is experienced by the participants. Subjectivity is generally not made problematic in constructionist accounts, and the liberal humanist version of the unitary rational actor is kept intact. It is assumed that the rational account of their social worlds is *the* account of that world. Poststructuralism, in contrast, seeks to understand the processes through which the person is subjected to, and constituted by, structure and discourse—and yet how it is that 'practice can be turned against what constrains it [such that structure can become] the object of practice' (Connell, 1987, p. 95).

Poststructuralist theory argues that people are not *socialised* into the social world, but that they go through a process of *subjectification*. In socialisation theory, the focus is on the process of shaping the individual that is undertaken by others. In poststructuralist theory the focus is on the way each person actively takes up the discourses through which they and others speak/write the world into existence *as if they were their own*. Through those discourses they are made speaking subjects at the same time as they are subjected to the constitutive force of those discourses. That force is, in part, achieved through the 'what' that is spoken, or the objects of discourse that are spoken about: 'You should be a good girl', for example. More forceful however, is that which is usually invisible, the *way* in which the subject spoken about is spoken into existence as that subject. In coming to understand 'goodness' and 'girlness', we desire the link between them in our own being without the imperative in the earlier sentence ever having to be spoken.

The concept of subjectification is not unlike Althusser's concept of interpellation. The difference is that Althusser emphasises that individuals *mistakenly* take themselves to be author of the *ideologies* through which various state apparatuses take them over. The concept of ideology is very similar to what poststructuralists mean by discourse. For example, Barrett (1980, p. 97) defines ideology as 'the generic term for the processes by which meaning is produced, challenged, reproduced and transformed'. According to Althusser, individuals, in learning to speak and to interact, come to see ideologies as their own, informing and stemming from their own desires and choices, and therefore not as something that they should either be wary of or challenge:

> I shall then suggest that ideology 'acts' or 'functions' in such a way that it 'recruits' subjects among the individuals (it recruits them all), or transforms the individuals into subjects (it transforms them all) by that very precise operation which I have called *interpellation* or hailing, and which can be imagined along the lines of the most commonplace everyday police (or other) hailing: 'Hey, you there!' (Althusser, 1971, pp. 162–3)

The concept of subjectification shifts the emphasis away from *mistaken* recognitions (which assumes the possibility of a correct recognition), to multiple possible recognitions. The substitution of the term 'discourse' for 'ideology' signals an important shift again away from Althusser's idea of *mistaken* commitments to multiple commitments. The mistake, for Althusser, lies in the fact that ideologies are not based on 'true' scientifically based knowledges. The poststructuralist use of the term 'discourse' similarly signals an understanding of the person as made subject through the discourses they have available to them. But scientific discourses are regarded simply as part of the array of discourses through which we constitute ourselves and are constituted, to which we may or may not make commitments, and yet which will have a powerful constitutive force in our lives.

THE APPLICATION OF POSTSTRUCTURALIST THEORY
TO THE DATA

The relation between the data and the theory is of particular interest in the writing of this book. The theory does not provide a frame or lens through which to look at the data (nor is the data a lens on a world which is thought to exist independent of that data) but a way of drawing attention to aspects of text and talk otherwise not visible. I use poststructuralist theory as a means of dislocating the press of more usual discourses, a way of unravelling old realities/perceptions and thus of making way for new ones. I draw attention to the text itself, not as it reveals a 'real', objectively knowable world to which the text simply points, but as it enables us to see the possible worlds that the text constitutes. Poststructuralist theory draws attention to 'the signifying matter, which, instead of making itself transparent as it conveys a particular meaning, becomes somewhat opaque like a piece of stained or faceted glass. Thus, in the most basic way the reader is invited to look at rather than *through* the linguistic surface' (Levine, 1991, p. xvi) .

This, then, is a study of the texts people produce about and from gendered childhoods. It is itself a text of gendered childhoods. Concepts from poststructuralist theory are drawn on to allow a different way of reading/seeing/understanding gender. The concepts do not dictate what is to be seen or written, but open up new possibilities that I, as author, have access to as a result of my reading/writing of feminist poststructuralist theory. There are a multitude of moments in the recorded conversations with the children, and in my memory of my own and others' childhoods and in others' writings of their childhood—far too many to be included here. These moments seemed, in the early stages of writing this book, like precious fragments of coloured glass, each one to be treasured, mused over, polished and placed next to other pieces in a pattern. Each piece of glass could be gazed at or looked through, so that the other bits took on a new hue. There seemed an infinite number of ways to order the pieces, each pattern making a different story, each piece looking different depending on what I placed next to it. The requirements of some linearity imposed by the form of the book limited the pictures I could make. I fancifully imagined putting all the pieces in a huge kaleidoscope so that the reader could turn them round and round and see with amazement each pattern as each jewelled moment fell into place in relation to the other moments. There is one sense in which each of the succeeding chapters gives you one turn of the kaleidoscope.

But it is not so simple. Each fragment is also like the shards of pottery, the fragments of other lives that archaeologists dig out of the earth, and through which they imaginatively construct lives other than their own. In this sense I too am an archaeologist, piecing together meaning from what the children say, from my own memories and the memories of others. And you as reader are the same, imagining life lived as a child, not just from the words on these pages, but using your existing ways of knowing, your immersion within, your subjectification through the same discourses out of which these children fashion their lives.

2 The Subjects of Childhood

Well I thought I'd never giggle again
             to tell you the truth
I felt really bad
sitting like this on the bench in the playground
after a minute you get totally bored
and wish you were with your friends
                    smiling
        We started laughing so much
                    we just couldn't stop
        We just couldn't stop and
        Mrs Brown told us to 'shut up'
                    it was just so funny
I always feel so different
             from everyone else

—Jennifer (Eastern Public)

THE PROBLEMATIC NATURE OF MODERN(IST) IDENTITY: BEING ONESELF AND BEING ONE WITH THE OTHERS

CHILDHOOD IS a time that is difficult to capture, so rich is it in new associations, emergent senses, connections, formings and unformings. As Virginia Woolf says in her own memoirs of childhood:

. . . the consciousness of other groups impinging upon ourselves; public opinion; what other people say and think; all those magnets which attract us this way to be like that, or repel us the other and make us different from that . . .

. . . the 'subject of this memoir' is tugged this way and that every day of his life; it is they that keep him in position . . . I see myself as a fish in a stream; deflected; held in place; but cannot describe the stream. (Woolf, 1976, p. 93)

A central tension in childhood as it is experienced in the modern world comes from the simultaneous struggles to be seamlessly meshed in the social fabric and to know and to signal oneself as a being with specificity. One's being must be able to be disattended by oneself and others, and at the same time be able to be identified as an individual, distinguishable from the rest. Further, that individual must achieve continuity of being and responsibility for his or her actions. One of the primary means for achieving this is through story:

We live immersed in narrative, recounting and reassessing the meaning of our past actions, anticipating the outcomes of our future projects, situating ourselves at the intersections of several stories not yet completed. (Brooks, 1984, p. 3)

Each child must locate and take up as their own, narratives of themselves that knit together the details of their existence. At the same time they must learn to be coherent members of others' narratives. Through stories we each constitute ourselves and each other as beings with specificity.

According to Phelan the concept of specificity:

Appeals to that in each of us which is irreducible to categories. It suggests that even after we have practised a politics which acknowledges certain categories of difference there will always be more to us than those categories. We are specific individuals as well as members of multiple groups. Thus, the demand for specificity provides recognition of the individual even as it refutes a unitary subject . . . However, a focus on specificity is not meant to remove the person from her context. Indeed it is opposed to classical variants of individualism which aim at abstraction from social context and suggest that the bearer of rights is an abstract being. Specificity as a methodological precept for social theory suggests that we must locate ourselves; our individuality does not substitute for social and historical position but resides within it. (1991, p. 136)

Benhabib defines the achievement of identity as 'how I, as a finite, concrete, embodied individual, shape and fashion the circumstances of my birth and family, linguistic, cultural and gender identity into a coherent narrative that stands as my life's story' (1987, p. 166). Porter adds to this: 'A narrative approach has two inseparable components. That is, *I am the subject of a history* with a particular personal meaning, and *I am part of others' stories*' (1991, p. 20).

In order to achieve these narratives of oneself and others, children must learn the ways of seeing made possible by the various discourses of the social groups of which they are members. This is not simply a cognitive process of language learning, but also an ability to read and interpret the landscape of the social world, and to embody, to live, to experience, to know, to desire *as one's own*, to take pleasure in the world, as it is made knowable through the available discourses, social structures and practices. Correct membership of the social order entails being able to read situations correctly such that what is obvious to everyone else is also obvious to you. It involves knowing how to position yourself as a member of the group who knows and takes for granted what other people know and take for granted in a number of different settings. Althusser uses the term *obviousness* to capture this taken-for-granted quality of the discursive categories, and in particular of the concept of 'subject', through which we construct our lives:

> As St Paul admirably put it, it is in the 'Logos', meaning in ideology, that we 'live, move and have our being'. It follows that, for you and for me, the category of the subject is a primary 'obviousness' . . . it is clear that you and I are subjects (free, ethical, etc.). Like all obviousnesses, including those that make a word 'name a thing' or 'have meaning' (therefore including the obviousness of the transparency of language), the 'obviousness' that you and I are subjects—and that that does not cause any problems—is an ideological effect, the elementary ideological effect. It is indeed a peculiarity of ideology that it imposes . . . obviousnesses as obviousnesses, which we cannot *fail to recognize* and before which we have the inevitable and natural reaction of crying out (aloud or in the 'still small voice of conscience'): 'That's obvious! That's right! That's true!' (Althusser, 1984, pp. 45–46)

Each person in a social group both shares a set of obviousnesses and is positioned in relation to them—the nature of the positioning depending in large part on their perceived category memberships. Those category memberships are most often conceptually and practically elements of an oppositional binary pair. So, for example, someone positioned as child (and therefore not adult), as student (and therefore not teacher), or as girl (and therefore not boy) must make these obviousnesses their own from each of these binary positionings. They must do this both as they make sense from within the categories in which they are positioned and from the position of its binary opposite, seeing themselves, not just from the inside out, but from the position of their binary opposite (Davies and Harré, 1990).

In *Frogs and Snails* I developed the idea of category-maintenance work, whereby children ensure that the categories of person, as they are coming to understand them, are maintained as meaningful categories in their own actions and the actions of those around them. In Althusser's terms, they were asserting the obviousness of those categories by signalling the unacceptability of activities that disrupt the obvious meaning of the categories (that meaning that 'we cannot fail to recognize'). In particular I observed them engaging in category maintenance work around activities that disrupted the obviousness that each of them was exclusively male or female. Male and female were achieved in this activity as opposite categories that take their meaning in a hierarchical relation to each other.

Social competence is thus fundamentally to do with appearing as normal or 'unpassremarkable' within the terms of the available, apparently transparent, categories. An ability to pass in this way requires the sharing of a set of obviousnesses. Sometimes the features that disallow this are outside of the control of the child. Names, for example, can be a source of constant attention if they are deemed too unusual. One of the children in the primary school study who had an unusual name was subjected to constant rhymes organised around his name:

Philo, cup of milo
Philo the dildo

Vulnerability to isolation and to teasing (the naming by others of oneself as inappropriate) if one does not achieve social competence as it is defined by those others, is a readily observable aspect of life in primary school (Davies, 1982). That teasing is most usually understood as 'peer pressure' where the group chooses to make the individual conform to a more or less arbitrary set of 'norms'. But it can be better understood as the struggle of the group individually and collectively to achieve themselves as knowable individuals within a predictable knowable transparent collective reality.

The following conversation with Jennifer took place in a one-to-one discussion with Chas. They were looking at the photos that Jennifer had taken as part of the project. This conversation readily makes visible the power she attributes to others in her struggle to inhabit the subject position of friend as she is positioned and positions herself within it. There is a tension between her access to specificity, with its attendant right to be different, and her access to group membership, which assumes and achieves sameness. There is, at the same time, a struggle to achieve the perceived requirement of a continuous and unitary self. She describes herself as usually cheerful and caught up in a pattern of expectations that she will always be so. Her explanations for this are that she is relatively new to the school, having come from New Zealand. She is different from the others in that they have better clothes and are slimmer than she is. She wishes her friends would recognise and accept her specificity and her variability as a being who is not always happy. She is intensely aware of moments of fear and unhappiness: 'I thought I'd never giggle again to tell you the truth'. Her friends, by contrast, appear to her to be persons whose specificity and variability can be acknowledged in this way. But because she fears being caught up in the storyline in which moody people are isolated, left with no position to occupy except as marginal outsiders, she shrinks from having her own moods recognised. The anxieties she experiences about how she is spoken into existence by her friends cannot be revealed to them because of the possibility that she will be marginalised, made peripheral to the group. Thus when Jennifer turns her reflexive gaze on herself, she refuses herself permission to take the freedoms that she sees her friends taking, for fear of not becoming one of them:

JENNIFER: At school you know I I've sort of got to be happy to everyone at school, 'cause I'm still really a newcomer. Well not a newcomer any more but if I sort of show me being moody they um they sort of don't like me any more. They can't stand me being moody, 'cause they can get moody but I can't. . . .

Well I thought I'd never giggle again to tell you the truth. . . . You know this morning I felt really bad, yesterday I felt really bad and then me and Stacey and Karen and Therese started laughing so much we just couldn't stop. We just couldn't stop and Mrs Brown told us to 'shut up' ((laughs)). All through class and we were, oh it was just so funny. And I always feel so different from everyone else. 'Cause you know I don't have much clothes, I don't have many shoes like them. And you know they have really coloured (   ) and everything . . . And because they're all skinny and everything and I'm fat. . . .

You see in the background of that one ((pointing to photo)), oh and there's another one, there. Well I always get scared of those boys, I mean they're no big thing or anything its just that I feel so different you know, that they could say something about me

CHAS: What—you feel really vulnerable?

JENNIFER: Mmmm

CHAS: In what way, physically or emotionally? How do you mean? Do you think they're going to physically hurt you or/

JENNIFER: No no/

CHAS: emotionally hurt you/

JENNIFER: I'd physically hurt them more than they could me

CHAS: . . . I wonder what it is then?

JENNIFER: If they said something about me I'd feel, you know quite bad

CHAS: . . . this thing of outward appearance is very important to you isn't it?

JENNIFER: Mmmm. I believe what other people say about me . . . |My friends| are a lot moodier than me and if I show my moody side then it all rocks. 'Cause I thrive on being cheerful and it's a lot nicer than being all sulky. And you know mixed up with your own feelings. It feels a lot better as well, 'cause you know sitting like this on the bench in the playground and after a minute you get totally bored and wish you were with your friends smiling and being cheerful . . . Therese who's, she's not really really skinny or anything and um, she's sort of got a half model build you know and sort of like that and she you know goes around calling me 'fatty' although she is quite, really, quite close really but, you know, she doesn't realise that she's so skinny that it wouldn't hurt if someone called her fat and if anyone does call her fat and you know Stacey goes 'You're not exactly that skinny Therese' she goes 'yes I am' . . .
(EASTERN PUBLIC—CONVERSATION WITH JENNIFER)

Jennifer is *afraid* of what the boys might say *because she will believe them.* This is necessarily so since they will speak her into existence through the same discourses through which she speaks herself into existence. She has no other discourse with which to resist their speaking. Her central strategy is to avoid the storyline in which she can be positioned as marginal to the group. Her preferred storyline is of the pleasure of being with her friends, of laughing, smiling and being cheerful. It is the achievement of this storyline that leads to the irrepressible energy of shared laughter that disrupts Mrs Brown's classroom order. This is her major defence against the awfulness of being alone, of being not like her friends, not liked, of vulnerability in the face of words spoken about her. The self is revealed here, not as an object or thing, but as an interactive, discursive *process*, fragile, capable of great pleasure in oneness with the group, in being competent within its terms, but always vulnerable to the discourses through which it is spoken and speaks itself into existence.

Being simultaneously the same and different (a member who knows and takes pleasure in the ways of the social group and a specific identifiable being) are difficult to hold in balance. The press towards sameness can be traumatic if the child loses control of the flow of action surrounding the difference. Claire, the daughter of a close friend, commenced school at the beginning of 1992. She had attended a child-care centre for several years and so was well used to, and competent in terms of, many of the features of schooling (Kantor, 1988). She nevertheless had a series of unexpected and traumatic events occur in the first week of school in relation to her positioning within the new group. In the summer holidays before school began, Claire had her hair cut in a short, stylish, 'unisex' fashion. In the ensuing weeks she was somewhat taken-aback when some people mistook her for a boy. At the same time, many people commented on how nice her hair looked. I told her about an article I had read in which the claim is made that in the world of art, the highest ideals of beauty have been closely linked with indeterminate sex. I suggested that she take claims that she looked like a boy as a claim that she was in this exceptional category. On arriving at school however, she found herself seriously persecuted by a number of older children who claimed that she was a boy and that she should go to the boys' toilet. In effect, the children were insisting that if she had a boyish hairstyle, she must also have male genitals. She should therefore have her right to enter the place where people with female genitals go without comment withdrawn from her. The obviousness of her category membership was questioned while the children worked to maintain the meaningfulness for themselves of the binary categories 'male' and 'female'. The segregated toilets provide a material, architectural sign of male and female as exclusive categories. Moreover, they are, in this instance, categories which have strong implications for the actions of each individual. Social competence involves not simply knowing how to read the signs that signal which toilet is female and which is male, but also knowing the implications for action of these signs. One door can be entered, and the other is forbidden—behind it lies that which may not even be seen. Knowing whether one has got it right depends on the visibility of everyone else getting it right, yet genitals are hidden behind clothes. People whose gender is not immediately obvious create an uncertainty in the correct reading of signs. The assigning of meaning to the pictures or words on the door is necessarily a collective action. Otherwise the signs have no meaning and the taboo cannot function. As a member of the collective, Claire too must be able to read the signs and practice in terms of the taboo. At the same time she has access to another discourse about the acceptability of short hair for girls and for defining the categories male and female as other than absolutely exclusive and opposite categories. It was nevertheless traumatic to be so loudly hailed by older girls as one who is incompetent, as one who does not know how to constitute herself as a legitimate person in the everyday world of her new school.

Confronted by these taunts and jeers Claire might have succumbed to the category-maintenance work being done, and positioned herself as unequivocally female, as opposite to male, as acceptable within the discourse of the taunters. Or she could have positioned herself, as she did, as one who sees and rejects the narrow-mindedness of people who perceive gender in this way. What she cannot avoid, however, is the experience of having been transgressive, of not having unremarked membership, at least in the eyes of the taunters.

The process of subjectification, then, entails a tension between simultaneously becoming a speaking, agentic subject and the co-requisite for this, being subjected to the meanings inherent in the discourses through which one becomes a subject. It is this dual process that is central in this study of the life world of children, in which gendered being is continuously created and sustained.

IDENTITY: A STORY WHICH CAN NEVER FULLY BE TOLD

Most theories of 'identity' dwell on the interaction between oneself and others, attributing much power to those others in their naming or shaping of the emergent self (Davies, 1988, 1989a, 1990a). Yet as Althusser (1984) points out, in modern(ist) conceptions of the person, one is *always already* a subject, even before birth. Prior to any interaction, the concept of the child as a being with individuality is already established. The child is hailed as such when it is born, and eventually comes to greet or hail itself in the same way, using the same discourses and storylines which it comes to take up as its own. Lacan (1966) has added an important shift to Althusser's idea of the humanist subject 'always already' having been. He talks instead of the 'inconclusive futurity of what will-always-already-have-been' or, in other words, a recognition that the story of who we take ourselves to be can never be concluded. The story of who we are can never fully be told since at any future point the apparent certainties of the present can be re-visited and re-vised. Because of this re-visability, any experience of oneself exists in a '"time" which can never be entirely remembered, since it will never fully have taken place' (Weber, 1991, p. 9). In this way, Lacan moves away from the deterministic element of Althusser's subject and focuses more on the processes of always becoming.

To illustrate this point about the necessarily inconclusive nature of who we each are, I draw on an experience of my own in relation to my father. When he died, this was an unexpectedly traumatic event for me. Unexpected, because I did not think I was in any sense close to him. His children were, by his definition, the responsibility and interest of their mother. He required of her only that she alert him to their activities if they were going seriously astray, at which point he might intervene with a lecture and in some cases a controlling action. I wept at his death, a seemingly endless weeping, as much for the absence of love between us as for the fact that he was now dead. Some months later I came across a photograph I had never seen before of my father holding a small baby and looking at it with great tenderness. My mother had placed it in a bag of oddments she thought I might want. I could not imagine that this baby in the photograph was me. I had never experienced my father either holding me or looking at me tenderly. Much of my life could be explained in terms of the pain I felt in relation to this absence. Perhaps the photo was actually of my younger brother, John, and my mother had made a mistake? But she insisted, when I asked her, that it was me. My story of always having been unloved by my father, of being born into a family where the father did not understand fatherhood to involve any form of tenderness, was called in question by this small faded grey and white image.

For days, even weeks, I was obsessed by the photo, not knowing how to incorporate it into my idea of my life. Even if he only held me and looked at me in that way once for the purposes of the photo, and at no other time, I could not maintain the certainty that he was who he had been for me until that point. I wanted to know, now, what had happened, how a man capable of looking like that became the man I knew. What he had always been, was no longer. My reading of the photo shifted who he was into an inconclusive futurity, even after his death.

What I now saw, was someone else who had come to exist, not only in the present, but in a now always present past. As for myself, a possible new perception of a person emerged who did not need to be defined primarily through lack of love. Maybe I could begin to see myself as someone who had in fact always been loved, though troubled by a

perceived lack of it from my father. Who I had always been now emerged too, in the present, as quite a different person. This was not because I discovered from the photo that I 'really' had been loved by my father. It probably was just that once, for the eye of the camera, that I was held and looked at in that way. Rather, my interrogation of the image in the photograph opened up the possibility of a new storyline that unhooked the old story of lack, and put another, more abundant, enabling story in its place. I also realised, on reading of Barthes' struggle to find a 'true' image/essence of his mother in photographs of her after her death, that my photograph was perhaps a means of ending the excess of my grief: grief at a lifetime of no love—no shared memories, no shared laughter, no shared intimacy. My father and I (unlike Barthes, whose memories seemed totally made up out of love) had given each other little more than the fact of a father, the fact of a second daughter. To find one moment of tenderness in the photograph, this I can choose to hold, not as a false representation of the whole, but as a moment that punctures the wholeness of the absence and alleviates the grief (Barthes, 1984).

To return to Althusser's image of hailing, then, the hailer does not *cause* the person so hailed to see themselves in a particular way. My father did not cause me to feel loved by looking at me tenderly on the occasion of the photo, nor did he cause me to feel unloved by not doing so on other occasions. Both the person hailed and the person doing the hailing are constituted through discourses and storylines, the constitutive power lying in the discourse and the ways in which it has been taken up. Sometimes discourses are shared. Other times they are not. My father had a discourse about fatherhood which kept him separate from me. I made that separation central in my emotional life through psychological discourses which defined it as a crippling lack. I longed for something that I perceived myself not to have had. I was hailed through one discourse and recognised myself through another. There were, at the same time, many shared discourses about the meaning of being a person, about justice, about gender and about class, through which my father and I managed to hail each other as knowable others, as father and daughter.

In order to know that one is being hailed as a subject, or as a particular kind of subject, in order to respond to that hailing it is necessary to share some obviousnesses about the nature of persons and the processes in which they are engaged. Each person must make their way inside the experience of belonging to the category of person as that is understood within their time and culture if they are to recognise themselves when addressed as such. It is also, as Lacan (1966) has pointed out, a process in which one must have an *image* of oneself as subject, to know oneself as such. Like a photograph, one's image of one's bodily self has a sense of being fixed and bounded, and can thus become a signifier of who one is. The fiction of a bounded unitary self, of a separate essential being, is established, through such images and through discourse, as real. At the same time as I learn to see other selves as they are spoken into existence, I learn to share in that speaking and in the speaking of 'myself' into existence.

The achievement of oneself as a speaking subject can be extraordinarily painful and alienating. It can also be a highly pleasurable experience. Virginia Woolf claims that her first and most important memory is an ecstatic experiencing of herself experiencing sound and sight:

> [M]y other memory, which also seems to be my first memory, and in fact is the most important of all my memories . . . is of lying half asleep, half awake, in bed in the nursery at St Ives. It is of hearing the waves breaking, one, two, one, two, and sending a splash of water over the beach; and then breaking, one, two, one, two, behind a yellow blind. It is of hearing the blind draw its little acorn across the floor as the wind blew the blind out. It is of lying and hearing this splash and seeing this light, and feeling, it is almost impossible that I should be here; of feeling the purest ecstacy I can conceive. (Woolf, 1976, p. 75)

For me, prior to the discovery of the photo, whenever I have tried to stretch my mind back as far as it will go, or when I have asked myself the question, if I were to write an autobiography, where would it begin, I think of the painful mental and physical harassment that was part of everyday life with my older brother Tony. But just as vivid is a particular memory of the flowering plum tree in my garden, which seems somehow to mark the beginning of my own awareness of myself as an experiencing subject. I think I was four or five. It was spring. It was a weekend and there was a sense of freedom and pleasure in the emergent day without plan or structure. I was in the sunlit garden and I think the grass was wet with the early morning dew. I noticed that the flowering plum tree was a profusion of blossoms and bees. I went up close to the blossoms and noticed their colour and shape and smell for the first time. It was a miraculous discovery, in the garden by myself, amazed at the exquisite flowers and the thronging profusion of bees. It was the tinge of plum brown colour in the flowers and the stalks that was most extraordinary given their pale delicate pink. I was, at the same time, intensely aware of myself standing there in the garden seeing and smelling the blossoms.

Layered behind that ecstatic image is another image of my father. He had lopped the tree back severely during the winter. Its shape was ugly and stunted. So there is, in fact, an earlier image of an ugly stuntedness by which I was affronted and to which I was opposed. The profusion of blossoms, I had been told by my mother, would come from the pruning. And here they were. My own for that moment.

And so we begin to create our own individual biographies, the stories through which there is an 'I' with something to tell, but with stories that can never fully be told. Those unfolding, shifting stories are embodied through smell and touch, through sight and sound. They are lived with more than the conscious mind. What poststructuralist theory enables us to see is that the very specificity of those experiences, and their intensity, need not be the markers of a bounded self, but, rather, the moments at which an experiencing being comes to know the possibilities being made available by virtue of their presence within the collectivity, albeit a collectivity which constitutes itself through discourses in which the individual experiencing subject is made the primary focus.

TAKING UP DISCURSIVE PRACTICES AS ONE'S OWN AND THE POSSIBILITY OF AGENCY

The children in the study groups talked about themselves as becoming particular kinds of persons. They sometimes defined this as a series of choices made out of the possibilities they found in their immediate environment. These choices were in terms of assent or dissent, being like, or not being like particular people. They were aware of the simultaneous power of others in their lives, and of moments of choice. Their choices stemmed from their access to particular discourses and their positioning within categories made real through those discourses. Having taken on as their own the discourses through which these memberships are articulated, the knowledge of how to belong in that category and the desire to be correctly located, no matter how painful that might be, are read as coming from one's 'inner' self. Woolf describes one such moment of choice in which she came to know her own powerlessness in contrast to her brother's power:

> Week after week passed at St Ives and nothing made any dint upon me. Then for no reason that I know about there was a sudden violent shock; something happened so violently that I have remembered it all my life . . . I was fighting with Thoby on the lawn. We were pommeling each other with our fists. Just as I raised my fist to hit him, I felt: why hurt another person? I dropped my hand instantly, and stood there, and let him beat me. I remember the feeling. It was a feeling of hopeless sadness. It was as if I became aware of something terrible; and of my own powerlessness. I slunk off alone, feeling horribly depressed. (Woolf, 1976, p. 82)

The question 'why hurt another person?' is owned by the child, Virginia, as her own, as is the overwhelming experience of powerlessness that follows. The question belongs to 'I'. It is asked by 'I', felt by 'I'. The I-as-girl is not articulated but nonetheless achieved. The desire for physical power and dominance is abandoned. Subjectification takes place in such a way that 'identity' is shaped through 'choices' which are understood to spring from and confirm that very identity, rather than through the apprehension of the discourses through which identity, personal choice, and inner and outer selves are made thinkable, achievable.

The following collective biography story, told by a young woman who was taking a course I was teaching on gender in New York State, provides an explicit example of desire being shaped in accordance with the gender categories to which one finds oneself assigned. It is also possible to see how apparently innocent *practices* which presuppose a gendered social structure can play a significant part in recreating that gendered structure. It is in the particular moment captured by this story, that her brother's penis specifically comes to be associated with his competence, dominance and power. The binary discourses through which her subjectification takes place make her brother's power specifically not her own, since, as girl, she is other-than-male, other-than-one-who-is-powerful. She achieves herself in this moment as girl. That is, she achieves herself as not powerful, and more significant, as not *desiring* power.

I don't remember exactly how old I am, but I must have been pretty young because my brother, Max, and I still took baths together. Each night we would urinate before going into the tub. I had never expressed any interest before, but tonight I realized how fascinating it was that Max could urinate standing up. I watched with obvious delight as he controlled the direction and force of the flow and pretended to bomb submarines in the toilet. He was clearly enjoying himself, and, as always, I wanted to play. I threw pieces of paper in the toilet and Max soaked them instantly. When it came to be my turn to urinate, I decided to try it standing up, like Max. I didn't know quite how to position myself. First I tried standing up just as Max had, but my little trickle missed the bowl completely. Then I tried squatting over the toilet. This time I managed to get it all in, but not with anywhere near the same amount of force and accuracy Max had exhibited. I most certainly couldn't aim at targets like he had, and I didn't have a penis to hold on to to control my stream. Whatever it was that I had, and I didn't know the name of it, was clearly inadequate. I was envious of the power and control Max had over his genitals. I was disappointed that we could only play the game when he was around, too. I cleaned up the floor and we got in the tub.

While we played in the tub that evening, my attention was predominantly focused on Max's penis. There it was in plain view. I felt different from him tonight, unlike I ever had. He assumed his usual position in the back of the tub so he could slide down on the incline and create waves for his toy boats. The object of his game was to shoot down any of my toys with his, or to go under the water for a sneak attack. Maybe it was just because he was bigger, older, and stronger, but he always managed to win. I felt dominated by him, almost powerless. The only way I could win was by outsmarting him, and then he would cheat. No matter how hard I tried, I'd never win. Why should I even bother to try? (COLLECTIVE BIOGRAPHY WORKSHOP)

Apparently harmless social rituals such as that of males urinating standing up and females urinating sitting down, combined with the binary divisions in the discourses through which male and female subjectivities are achieved, can thus be seen to constitute the experience of male superiority and female inferiority. The boy's penis is something that is named, recognised, touchable and usable, not only for urinating but also for play and, in this case, for powerful play, making 'obvious' the usually symbolic connection between penises and powerful destructive missiles. This particular practice provides Max with a powerful subject position that he can take up, with his penis as central to that power. He *recognises* the obviousness of his power and uses that power in the ensuing play. In contrast, Jean's attempts at urinating standing up or squatting fail. She has no named, known, touchable part of herself that she can use in her efforts: 'Whatever it was that I had, and I didn't know the name of it, was clearly inadequate'. Jean's lack of aim seemed 'natural', that is, to do with the physiology of her body. She did not realise boys' aim is the result of much practice, often with not very successful outcomes, and that girls can learn to hold their labia in such a way that their aim and force is at least equal to any boy's. Without access to this information and this practice, her powerlessness was understood in relation to an absence, a lack, a no-name.

> Silence itself—the things one declines to say, or is forbidden to name, . . . is less the absolute limit of discourse, the other side from which it is separated by a strict boundary, than an element that functions alongside the things said, with them and in relation to them within over-all strategies. (Foucault, 1980, p. 27)

Haug et al., writing about the collective biography or memory work they undertook in Germany, also discuss silence and, in particular, the silences that surround female genitals. Following a story in which a girl talks about the struggle to learn to keep her legs together as 'good girls' should, Haug et al. say:

> Clearly, then, something 'sexual' is being signified through leg posture. In expending such large amounts of energy on keeping our legs together, we begin to feel there is something we must keep hidden . . . It is through the activity of concealment that meaning is generated . . . 'Sexualization' is acquired without sexuality itself ever being mentioned. (Haug et al., 1987, p. 77)

Thus the lack of naming, this sense of absence created around female genitalia, is also fundamental to the social practices through which femaleness is constituted. It is to the absences and silences in children's talk, as well as to the discourses and practices through which they articulate their experience, that any analysis must look.

As well as the male–female binary, the child–adult binary is a powerful constitutive force in children's lives (Baker and Davies, 1992). The children in the study groups often constituted themselves in their talk as *children*. They constituted adults, in contrast, as people with agency who are in control of their own lives and the lives of children. Adults give children information that will enable them too to become agents. At the same time they nevertheless manage to constitute themselves as agents, as people not pressed into being, but as recognising possibilities, as making choices in relation to the possibilities presented to them:

JAMES: Like the brothers mainly when you are getting, when you are fairly young your brothers mainly have an attit- ideas about one thing and you gradually grow up to get your attitude, you either go one way or the other

ZAC: You get help from each person, is that right?

PHILO: Yeah you look at people and like if they're um like if they are boy and girl, you act like they look and they acted and things

ZAC: You mainly learn off your mother and father

PHILO: Yeah

CHAS: How do you learn it off your mother and father, Zac?

ZAC You you are mainly always with them when you are a baby and you get/

JAMES: They tell you what's right and wrong/

ZAC: just like ( )

CHAS: They tell you what's right and wrong?

JAMES/ZAC: Yeah

CHAS: Right, right, so you think that this little baby ((in the photograph)) will learn about itself and the world mostly from its parents and from its brothers and sisters

JAMES: From its family

CHAS: From its family/

PHILO: Everyone they see/

CHAS: from everyone

JENNIFER: Like we all have people, kind of like girl friends

STACEY: And maybe from advertising and TV and things like that/

CHAS: Right/

STACEY: 'cause they might see other kids their age on TV commercials and they say 'ohhh'

(EASTERN PUBLIC)

The children thus recognized the multiple possibilities that were presented to them, from different cultural sources. In the following conversation they discuss how even children with very strict parents, with very definite views, are capable of seeing other possibilities:

CHAS: What do you think makes a good child?

PHILO: Have to be quiet

ZAC: Well behaved

CHAS: Well behaved yes

PHILO: 'Cause some of the/

STACEY: Religion

JAMES: Religious?

STACEY: Yes some people with religions as well like if you have the uh, Jehovah, one of the ones that you don't think about every day and you've got really special rules that they have to stick to and they won't do something . . . if they are naughty they will get in trouble and you will be sent to hell or something like that . . .

JENNIFER: Sometimes the more a child is told not to do something the more he will have the desire to do it

CHAS: That's right

CHARLOTTE: 'Cause he wants to be outrageous, to do something that no one, that he's not s'posed to do

JENNIFER: He doesn't want to be kind of molly-coddled by his mother

CHAS: Right

CHARLOTTE: It might be more that she's by saying that she is tempting him into doing it.

(EASTERN PUBLIC)

In any naming of direction, its opposite is also opened up as an unstated possibility, particularly where that naming is done with force. Moreover, there are readily accessible storylines through which those who act only in accordance with adult directives are inadequate, in this case 'molly-coddled'. Direct displays of adult power are nonetheless a prominent feature of children's lives. These displays are different from the more subtle power entailed in teaching a child to share the same set of obviousnesses, and the positioning of the child in terms of these.

Many of my own most vivid memories of my parents are of them wielding power over me in ways that caused extreme discomfort and yet in which I came to conceive of myself as a being who could position herself in opposition to the impositions of others. I was, like any child, made subject and subjected to their storylines—good parent storylines, storylines about responsible adulthood, or hard working fathers needing peace and quiet from the noisy prattle of children. Their rule that we must eat everything on our plates was an example of their version of being responsible parents. As part of that same storyline my mother occasionally attempted to deceive us about what we were eating in order to get us to eat things that were good for us. I remember eating a delicious steak and kidney pie, only to suddenly find myself chewing something that had a strange leathery texture and was foul tasting. I exclaimed in involuntary horror as I struggled to swallow it. My mother said, 'Oh, that was some liver, I thought you wouldn't notice'. Having caught her out in her trickery made no difference, though, as it all had to be eaten. 'Think of the starving children in India' she would say. I couldn't comprehend how my eating food I didn't need or want would help the children in India. One thing I really hated to eat was the thick ridge of shiny fat on lamb loin chops. One dinner time, having struggled for some time to eat the fat, I quietly got up from the table and took my plate out to the kitchen and scraped the fat into the garbage. When I returned my father asked what I'd done with the fat. With some fear and embarrassment, I told him what I'd done. He ordered me to go and get it out of the garbage and eat it. I had no choice but to obey him. I left some of the fat in the garbage though, and felt a small point of satisfaction. While he was being clearly outrageous, and I was having to do something utterly intolerable, at least I was not eating all the fat that had originally been on my plate.

There are three further stories from my childhood that are closely related to each other in my remembering of them. They tell a story of 'discovering' myself as agent.

My brother Tony was two years older than me. He was tall and very strong, good at sport, good looking, but very poor at school work. He was a very disruptive and difficult person to grow up with. He had had polio when a small child, soon after I was born, which had paralysed half his soft palate, making his speech incomprehensible until he had learned to use the unparalysed half. He was a child hungry for love, but so difficult and destructive that it was extraordinarily difficult to love him. I remember him hugging my cat to him so tightly that it struggled and clawed against him until finally he was forced to let it go. By the time it had sprung away from him he was filled with anger and hate for this cat who did not love him. He wanted to kill it.

My father allowed Tony freedom and space that the rest of us could not have. If Tony had harmed any of us, or even my mother, it was not his fault. Tony was often given board games for Christmas, which then meant we had to play them with him, however awful that might be, given the combination of his aggression, his uncontrollable tantrums and his need to win. One day Tony and I were playing snakes and ladders. He had developed a way of sniffing that made my stomach heave every time he did it. It was a loud long gurgling sound as he sniffed the snot from his nose into the back of his throat, followed by a throat clearing sound as he forced the snot into his mouth. He would then swirl it around his mouth before swallowing it. I begged him several times not to do it, but he ignored me. I said I couldn't keep playing if he sniffed like that. He leant over and hit me very hard on my bare leg. I declared I would no longer play. Tony ran to my father who told me I had to play with him and that I shouldn't upset him. I showed him the red mark on my leg which was in the shape of Tony's hand, but he said it was my fault for upsetting him. My indignation was almost overwhelming but the ethic of care, no matter how difficult to carry through, was absolute.

In fourth/fifth grade we had a girl in our class called Robyn whom the school had decided could go no higher than fifth grade. Each year she joined the new cohort of fourth/fifth graders. She was about fifteen, had buck teeth and a slight speech impediment. She mostly spent her time drawing. I don't remember her ever joining in the lessons. There was another girl in the class called Sue, who was tall, good at sport and pretty. At the beginning of the year she decided that Robyn could not be a social member of our class. She told her to sit on her own at lunch time. I saw the look on Robyn's face and her slightly hunched body as she walked away from us to the part of the school yard that Sue had ordered her to. I struggled with myself, thinking how cosy it was and what fun to be part of Sue's group, then hotly declared that it was not fair to exclude Robyn and that I was going to have lunch with her. I invited anyone who wanted to join us to come to the spot allocated us by Sue. Several of my friends came and we formed a splinter group until Sue relented. This stood in my mind as an indication of me as a moral person; the event was evidence of my strong moral principles. That is who I took myself to be. I had positioned myself as someone who could disrupt the actions of powerful others, who were failing to care in appropriate ways, and succeed.

The following year I was elected as class captain. One of the impossible tasks of class captains was that they had to keep the class quiet if the teacher was late for class. That year we had a teacher who was chronically late for class after morning recess. The class was restive and the chatter impossible to stop. In despair at my own powerlessness I called a class meeting at morning recess and put the problem to them. I said I had been elected by them as class captain, but they obviously didn't accept or want my authority. It would be embarrassing and difficult for the class to ask for a formal re-election since that would involve an admission to the teacher of their failure to follow the rules. I said that I was prepared to continue to carry out the formal duties of the captain, such as taking the absentee list to the school secretary each morning recess, but that they should privately elect a new person whose authority they respected and who they were prepared to listen to in the teacher's absence. I left the classroom to allow them to vote for a new captain. I waited outside, feeling relieved at having found a solution to my intolerable situation. The class sent a messenger to me to return to the class. They had written in big letters on the blackboard 'WE WANT BRONWYN' and cheered when I walked in. I was totally overwhelmed at this unpredicted and extraordinary moment of power.

All three events are organised around an obviousness that women gain acceptability and perhaps some form of power through self-negation and concern for others. In the first story I am positioned by my father as one who must negate my own wishes for Tony's benefit. In the second story I choose to do so for Robyn's benefit. In the third, I am unexpectedly positioned as one to be given power in response to shedding it. Not aware of the growing centrality of this connection between self-negation and agency in my own lived narratives, nor of the suffering it would lead to, I was happy to constitute myself as someone with power and agency and made some considerable investment in the idea of myself as the moral person to whom such power might be given.

From the point of view of some of the children in the primary school study, their resistance to adult power is understood as fundamental to being in the category *child* rather than anything to do with the specific kind of person they are or want to be—though the moments of dissent *may* be fundamental moments in the recognition of themselves as beings with specificity. The children generally tended to assume that adults, in contrast to children, have taken over their lives and so have become agents by virtue of being in the category of adult. They define adults as not being caught up in the same patterns of assent and resistance that they perceive themselves to be:

STACEY: As you get much much, older like you're heading into the 30s, 40s, you're not influenced by anybody then/

JENNIFER: 'Cause you're/

STACEY: because you've sort of taken over your life, finally

ZAC: At school you're being taught by teachers and at home you're being told by mothers

JAMES: You've got certain guidelines for things, separating one from the other by yourself and probably you are your own boss, you you probably don't have very many guidelines

JENNIFER: That's the problem with teenagers, they start thinking that they own their life and they shouldn't be influenced by anyone else any more 'cause they're older.
(EASTERN PUBLIC)

Yet, when these same children perceive adults to be behaving outside the range of behaviours appropriate for the category the children take them to be in, they rapidly move to censure the behaviour, bringing whatever category-maintenance skills they have to bear on the adult's talk or action. During the discussions with the study groups, for example, Chas asked the children what they envisaged for their future lives. She asked them whether they imagined having a partner and called into question the obviousness of heterosexuality. They protested immediately, letting her know that her own competence would be called into question if she persisted in such a line of talk:

CHAS ((TO JAMES)): What else, apart from being pretty and help you to lose weight will this person [your partner] have and I'm assuming its going to be female?
    ((Uproar–laughter))
JENNIFER: *Oh Chas*, you shouldn't say such things
CHAS: Well go on
JENNIFER: We all know nuns' games ((laughter))
CHAS: I'm not going to presume anything
JAMES: And I'd presume you're a leso
(EASTERN PUBLIC)

Thus the children, having taken up the dominant heterosexist discourse as their own, move rapidly to maintain that discourse as valid, without necessarily seeing how forcefully they close down the possibility of agency for those who step outside the categories legitimated by that discourse. The romantic storyline is one of the discursive means through which the oppositional, hierarchical male-female binary is held in place. Chas's gentle disruption of the obviousness of heterosexual marriage as what they should desire for their futures is, here, jokingly, but nevertheless forcefully resisted. In this case they refuse her adult power to call any aspect of the dominant gender order into question. It is interesting to reflect on the ways in which children resist adult power, or work around it.

One of the forms of resistance that has been handed to children by adults over the last decade is to do with the right of children to refuse sexual abuse. In the following transcript from Karobran Public, the study group tells Chas about a gardener at their school whom they take to be a 'perv' (sexual pervert) who is interested in them sexually. One of the strategies in the anti-abuse campaign was to tell children that they had the right to say 'no' to sexual abuse and to provide them with sets of words and imagined situations in which they could do so. It is interesting to observe how they have taken this up. Their refusal of sexual abuse involves a combination of careful avoidance and sporadic guerrilla warfare. Both these forms of resistance are under the children's control. This is not to say that they do not still feel vulnerable and deeply affronted by the gardener's actions and at the failure of adults either to protect them from it or to hear what they have to say:

CHAS: (   ) What is it about Mr Molner that is the problem

ANNA: Well he tries to perv on you, like, we are doing the dance, right, and we have to get changed and every time just before you get changed, like he walks out and then quickly walks back in again. And every time like, after he's seen us do our dance in our clothes, he says, he keeps asking when we're doing our dress rehearsal

ROSIE: So we don't tell him . . .

CAROLYN: He's a perv . . .

MAL: Anthony Herbert, he used to go to this school, um well he was sitting in the toilets when we were going out to the oval out near the ABS [Anglican Boys School] and um Mr Mol- we had to get changed because we all had to play football out there and we Anthony was getting changed ((starts to laugh)) Mr Molner walked in um ((laughter)) . . . Anthony called him a 'perv' and he he then when we Anthony was the last one to leave and we saw Mr Molner's head go over the ah wall. He's got this little room in the toilet and we saw his head come under the ((laughter)) and he looked at Anthony ((laughter)). Anthony didn't spot him until he got out and we told him and we were all laughing at him ((laughter))

ROSIE: Yeah, there is this little room in the toilet in the middle

MAL: Have you got one too?

ANNA: Yes, we've got one too and it's just in the middle eh ((All talking together))

ANNA: Yeah, 'cause there's a gap *that* big . . .

ROSIE: I'll be waiting for the bus out the front there and I'll ask the teacher if I can go to the toilets and I come back to the toilet and he's in the toilet and I'll run back up there and I won't go to the toilet

ANNA: I won't go to the toilet after school or even during school in the afternoon 'cause he's always there hanging around the dunnies

ROSIE: If someone pervs at you you shouldn't laugh at it because if like if it happened to you then you'd be really upset if someone laughed at you

ANNA: It makes you weird when you tell someone

BRIAN: Yeah

ROSIE: Yeah . . .

ROSIE: He's old

MAL: He acts really like a girl . . . He goes around 'oh'

ANNA: 'Oh hello sweet heart and darling' and goes like that and you just go ((shrugs)) well that's what I do

ROSIE: I keep at least six metres away from him

CHAS: How does it make you feel?

ROSIE: It makes you feel unprotected sort of

ANNA: With him around how can you be safe when you are worried about him staring and things like that, perving

BRIAN: Sometimes he comes up and pinches you on the bottom

ROSIE: Yeah

ANNA: Or he puts his hand like, or he puts his hands like that like on ya so I just punch, I just elbow him

BRIAN: That's what I do. We nearly double banked at one time . . . We put him on the ground and ran away from him.

CHAS: God

KEN: That's why he doesn't like us much . . .

ANNA: . . . he just looks in every toilet as he goes along

BRIAN: Sometimes he will just turn the hose off so he can see

ANNA: I always, if I ever go to the toilet I go to the ones with the real big doors

CHAS: Right

MAL: If I see water in the toilets, I won't go in there

BRIAN: Yeah, I know

ANNA: Like on the last day um he went into the toilets and he was hosing out the toilets and I like I was just and he was hosing out the toilets and/

ROSIE: He was trying to wet us

ANNA: yeah, and he did try to wet us and he, so we all went around and stopped the hose ((All loudly talking at once))

ROSIE: . . . no one's told um any teachers

BRIAN: We have, we have

CHAS: Why haven't you?

ROSIE: Well um/

BRIAN: I have I have

ROSIE: Well we've got no evidence

BRIAN: I have

ROSIE: we have nothing to prove it

ANNA: And like sometimes adults don't believe kids

BRIAN: Yeah mine don't

ANNA: Even if there's heaps of them

(KAROBRAN PUBLIC)

The children reveal the empowering effect of the anti-sexual abuse discourse that they have taken up as their own. With it they can resist the dominant discourse which constitutes children as powerless objects, subject to adult power and control. They act as agents who can thwart the desires of Mr Molner, while recognizing at the same time, the lack of agency that comes with being children who will not be believed by adults.

In the next chapter I further explore the complex issue of adult authority in children's lives. In a complex double move, adults who want to enable children to deconstruct the obviousness, the inevitability, of the dichotomous hierarchical gender order, must give them access to new discursive possibilities (which they may well resist) *and* undermine their own usual embeddedness in the authority of adult–child relations.

3 Knowledge and the Subjects of Reading and Writing

> *(We) need postmodern insights in order to know how meanings and bodies get made, not in order to deny meanings and bodies, but to build them with a chance for life.*
>
> —Haraway (1988, p. 580)[1]

IN PRIMARY school classrooms formal ownership of knowledge is assumed by teachers—they have the authoritative codes for interpreting meaning and their task is to give children access to these codes, or rather, to subject them to them. This is an obviousness about teaching that is not usually attended to by teachers, it is simply part and parcel of the way teaching is done—of knowledge one has about teaching. This knowledge about teaching-as-usual is often in tension with other ways of knowing that each teacher has, these other ways of knowing being informed, for example, by the humanist knowledges and ideals that are so often made relevant in classroom discourse. But these

---

[1]This quote from Haraway uses the term 'postmodern' rather than 'poststructuralist'. There is no simple way of distinguishing these two terms as their usage varies from one country to another, from one discipline to another and from one writer to another. They are used interchangeably in the US, but there are some distinctions that I think are worth making. Poststructuralism is most usually used to refer to concepts developed by a diverse range of French writers working across historical, literary, philosophical and psychoanalytic areas of study. These writers, while holding on to some aspects of structuralism, have nevertheless disrupted many aspects of it. The human psyche is no longer seen as being determined by the structures of language, or of social structure, or of the brain, but as being in process, as capable of multiple possibilities as it finds itself positioned now one way and now another in relation to its own history and context,

tensions are not enough to disrupt the obviousness of the usual authority relations in classrooms. The authority of teachers over students and the teachers' authority in interpreting text are generally understood as a necessary basis for the management and control of classrooms. Yet that authority and control of the group may contradict and undermine other unquestioned assumptions about what teachers ought to be doing in classrooms—for example attending to the needs of each individual child (Davies and Hunt, 2000).

Despite the multiplicity and variability of teacher knowledges, children do not have freedom to innovate with or to reject teachers' interpretations. While teachers might want children to bring 'something of their own' to the classroom or the lesson, what it is that is brought must conform to tightly set knowledge boundaries and to acceptable forms of saying or knowing, and will be subjected to teachers' authoritative scrutiny, interpretation and evaluation. Whatever children have come to understand prior to their schooling in the process of learning to engage in discursive practices, is subjected to authoritative teaching when they go to school. The categories to which they have been assigned are now potentially subsumed under educational categories of success and failure. Getting it right is not just a matter of being able to converse competently, but a matter of becoming competent in the terms that each teacher designates as competent.[2]

The disruption of knowledges advocated in feminist poststructuralist writing runs counter to this culture of the classroom. For teachers to introduce critical literacy into their classrooms and for students to begin to deconstruct the text and to talk through the ways in which they are constituted, a great deal has to change. Assumptions about the teachers' interpretive authority and the authority of texts, assumptions about the nature of authorship, the nature of student-

spoken into existence through multiple and contradictory discourses. The humanist, enlightenment version of the person is called into question. The rational mind is no longer seen as having control and the personal/social binarism is disrupted. The various versions of postmodernism cast a wider net and include disciplines which focus on the structure of the physical environment. Postmodernism can be said to disrupt the certainties of modernism, to enjoy the shock and surge of juxtaposing one discourse against another, one way of organising space against another, one set of rules against another. In the various forms of both poststructuralism and postmodernism, modernist concepts such as the human subject, the author and authority are deconstructed, disrupted and partially abandoned. Such disruption can be quite nihilistic. In contrast, feminist writers have picked up on the surge of energy created by these disruptions and have seen the possibility of breaking down old oppressive structures and of locating and experiencing themselves differently, of moving outside fixed structures. A good reader on postmodernism is Nicholson (1990).

[2]In middle class homes, in particular, much of the same kind of teaching that goes on in schools will already have begun prior to school age (Walkerdine and Lucey, 1989). The major difference at school is that the authority of the teacher as one who knows is a central feature of who s/he is taken to be.

teacher interaction, the texts made available to students, methods of assessment and the understanding of the relation between knowledges and the person must all come under critical scrutiny. They must be subjected to substantial re-ordering if students are to be given access to the means whereby they can constructively resist the imposition of binary knowledges and so begin to read and write their way out of the limiting subject positions currently available to them. Critical, deconstructive reading and writing cannot be added in as an extra, but must be fundamental to the curriculum itself.

A constant question asked me by those students of mine who are also teachers, is 'but how can I use this knowledge in my classroom?' At first I was nonplussed by the question, since I was, I thought, demonstrably using it in my teaching with them, and, further, several articles I had written on feminist poststructuralist theory and classroom practice spelled out the answer to the question I thought they were asking. I could not understand why they couldn't use their own experience as students along with these ideas to implement change in their own classrooms. But I now see that there are some prior questions: 'How do I undo those aspects of my teaching that run counter to critical/deconstructive reading and writing?' and 'What are those aspects anyway?' The obviousness of everyday teaching makes it difficult for both teachers and students to interrupt it. The knowledge that they have about being teachers and being students is not knowledge they attend to; it is disattended in order to attend to the contents of teaching and learning. The purpose of this chapter is to look at the way in which the obviousness of classrooms is both put in place and maintained in place. The point of so doing is to make the non-visible sufficiently visible that teachers can learn to *see* the details of their own practices in order to begin to change them.

Prior to going to school children learn to talk, to observe, to register their own bodily experiences in particular ways. They come to certain conclusions about the way the world is. One of the early things they inevitably learn when they go to school is the apparently infinite revisability of these conclusions in the face of superior and more powerful school knowledges. They learn to see in ways deemed legitimate by people with access to those authoritative knowledges.

I vividly remember walking home from school one hot summer afternoon when I was six years old and suddenly seeing all the silvery leaves on a tree shimmer together. A moment later I felt a breeze on my face. I was filled with wonder at my discovery that wind was created by the waving of leaves. For a long time I puzzled over how all the leaves knew to move together at exactly the same moment in time, but I presumed that it was something similar to a flock of birds wheeling simultaneously in the sky. I also remember the look of puzzlement on my teacher's face when I asked her how all the leaves knew to move at the same moment. Her incomprehension clued me into the fact that I had asked an apparently non-askable question and I dropped my questioning immediately. But why was I so ready to abandon my observation, at so minute a signal from the teacher?

From the beginning of schooling, children are actively taught to defer to teacher and to textual authority (Baker and Freebody, 1989). Indeed, narrative plays a central part in establishing and maintaining dominant social relations. This chapter is devoted to teasing out some of the detail of how this is done, in particular through the subjects of reading and writing. At the same time I will look at the way in which the children are subjected to, made subjects through, this exposure to school-based knowledges. In learning to read and write children are simultaneously learning to exist inside the authority relations of the classroom and a different way of inserting themselves and being inserted into the storylines of their culture.

Teachers, like everyone else, interpret and make sense of the world through narratives, that is, through the storylines of their culture. Story is one of our predominant modes of sense making. As Richardson (1990, pp. 117-118) points out:

> Narrative displays the goals and intentions of human actors; it makes individuals, cultures, societies, and historical epochs comprehensible as wholes; it humanizes time; and it allows us to contemplate the effects of our actions, and to alter the directions of our lives . . . Narrative is both a mode of reasoning and a mode of representation. People can 'apprehend' the world narratively and people can 'tell' about the world narratively.

Thus we not only read and write stories but we also live stories. Who we take ourselves to be at any one point in time depends on the available storylines we have to make sense out of the ebb and flow of being-in-the-world along with the legitimacy and status accorded to those storylines by the others with whom we make up our lives at any one point in time.

At the beginning of 1992, Chas's daughter, Alexandra, began school. Her teacher asked the children to bring their favourite version of Cinderella to school. Her plan was to look at and discuss with the children, culturally different versions of the story, since there were Korean, Aboriginal and Malaysian and Chinese as well as Anglo-Australian children in the class. On reading one version of the story, when she came to the picture of Cinderella dressed like a bride, she said to the children, 'Oh, isn't she beautiful! Who wants to have a wedding dress like that?' Alexandra replied, 'No way!' 'Why not Alexandra?'

asked the teacher. 'I *might* get a boyfriend when I grow up but I don't want to get married!' replied Alexandra. The teacher was highly amused by this, and later told Chas to ask her what she had said about Cinderella's wedding dress.

Alex thus found that the expression of an opinion that went against the teacher's and the text's version of gender relations was something that adults would talk about and report to each other with amusement. Although she had not been told she was wrong, she had been constituted as different, as one to tell stories about. While Chas praised her for 'sticking up for her own beliefs', Alexandra discovered that what seemed obvious to her (that marriage is not necessarily a good or desirable thing) was not what her teacher thought was obvious. The teacher, without necessarily planning to do so, had imported into her lesson through the stories and her own unexamined relation to them, her ideals of romance and marriage and she had invited the female children to position themselves as ones who belonged in that storyline and who longed for a beautiful wedding dress. She did so as if this were perfectly normal, that is, not something to tell a story about. Alexandra's response, which disrupted the obviousness of the pattern of desire being made relevant for girls by the teacher, was constituted, in contrast, as something to tell a story about, something which stands out from the everyday flow of events.

When my own children first went to school, I found their willingness to accept the authority of the teachers quite startling. During the first week of school Paul came home with the story of creation. I told him it was only one story among many and that since we weren't there at the time we couldn't know for sure. I drew two comic strips for him, one telling the story of creation and the other the story of evolution. He was delighted with both stories and asked could he take them to school to show his teacher. She informed him that the creation story was the true one. He came home announcing this triumphantly. He had found someone who knew more than I did and who would give him her knowing. He told me, as I was writing this story, that he used to regard knowledge as a vast, unknowable and terrifying sea. If you put one toe in you could get sucked right in. If someone gave him definite knowledge, that was one piece of the sea he had tamed and he was highly exhilarated by that. The teacher had had no hesitation in positioning herself as the one with access to authoritative truths with which to tame his ocean (*sa mer(e)*?).

But that certainty comes at a price. Because he did not know how the teacher's knowledge was arrived at, the intimidating vastness of 'true' knowledges seemed much greater than it actually was, the task of acquiring them seeming to him to be outside the capacity of any one person. As children discover that *their* knowledges and their parents' knowledges are re-visable and that school knowledges are not, deference to the teachers' knowledges becomes almost inevitable, along with a high degree of uncertainty about independent perceptions and reasoning.

But in each of these stories, of Alex and Paul, the transmission of authoritative knowledges is visible, we can tell a story about it. The possibility of disagreement is there precisely because the transmission is made visible. More often, the transmission is of an obviousness to which no conscious attention need be paid once the point is understood. In the following reading lesson, taken from Baker and Freebody (1989, p. 164), for example, the teacher is reading to the children, giving them her interpretation of the text as the authoritative interpretation at the same time as she teaches some of the mechanics of reading and of story. In attending to the story the children are incidentally learning to perceive as obvious both the teacher's authority and the teacher's authoritative knowings:

T: (1) ALONG CAME MRS WISHY WASHY. Dear she has a funny look on her face now.
(2) JUST LOOK AT YOU SHE SCREAMED. She's definitely not very happy.
(3) But I wonder what she's going to do about it. Let's find out.
(4) Turn over the page.

In (1) the children are shown that illustrations and written text are closely related. They can find out about the 'Mrs Wishy Washy' in the words from the accompanying picture. By implication, they should *want* to know more about the person named in the text and so look for clues. The teacher will tell them what clues to look for. One kind of clue that they can look for is facial expression, particularly unusual expressions. In (2) the children are given the teacher's reading of Mrs Wishy Washy's expression as an authoritative interpretation of that expression. In (3) they are shown that part of the task of the reader is to anticipate what happens next. There is a relation between what happens here, to what happens next. But the only way to find out what happens next, is to turn the page and to see what the author has to say. Teacher and students are dependent on the author for the unfolding of the story, a story which will, moreover, occur in a particular sequence. In this excerpt we see students gaining access to the complex interleaving of teacher and textual authority. While learning how to consciously attend to the story (to find out what happens) they learn to put to one side or bracket their own perceptions in favour of what the teacher tells them. In their analysis of this excerpt Baker and Freebody point, in particular, to the imbrication of learning to read text with learning about teacher–student relations:

... we can see how the teacher assumes an interpretive posture between the story and the child, inserting comments into the reading of the story ... These insertions comprise the teacher's metacommentary, which is a feature of reading instruction throughout school life. Such metacommentary does not appear merely to parallel the text, but, at this very early point in reading instruction, to penetrate and shape the text. Thus it is a metacommentary not only on the text itself but on the social relations in which school learning from text will occur. (1989, p. 164)

In becoming competent participants in the culture of the classroom, students thus learn to regard the authority of the teacher and text as an obviousness, rather than as anything that can or should be called into question.

That stories are sequential, that to understand them you need to ask what happens next and attend to the clues in the text in order to anticipate and read the further clues on the next page, are fundamental knowledges for reading the traditional narrative form.[3] Also being taught are school-based versions of reading narrative which are useful for establishing and maintaining the authority relations of teacher over child, rather than for giving students the knowledge they need to interpret text. For example, the children are being taught that it is the author who will tell us, who is the authority, rather than that we must each bring our own knowledges to bear on the text in order to comprehend it. They are being taught that it is the author's intentions to which the teachers will give us authoritative access, rather than that these intentions are not knowable and that we can only guess at them from the clues in the text combined with our own knowledges of possible storylines and the meanings we have learned to give them. They are being taught to attend to the 'real story' that the author intended, to attend only to the text as a transparent medium for giving us access to that story. The alternative, that the text visibly draws on cultural/discursive resources through which the world can be seen and felt and understood in particular ways, and through which we are positioned and come to feel and desire in particular ways, is not made a possibility here (Foucault, 1977b).

---

[3]So obvious are the learnings here that we usually interpret them as 'natural'. Children who are read stories in this way learn to want to know what comes next. I would not have understood this if I had not worked with a boy in the course of gathering data for *Frogs and Snails* who had not learned these obviousnesses. He would randomly turn to any point in the book and start to talk about his interpretation of the picture and was not at all interested when I offered to tell him what the words said about the picture. His mother could not read English and his younger brother always pushed the pages back and forth when they sat together to 'read' a book. His mother would 'read the pictures' to him, that is, make up a story in relation to whichever page happened to fall open. Thus what was obvious to him, that you could tell whatever story you liked in relation to any picture the book happened to fall open at, was very different to the set of obviousnesses that children who have been introduced to books in the way that is happening with Mrs Wishy Washy.

Through interactions such as these, teachers give students access to the knowledges through which they will be judged as competent or incompetent and treated accordingly. Taking these knowledges on as one's own is essential for survival in the classroom and for opening up the possibility of being positioned as one who is worthy of teacher respect. Maintaining perceptions and knowledges at odds with the teacher's is to position oneself as marginal in educational terms and to risk being positioned as a failure.

In another reading lesson, also taken from Baker and Freebody (1989, p. 17), a subtle exchange of information about reading along with a positioning of teacher and student takes place. This time the student is reading the text:

1 S: 'IT LOOKS COLD OUT THERE' SAID NICK. 'I DO NOT/
2 T: Alright it *means* do not/
3 S: I *DON'T* HAVE A COAT, I CAN'T COME WITH YOU/
4 T: Good ((said quietly))

The student displays to the teacher several complex pieces of school knowledge, over and above an obvious ability to decipher text. S/he reveals (1) that s/he knows that 'don't' is an abbreviation of 'do not', and that school reading texts and formal classroom talk privilege the unabbreviated form. The teacher recognises this display of knowledge with 'alright', but draws a distinction between meaning and the written/spoken form ('it *means* do not') (2). The student quickly reveals that this distinction is understood and proceeds to read the word 'correctly' (3); correctly now having been defined as what is on the page rather than the form that has been defined as correct in classrooms. The teacher thus reveals the authority of the text along with her authoritative knowledge of how reading is done. The student is able to engage in an unflawed reading performance (3) and to receive the teacher's praise for doing so (4), by taking these knowledges as her/his own and without calling them into question. The teacher is thus positioned as one with unquestioned knowledges who can give the student access to those knowledges and who can at the same time evaluate students in terms of the extent to which they display those knowledges. In this case, the student is positively evaluated as one whose access to these knowledges and whose take up of these knowledges is good.

When any teacher asks students what they think, they rapidly discover that what is being asked is what they *should* think, even if, as in the following reading lesson (Baker and Freebody, 1989, p. 181), the teacher appears to be asking specifically what individual students think:

T: . . . What do you think is the thing about the story you like most?

S: ((whispered eagerly)) I know!

Evident in such a response on the part of the student is the knowledge that what the teacher says has to be interpreted within the framework of teachers asking students to display school knowledges. The hearing of teacher requests, invitations, suggestions and orders is always done in the *context* of the classroom, and the context is obviously critical in determining what is meant by what the teacher says. In the following transcript taken from Luke (1991, pp. 140-144) it becomes evident that the teacher's request to the students to 'help me write a story' actually means 'facilitate *my* telling of *my* story *and* in the process learn from me the obviousnesses of story writing'. In this case, the children's occasional attempts to actually contribute to the story lead to explanations on the part of the teacher that she is the author and therefore has total authority over the story. Their position as 'helpers' requires them to facilitate her display of how one must think about the writing of stories in order that they may then write their own:

1 T: Now . . . We're gonna do something now, you're gonna have to help me . . . because I'm going to write a story, and you're gonna help me write the story, and afterwards, you might go and write yourselves a story. But help me first. OK, and now, seeing we've been doing lots of stories about princesses and things like that

2 S1: What we're gonna do?

3 T: What we're gonna do today is a story about a princess

4 S2: Princess

5 S3: and a prince

6 T: Come in a bit boys over there

7 S2: And a prince

8 T: You reckon we should have a prince in it?

9 Ss: [unison] Yes

10 T: Aw I was thinking of a dragon

11 Ss: NO . . . [unison, laughter]

12 T: And a prince too?

13 Ss: [inaudible commentary]

. . .

14 T: I thought, what'll I call my story?

15 S1: Princess of the World

16 T: ((gesturing to Aboriginal girl)) Just sit down anywhere there Kay

17 S2: Ninja Turtles

18 T: No, no Ninja Turtles in my story. This is called/

19 S3: Princess of the World

20 T: The princess

21 S3: Aw

22 T: and the Dragon

23 S2: Swwssh

24 T: Now, Jake. This is my story and I can write what I like in my story, when you write your story you can put a Ninja Turtle in it if you want to because that's your very own story. You're going to help me with my story, but you're not going to write it

25 ((a 'story starter' is then collaboratively worked on))

26 T: A LONG LONG TIME AGO THERE LIVED A PRINCESS. I think I can make it a bit better than that

27 S1: A dragon too

28 T: No, no. No. What. How 'bout: when you think about a princess what do you think about?

29 S2: A prince . . .

30 T: No

31 S2: A prince

32 T: no what do you think she'd look like?

33 S3: A

34 T: With long hair? What colour?

35 S3: Yellow, black [chorus laughter]

36 T: What about long, long golden hair? A LONG LONG TIME AGO THERE LIVED A PRINCESS WITH GOLDEN HAIR. Now if she had long hair, what sort of a princess do you think she'd be? What would she look like?

37 S1: Nice

38 T: Nice. Oh yes, wonderful, that's very good

The teacher begins by reminding the children that they have been 'doing lots of stories about princesses and things like that' (1) thus tying this event to specific previous events. She announces that they are going to 'do' 'a story about a princess' (3). The children instantly display their knowledge of 'princess' as belonging in the binary pair of 'prince and princess' (4-12 and later 28-31). Presumably this was central to the previous lessons. But today the teacher appears to want something different, not to disrupt the binarism, but to further establish it by inserting information about what the princess looks like, that is, her object status within the binary pair (32). She also appears to want to rehearse the structure of story, to display the naming of story as the beginning and the need for a 'story starter'. She teaches these as linear, that is, as if authors produced the texts we read from beginning to end. She also presents story as belonging to and coming out of the mind of the author. No mention is made of the way in which images, storylines and binary thinking are cultural/discursive products which writers may use to construct familiar stories or which they can use to invert, invent and break up old storylines and thus begin to make new ones. Nor is any mention made of the way in which the traditional storyline she is constructing is implicated in the patterns of desire the children will develop (Walkerdine, 1984). Instead, associations and images are not made visible or problematic, their presence is justified in terms of what the author wants (14-24). The image they produce of the princess as having 'long golden hair', and of this feature indicating that she is 'nice' (36-38), is inserted into the telling of the story without attention to the politics of that association, despite the fact that, as Luke points out, there are many Aboriginal girls in this classroom. At least some of the Aboriginal girls in this classroom went on to write stories about nice looking princesses with long golden hair. The lesson they have learned is of the importance of appearance of the female character and the correctness of the association between long golden hair and looking good. They have also learned, by implication, that looking nice and being located in the storylines they are learning to write is not for them. While this might seem, at first glance, a good thing, their Aboriginality protecting them from being drawn uncritically into the romantic storyline, at second glance it is much more problematic. The girls want to write a story about a golden haired princess despite her description precluding the possibility of any straightforward positioning with her. Their imagination is thus caught by the images, the associations and by the patterns of desire made relevant in the romantic storyline at the same time as they are positioned as marginal to it; they are both learning authoritative knowledges and being split off from that knowledge at the same time. And they are being given neither the resources to see and name this process nor the knowledge with which to resist it.

Luke's analysis of this lesson demonstrates 'the discursive construction of the consequences of literacy, specifically the cultural logic prefigured in "doing" narrative in an early childhood writing lesson' and the way in which 'stories are a key moment in gendered regulation' (1991, p. 138).

Scott makes a plea for teachers of literature and people writing in the disciplines such as history to make visible the creation of subject positions, such as that taking place in this lesson, not, she says:

> . . . in the sense of capturing the reality of the objects seen, but of trying to understand the operations of the complex and changing discursive processes by which identities are ascribed, resisted, or embraced, and which processes themselves are unremarked and indeed achieve their effect because they are not noticed. (1991, p. 792)

Instead, the acquisition of school knowledge is a twofold process of reading signs correctly and inserting your individual self inside the scenes made possible by these correct readings. One of the additional complexities of school knowledges is that the form can differ from teacher to teacher. The following conversation (taken from Davies, 1983, pp. 63-65) took place between a teacher and his students in the first lesson on the first day of school in a sixth grade classroom. The teacher is writing on the board the things the children will need to buy. They have just discussed what a botany book is and how much it will cost:

T: OK. But get that Botany book. Ah, other things you will need, I don't like your using, well, textas aren't *too* bad, but I prefer coloured pencils, how many have textas? ((A few children put up their hands.)) Ah huh! alright then, you don't have to chuck them away, just be very careful. Textas tend to ah/

S: Smudge

T: Smudge a bit, but if you're careful they'll be alright, OK? But textas or coloured pencils ((writes 'coloured pencils' on the board)). I'll supply the ruler. If you haven't got a pencil I'll even give you a pencil, ah, today. In fact I'll give you a pencil whether you've got one or not then you can't say you didn't get a pencil. Um, I would suggest for this week, kids, that you do all your work in pencil. There is a reason for that, because if you make a mistake ( ) or something like that, then it is easy to correct. Just for this week and we'll start the biros next. ((Sarah raises hand)) Yes Sarah?

SARAH: What kind of pens do you need, like what colour pen?

T: Well, I think either blue or black, ah, I only use red here for underlining, ( ) I but never write for me in red because then it becomes confused with when I write in red, OK? So either blue or black, right? ((Terri raises hand)) Yes?

TERRI: Do you do a margin in red pen Mr X?

T: Ah good question that, that's a good question, Terri *no* not for me dear, would you do *all margins for me*, in pencil. I think that's safer, right? All margins for me, in pencil. You can do underlining, see, for example, the date, you could underline that in red, OK?

Terri receives high praise from the teacher here because she has read the scene well. She has understood his passionate commitment to form and to tidiness. The details of how things are done are not always spelled out so clearly, and each of the three students in this interaction realises that the minute details are of particular importance to this teacher. Their comments and questions are not simply information seeking but displays that they understand what is important in this classroom. For this they are rewarded by having their words taken up, by being given careful detailed answers, by being praised for the goodness of their question and by being addressed with a term of affection.

On the other side of this is the pain of getting it wrong. I remember, for example, doing sums in first grade. We had a relief teacher. I had done my sums quickly. They were easy and I felt good. While waiting for the others to finish I decided to make the answers look better by closing up the ends of the two answer lines to form a neat little box. When I took my book out to be marked, the teacher marked them all wrong. I was shocked and amazed to see the page covered in crosses. I went back to my desk to check them and they were right. Heart beating wildly, I took my book back out to the teacher and asked quietly why they were wrong. She looked at my book again and said she thought the lines I had drawn in were part of my answer and I should rub them out. I was both angry and ashamed. How could she think something so obviously stupid? Quietly I returned to my desk to rub out the lines that she claimed to have thought were 'ones'. She had the power to position me as one who does not know how to work properly. My quick correct answers were useless if I did not know the correct form to present them in. If innovations, or something of one's own were welcomed by the teacher, answers to sums in boxes was definitely not one of them.

I remember, too, a writing lesson in fourth or fifth grade. I cannot remember what we were writing. That year I had developed a passion for writing stories and filled page after page with long complex stories that were first scribbled into work books and then written out neatly into composition books. But this was a lesson on writing style. The teacher had told us that the way we wrote, the way we sat, and the way we held our pens was a very personal expression of ourselves, and she asked us to think about our bodies in relation to the desk, the book, and the pen. I tried turning my book around at a strange angle and wrote with the words running away from me from the front of the desk towards its back. This experiment filled me with pleasure. But the teacher disallowed it. It would not do. I must turn my book back to the correct 45 degree angle. I tried to argue with her, to tell her that it felt like a very personal expression. In desperation, I even lied about this being the way everyone in my family wrote. But she would not be persuaded—and so I capitulated. I turned my book round to the right angle. And I felt as if something terrible had happened. As I sat there, squeezed into the correct posture, with my fingers cramped tight around the pen, a terrible, loud, embarrassing sob came heaving and snorting out of my aching chest. I held my breath and checked my tears and forced my body not to cry, and each time I though I had it under control, another sob would come lurching out of me, hideously loud in the silence of the classroom. Eventually the teacher told me to go out to the water bubbler and wash my face and not to come back in until I had control of myself. I was terribly ashamed. I had misread the situation as one in which an idiosyncratic response was legitimate, and it turned out not to be so. My shame was connected to that misreading, my stubbornness an attempt to maintain the legitimacy of my reading of the situation. My competence was called into question, not as a writer, but as one who cannot read the obviousnesses of a classroom scene.

But there is another layer of meaning here, to do with the relation between writing and the self. To have fought so hard over something so apparently trivial, to have cried like that when self-control was so important to me, suggests something more than a misreading of the scene. An image from Woolf's holograph of *The Waves*, provided by

De Salvo (1991, pp. 250-251), gives me a further way into my remembering of this event. In this early version of *The Waves*, Woolf actually describes each child in terms of the way s/he writes, taking the way of writing to be a clear signal of the character of each child:

> They sat in rows, yawning or writing very laboriously, for already, though that might have seemed impossible, they had their minds, their characters. There was, for instance, one most solemn child. He never dipped his pen without deliberation; often hesitating half an hour perhaps. But when he wrote the letters were firm & clear. Compare him with that moody fitful little girl. She swayed at her task, as if she despaired of ever getting it done; & then suddenly made a dart & wrote something very fast; & then there was a boy who gaped at the page; & rolled in his seat & rumbled his hair. And the eel-like boy; so fastidious so agile. One after another they dipped their pens.

In my case, having chosen to be so good, to always read in careful detail what was required of me by the adults in my world, writing stories provided an important possibility of otherness to that over-determined being. I could please the teachers with my prolific production of stories while at the same time drawing together and naming some threads of my own history of being in the world, and of tapping the possibilities made available in the culture for the telling of story. Creating my own stories gave me voice, a sense of my own specificity. The physical bodily act of writing had become significantly tied to that specificity, to the person I was beginning to (re)cognise as 'myself'. It was that specificity, however experimental and fluid it may have been, that I was so loathe to let go of, to let the teacher have control of.

MORAL KNOWLEDGES

Teachers' authority does not just relate, then, to the determining of correct outer forms. It is brought to bear directly and indirectly on the being who is learning and experiencing those forms as ways of being in the world, as a being making sense of the world, as a being occupying subject positions made available in that world. Not only moral identities but the ways in which one learns to read what a moral identity is are learned in the interaction between student, teacher and text. Incidents such as those I have been describing mean that learning to read the scene from minute details becomes a childhood obsession, preventing them from admitting areas of ignorance and leading them to attempt always to achieve correct or acceptable presentations of self. The primary school children that I had spoken to in an earlier study (Davies,

1982) talked about this a lot. They had had several changes of teacher during the year and were very aware of the changing rules with each teacher. On one occasion their Headmaster, whom they admired and trusted, became very angry with them, punishing them severely for something he had never previously defined as unacceptable. The school clinic had just been turned into a music room. The children draped clinic blankets over the desks to make a cubby, put some pop music on the tape recorder and climbed in under the blankets. When Mr Bell discovered them there, his outrage knew no bounds. He stood the children up in front of school assembly, telling the assembled children that these were the kinds of people that they did not want to become. The girls were stunned and the boys were outraged. In Mr Bell's eyes they had transgressed the child-adult boundary and the taboos had to be heavily reinstated. From the boys' point of view they had been robbed of their ability to position themselves as competent students. They had been judged in terms of an unstated law and so it was Mr Bell and not they who was in the wrong:

BRONWYN: Do you think he was wrong to get mad?

GARRY: Yeah

RODDIE: He had no right to get mad at us. He could've given us a warning first, but ah no! straight to the office!

GARRY: We've had warnings before, tons of warnings

BRONWYN: About what?

GARRY: About five warnings we get in class before we go out

RODDIE: But not about going under the blankets

BRONWYN: So you're saying that normally Mr Bell warns you but this time he didn't

GARRY: No ((In agreement, i.e. no he didn't warn us))

BRONWYN: So that's a bit tough you reckon?

RODDIE: Yeah!

BRONWYN: So even if you think it's just a good fun thing to do and Mr Bell tells you that it's not allowed here, then you would agree with him and not do it?

RODDIE: Yeah! But he didn't have to blow us up first . . .

RODDIE I don't think it's wrong 'cos we wasn't doing nothin'! I was sittin' near Warwick

GARRY: Yeah, the girls were up one end and the boys up another!

BRONWYN: But just say you were doing something, would there be anything wrong with that?

GARRY AND RODDIE: Yeah

BRONWYN: Why?

RODDIE: Dunno. 'Cos you're not meant to do that at school

Roddie doesn't know *why* whatever they were alleged to have done under the blankets was unacceptable. This is never spelled out. His 'dunno' suggests he neither knows, nor particularly wants to know. The boys' anger relates to the injustice of being positioned as wrong in relation to something not defined as wrong at the time of the act. Once defined, however, they define it as law. The girls' response was quite different. In a different conversation Suzie described her bodily emotional reaction to the public humiliation: her body shook all over and she felt shock at what was happening to her. These are profoundly gendered ways of responding to the crisis brought on by Mr Bell's reaction to their action. The boys have taken up as their own a powerful discourse with which they can place Mr Bell in the wrong. Their moral identity is not in question since they can read the scene as one in which they have not broken any law. The girls cannot do this. They take on in their own bodies the shock of being positioned as bad. The powerful male principal can readily position them as powerless, as vulnerable, can locate their interest in sexuality as a badness and a wrongness located in their very persons because these are the very authority relations and storylines through which the girls have come to know themselves as beings in the world.

This event thus constitutes a violence to the girls not experienced by the boys.

BINARY KNOWLEDGES

A closely related violence experienced by both is achieving the ability to see in simplistic binarisms—to squeeze the multiplicity and variability of everyday life into the binary categories through which school learning is done. Zac, for example, having learned to think in terms of the male–female binary in which men belong outside in the public world of work and women inside, in domestic scenes, creates this division in his photographic project. His mother is represented as inside and his father as outside the house. As he arranges the photographs, he further establishes this difference by grouping the photos of his mother in the middle of the display poster, with the photos of his father outside, around the outer edges, making the outer boundary of the text he is creating. Chas's questioning reveals something quite other than this binary spatial division between his parents. When he sees this, he explains that it *would* be the way it ought to be, that is the male–female binary would be being lived out correctly, if circumstances were different. The following conversation takes up where Zac has just explained that his mother doesn't 'really' play cricket, she only 'tries':

1 ZAC: . . . she does try, she tries playing cricket or soccer or hockey and we play all them out the back garden

2 CHAS: Do you play games with your dad? Does he ever play with you?

3 ZAC: Oh he usually, he doesn't now 'cause he's always usually working but and he's getting older and but he used to muck around with soccer and play cricket. He still plays cricket, his grandfather was A-Grade and he used to play for Dungowan and everything

4 CHAS: Really?

5 ZAC: He teaches me strokes and everything

6 CHAS: Right, but he spends quite a lot of his time working and earning money to keep the house repayments up ((referring back to an earlier conversation)) and/

7 ZAC: Yeah/

8 CHAS: and that sort of stuff. And your mum stays at home does she?

9 ZAC: Yeah

10 CHAS: But she's looking for a job

11 ZAC: Oh she isn't really now

12 CHAS: Has she always stayed at home?

13 ZAC: Yep

14 CHAS: She has?

15 ZAC: Oh when we were young, about 1, 2, 3 she used, she worked at a stock station agents

16 CHAS: Mm. Notice that these shots of your dad are outside/

17 ZAC: Yeah/

18 CHAS: and these ones of your mum are inside. Is that fairly typical of the way they operate?

19 ZAC: Yep

20 CHAS: It is?

21 ZAC: Oh but mum really, usually does help outside with the garden, she does the gardening a lot

22 CHAS: Does she do the flower part of the garden or the vegetable part or/

23 ZAC: All

24 CHAS: She does all of it does she?

25 ZAC: She mows, and does things

26 CHAS: Right, so she's very capable

27 ZAC: Yep

28 CHAS: Do you get on well with your mum?

29 ZAC: Yeah

30 CHAS: Are you as close to your mum, closer to your mum or closer to your dad do you reckon?

31 ZAC: Oh (I'd be) closer to dad if he was at home more probably

32 CHAS: Would you?

33 ZAC: Yeah

34 CHAS: Why do you think that is?

35   ZAC: Oh because I like working outside on cars and that sort of thing. Not
        really sitting inside doing nothing
(KAROBRAN PUBLIC, ZAC'S INTERVIEW)

Through his talk Zac achieves a number of iterations of his
mother and himself as existing as different, opposite kinds of being and
of femininity as the abject other which he is not (35). He aligns himself
with the absent father with whom he can identify, as the one he would,
hypothetically, be close to if he were present (31). Men (and Zac) are
constituted as people who work (3, 7, 35) and women are constituted as
people who do not work (9, 11, 13), the exception taking a number of
conversational turns to elicit (turns 8 to 15). Men (and Zac) are
constituted as active in ways that matter (3, 5, 35), while women are
distinguished as the abject inactive other (19, 35), again, the exception
taking some work to elicit (turns 18 to half way through 21). In
describing the ways in which this binary is disrupted by actual practice,
he uses words to minimize his mother's work and activity: she only *tries*
to play (1), she only *helps* with the garden (21), and she didn't *really* work
in any way that matters (13). Zac establishes himself in terms of an
always-possible futurity, in which he is unquestionably male, like his
heroic grandfather and his hardworking dad, who he would be close to
if he was present. The closeness with his mother that is evident in his
talk—she plays with them in the garden at cricket, soccer and hockey,
she is the one who is there—is made unproblematic in this division
between himself and his mother, and the establishment of himself as
not-female. The male–female binary has been taken on as his own, both
as a way of telling about the world and as a way of feeling and of
positioning himself in relation to the world and of knowing his own
maleness. As well, the privileging of the abstract over lived experience,
so common an aspect of male thought, is visibly achieved. Although this
binary thinking does a violence to the detail of Zac's life, it also
privileges him in its achieving of the male as the ascendant or
foregrounded element of the male–female binary.

For girls, binary thinking is a double violence, since it obscures
the detail of their lived experience and places them in the negative half
of the binary. Girls' partial refusal of abstract thought and their
maintenance of their knowledge of their lived experience may well be
related to this in some way. But their refusal is necessarily partial and
incomplete, since the category of good girl does not include resistance.
To be accepted by adults, girls recognise the centrality of obedience and
conformity, even where this might be to their own detriment. In the
following conversation, Chas queries Jennifer's use of hegemonic values
to see/experience her own body, but Jennifer resists. These values have
been taken up as her own, and are not to be given up easily. She locates

her holding to these perceptions and feelings in her relations with her mother. She is caught between the knowledge Chas is giving her, which opens up the possibility of a different way of experiencing her own body, and the knowledge her mother gives her which does not include what she now shares with Chas. This conversation takes place around the photos Jennifer has chosen for her project:

CHAS: Now if you would just into the microphone, tell me what it is about, it 'doesn't show your legs' nonsense. You said that you chose them because none of them showed your legs/

JENNIFER: 'Cause my legs are fat

CHAS: But we've done all that work on discourses of resistance, how come you're still gonna accept that and not develop some sort of discourse of resistance to the way a girl's body should look Jenny?

JENNIFER: Because, because everyone else looks good and I look bad

CHAS: Well that's only looking bad if you're accepting the dominant discourse about what a girl should look like

JENNIFER: Mmm, that's right

CHAS: So you're gonna accept that are you?

JENNIFER: Yep. I've been taught not to fight, I 'sit down and shut up' says mum. ((Chas laughs)) That's how I've got to stay

CHAS: Nonsense Jennifer

JENNIFER: Well you go and tell my mum that

CHAS: I'm sure your mum doesn't want you to take on board a discourse that's going to make you feel bad

JENNIFER: Doubt she even knows what discourse means Chas

(EASTERN PUBLIC, JENNIFER'S INTERVIEW)

As Jones points out, when authority is conceptualised in the traditional way, it has a boundary making function which can only be disrupted by 'working to transform radically the mode of interpretation and communication, that is, the mode of authority itself' (1991, p. 109). She goes on to say that authority understood in the traditional sense:

> . . . closes down inquiry into the nature of relationships that authority stabilizes. In a very strong sense, that is precisely what traditional notions of authority are intended to do: suspend the process of judgement and decision-making as an ongoing, conflicted, and collective process, and locate it in one ultimate sovereign point. (Jones, 1991, p. 109)

THE POSSIBILITY OF MOVING BEYOND FAMILIAR KNOWLEDGES AND AUTHORITY RELATIONS

Given the detailed knowledge that students gain about how school knowledge is done, and the invisible ways in which they are given them and in which they take up these knowledges as their own, it was almost inevitable that these knowledges would be made relevant in the study group sessions. Both Chas and the children brought with them to the research a set of school-based understandings that made the work she was trying to do with them extraordinarily difficult. Since she was doing 'research' with them, they resisted anything that seemed like work, especially reading and writing. When she attempted to get them to write stories for the photos of their childhoods or of their current lives, they often constituted her as teacher, and the writing as something to be avoided if at all possible. The idea that they could learn to read the texts of the photos, and to see how the stories they bring to the interpretation of those texts create the versions of the texts they see, or that they might disrupt current perceptions and find something new, was often lost in a running battle simply to get them to commit words to paper.

The possibilities that Chas wanted to open up for the children were generally not seeable by them in the context of school as they knew it. Even though the situation with Chas was not 'school' but 'research', in which their ideas and thinking were highly valued resources, the moment she shifted from talk (which they were happy to do endlessly) to reading or writing, the situation changed. Chas positioned herself and was positioned as the authoritative teacher, though with questionable authority, given her non-teacher status and her brief time with them each week. She was thus constituted, in part, as someone to resist. Chas often felt deeply frustrated that the children were not willing or able to discover what they *could* do and think if given access to deconstructive/ reconstructive skills.

One of her strategies was to get them to keep journals in which they could reflect on the ideas they discussed each day. In the following conversation, which took place when the journals were introduced to the Eastern Public study group, it is possible to see how her use of teacher/adult talk means that she inadvertently takes control of what the children are to do in their journals, robbing them of the reflective freedom she wanted to give them:

1 CHAS: . . . You see this book here, this is a book I want you to use as your journal. Each week what we will do is we'll just write down some um just keep like a record, a personal record of what we do in our sessions. You can do pictures and whatever you like? ((She hands them out a book and a nameplate for each book that she has printed out on her Mac))

2 JAMES: Do you have a Macintosh?

3 ((discussion of computers takes place))

4 CHAS: Yeah, they are fun aren't they. Look what sort of, I've got a bit of paper here 'cause we want to just brainstorm, what sort of things do you reckon we should put in our journal? ((sticks butchers' paper up on the wall))

5 PHILO: Like um, I don't know

6 STACEY: When, instead of writing your name telling yourself all about you, you could put yourself down as this person/

7 CHAS: Yeah alright you can do that. But what sort of things do you think I want you to write about do you reckon?

8 JENNIFER: I can't remember much about what we were talking about

9 CHAS: What's happened. Yes what else?

10 CHARLOTTE: What other people think, what other people in the group have suggested

11 CHAS: Mm

12 JENNIFER: I can't remember any of it though

13 CHAS: You can remember the general topic though that we have talked about can't you?

14 JENNIFER: Yeah

15 STACEY: If boys put you down you say, 'Oh this boy and this boy'

16 CHAS: Yes good, good things like the sorts of/

17 STACEY: Comments

18 CHAS: comments and conflicts

. . .

19 ZAC: I really can't remember

20 CHAS: Oh that's all right we can talk about it you see and then you can write down. It is very easy, don't don't worry 'cause the journal is going to be lots of fun because it is your private record. What else? Like for example today I've got a headache, so I would put something like that in my journal, just something about myself, about yourself

21 JENNIFER: How you are feeling?

22 CHAS: Yeah how you are feeling. Yep that's right, your feelings. For me it would be about my health because I have a headache. I have got to take Alex to Sydney on the plane as soon as I leave here and I hate flying and I always get, I hate it, I hate getting on the aeroplane

23 JAMES: I'm going down too, I love that

24 ((discussion about trips to Sydney. Chas tells a story of her daughter and James tells a story about his brother))

25 CHAS: I would really like you to write down how we could make it more interesting, I want your general comments too

26 CHARLOTTE: How we could improve it

27 CHAS: Yeah

28 CHARLOTTE: Get the kids to say what they really think and so on

29 CHAS: And what it was like

30 CHARLOTTE: Yeah and how you felt and stuff

31 CHAS: Yeah, was it hideously boring, you know was it, would you prefer to be doing your class work

32 JAMES: No way ((laughter))

33 CHAS: How was it. You know, boring, fun, could it be improved. That is the sort of thing I want you to write. Now I detect that you are very reluctant to write. Don't you like to write Zac?

34 ZAC: No not really

35 ((discussion about another boy who didn't like writing and how Chas wrote for him to get him unstuck))

36 CHAS: Now if you want to draw I've got some textas in here, if you prefer to write with a texta and I've got some coloured pencils because I want you to draw pictures and things too if you want to decorate it

37 JAMES: You could do cartoons?

38 CHAS: Do cartoons

39 PHILO: I'd rather do cartoons than write a story or

40 CHAS: You don't have to write a story. Have you heard of people keeping a diary, it's just a/

41 PHILO: Yeah/

42 CHAS: diary, it is for your own benefit.

43 CHARLOTTE: Dear Diary, today I got up/

44 CHAS: Yeah

45 CHARLOTTE: and felt really yucky

46 CHAS: Today was the first session

47 ZAC: Dear Journal

48 CHAS: Dear Diary, speak your mind, it is up to you

49 JAMES: Dear Diary

50 PHILO: Dear Journal

51 JAMES: Today I got up and fell over

52 CHAS: Yep

53 JAMES: Then I went back to sleep

54 CHAS: Yep. Do whatever you like

55 STACEY: Today is the 25th isn't it?

56 CHAS: Yep it is the 25th

57 JAMES: So we can draw cartoons?

58 CHAS: Yep, it is your book, you can do whatever you like James ((silence))

59 JAMES: I can't do cartoons side on ( )

60 CHAS: If you want to get up and have a little stretch or something that is quite acceptable

61 JENNIFER: Is embarrassed 'im' or 'em'

62 CHARLOTTE: Em

63 JAMES: Everybody knows how to spell ((laughter))

64 CHAS: What are you doing Philo, thinking? Right, fair enough

65 JENNIFER: Thinking about what cartoons he wants to draw.

. . .

66 CHAS: Come on James what happened today? What is the session? Explain why you are writing in the book anyway, perhaps to begin. Why are you writing in the book?

67 JAMES: Because we have to

68 CHAS: ((laughs)) Because I've asked you to. But it is a wonderful thing for you 'cause I'm hoping that you'll be able to see perhaps some changes and things that are going to occur. What did we talk about, we talked about the differences and similarities between girls and boys didn't we?

69 JAMES: mm

70 CHAS: And we started off by saying that they were perfectly similar but it seems to me by the end of it we discussed quite a lot of things that were different between boys and girls

71 JAMES: Do you have to write 'Dear Diary'

72 CHAS: You write whatever you like

73 JENNIFER: I wrote 'Dear Journal'

74 CHAS: You can write/

75 PHILO: I wrote 'Dear Gremoremscis' ( ) ((joking))

76 CHAS: I will not read it unless I get your permission at the end of the project. I will not read it, it is personal/

77 JAMES: Dear Mother do not read this book ((laughter)). Dear Mum don't read this. You write that on the first page and then you go to the middle or something like that. And then you start writing
    (EASTERN PUBLIC)

Chas begins by handing the children the books she has brought them to use as journals. The boys make their knowledge of computers relevant, presumably in relation to the nameplates (2). Chas goes along with this digression (3) and then she draws the conversation back to the journals, suggesting a collective exercise, including them in as ones who share her desire to brainstorm what they will put in 'our' journal (4). Philo doesn't know (5) but Stacey comes up with an idea not unlike Haug's collective biography writing, where the experience of becoming gendered is told in third person stories (Haug, 1987) (6). Chas accepts this offering, but then slips into teacher talk, revealing that the exercise is actually one in which the children have to discover what she wants. The original 'What do you reckon we should put in our journal' (4) is now overlaid with 'But what sort of things do you think I want you to write about do you reckon?' (7). It is now her brain that is to be 'stormed', not theirs. Given what children know about school knowledge there is now probably little that Chas could say to retrieve this as the sort of situation she wants. The children define it as a remembering exercise (8), Chas confirms this (9, 13, 20) and suggestions are offered up along these lines (10, 15, 17), with the children noting along the way that 'remembering' is a problem (12, 19).

In turning their reflexive gaze back on their talk, Chas wanted them to ask themselves what they now understood and to use writing to express this. The children understood this instead as 'what are we supposed to have understood—what am I supposed to remember?'. Chas tries to retrieve the situation, seeing their concern about remembering. She tells them it is fun, it is personal and private and introduces personal 'feelings' as relevant (20). This leads to an exchange of stories (21) and then Chas adds to the list of things the journal might include: an assessment of the study group sessions. This is an attempt to give authority back to the children, to constitute them as knowers, as people with the right to critically reflect on her activities. Charlotte rapidly picks up on this, hearing it as an invitation to say what they 'really' think (28). Chas then focuses on Zac's reluctance to write, asking if he would rather be doing 'class work' (33-35). This is laughingly rejected, but there is no enthusiasm for this 'non class work' project which has become remarkably like class work. The possibility of drawing rather than writing is raised, as opposed to story writing (39). Chas distinguishes between story writing and the genre of diaries, negating once again the possibility that Stacey had raised at the beginning (40). The children then play with the task, now defining it as the traditional form of diary writing and therefore a superficial and somewhat pointless class exercise (43-52). The date is followed by Dear Diary (with variations on that theme) and questions are raised about correct spelling. But James doesn't commence. He sees it as a situation in which there are a set of rules that he has not yet figured out (65-71). The others help him with their beginnings (72-74). Chas tells him his focus is wrong, he shouldn't be worrying about the form since it is both exciting and personal. James plays around with the idea that they can have something personal and private, knowing how difficult that is for children to achieve (76) given the rights adults have to scrutinise and evaluate what children are doing.

Looking into the children's journals, then, to see just what they did write down, the same pattern is repeated. At the end of a discussion on positioning within story, for example, the children, more often than not, wrote about the legitimate authority of texts and how they must learn to position themselves correctly as male or female. They struggle in their writing to articulate, in abstract terms, the concept of positioning. They use the war-like metaphor of taking sides, appropriate to the battle of the sexes as they understand it. At the same time they position themselves as good students, as able to learn directly from the stories how to correctly place themselves inside the male–female binary:

Today we learnt about consaquenses. Story's tell us what we can be or do and you can take sides, positioning ourselfes, like as if you take Snow White's positioning you are nice, kind, pretty, and have lots and lots of friends like the seven dwarfes. but if you position your self as the evil queen you are ugly and selfish and might not have a lot of friends.

Yes I think that it is true.

Aleisha

Stories tell us about taking sides and having a good live. Taking sides makes us to have a good live and be brave, nice, good, happy.

Books do help us to have a good live and they give us a message.

Ken

When you possion [position] you take a side as one of the characters in the story and story's can teach us to be kind and loving and brave how to behave. we try to be like the character. I agree stories give us guidance for when we grow up.

Rosie

Today we was talking about books what they teach you and do. Books teach us about leading our life and stuff.

And they make you want to position yourself with a character like if their beautiful and have lots of friends. They make you want to be like them.

I do think that they make you want to be like they are when we grow up.

Carolyn

Anna was one of the few who did not take as read the authority of the text. She appears to resist the implications of positioning within story for herself. Her brief journal entry does not indicate that she understood Chas to be encouraging such resistance. Rather it would seem she had read Chas as teaching text as legitimate and herself as resisting this:

Posisionly [positioning] means when you read you take a side. I don't agree.

Yet Chas's intention was to introduce the concept of positioning in relation to story in order for the children to see how they are drawn into stories, how different readings are possible depending on the position the story is read from. She talked with them about the way in which desire can be constructed in limiting and destructive ways through the positioning of self within gendered storylines. It is significant that the understanding that sometimes appeared in their talk, disappeared in their writing. The formal task as they understood it made the questioning of textual authority too outlandish, not even thinkable, certainly not writable, at least not yet, by these children, in this school context.

Writing is experienced here as a rather painful display of oneself as having listened to one's lessons and understood the messages about being the right kind of person. The fluency of talk is lost, partly due to the technical difficulties to be overcome in the task of writing, but also as a result of the definition of the task. A story that Anna wrote on computer is infinitely more fluent, for example, than her blunt brief journal entry. The story, in contrast to the journal, she defined as an opportunity to tell something of her own and with the aid of the computer the technical problems of writing were removed. I will return to Anna's story in the final chapter.

School knowledge can take us over, both as students and as teachers. It becomes an obviousness that can undermine what we set out to do. The work with the study groups was an attempt to disrupt some of those obviousnesses. The purpose of that disruption was to enable the children to see the relation between themselves and text differently. Instead of being informed by an authoritative text, or of deciding whether or not they like a text, or whether or not the text is 'realistic' (bears any relation to the world as they understand it), critical/ deconstructive writing, as I am conceptualising it here, enables children to see the text as shaping them and shaping worlds in ways that have previously been invisible to them. According to Luke:

> . . . this requires a reworking of: (1) the very games of talk around text with an eye to making explicit the possibilities of what can be done, said and meant with texts; and (2) a critical exploration of elasticity and difference of texts, genres and discourses at the earliest stages of literacy training. (1991, p. 150)

It involves finding a way to make the shaping process visible, to 'catch the text in the act' of shaping. This requires a complex cognitive shift away from an apprehension of the text as transparently revealing a real world, to a simultaneous apprehension of:

- the world evoked by the text;
- one's own subjective response to the text;
- and at the same time an evaluation of the discursive effects of that relation between oneself and the text.

In effect, teacher and students both need to immerse themselves in text and distance themselves from that text at the same time.

And in classrooms, there is a further layer of complexity to be attended to. The obviousness of the teacher's authority must be undone such that it does not intrude on the students' ability to track their own involvement in the text, such that the deferral to teacher authority does not interrupt the immediacy of involvement in the text. The teacher must therefore achieve an extraordinary balancing act between being one who does have a wealth of information and ideas to pass on to the students (including the idea of learning to interact with text differently) and creating a situation in which that greater store of knowledge does not interfere with, or interrupt the students' immediate involvement in, the text. To do this we need to find a way of constituting authority not as an end to discussion but as a way of providing multiple voices whose speaking can begin the conversation. As Jones says: 'We can think of authority not as border-patrolling, boundary-engendering, but as meaning-giving; and as with all gift giving, we should prepare ourselves for the disappointment of possible refusal' (1991, p. 123).

In the chapters that follow, I explore the students' work with Chas in which they explore the possibilities of becoming critically literate, of catching texts in the act of shaping them. At the same time, what the next three chapters make painfully clear is that the oppositional and hierarchical gender order is constituted in violent ways, and in patterns of relentless reiterations of male dominance—over girls and over weaker boys.

4 A Vision of Femininity?

There are puddles on the sidewalk. We stop and look into one. The wind has died and we see ourselves by moonlight, enraptured by our smiling faces, made very self-conscious by all this talk of consciousness of self. A breath of air and the reflection breaks up.

(Myerhoff and Metzger, 1980, p. 101)

I WAS TEN and John was seven. I loved him dearly, this little brother of mine, but now we were fighting over the toaster, each trying to cook our breakfast toast in order to get ourselves to school on time. As the fight escalated he punched me in the stomach. I angrily told him that our father had only recently forbidden this, though why it was forbidden was a total mystery to me. He punched me again in the stomach and I threatened to tell. And he punched me again. I marched off to our parents bed-sitting room, terrified at what I had said I would do. Knocking on their door was not something my father encouraged. Adults should not be disturbed by children. I knocked on the door. My father appeared and I told my tale with some trepidation. He walked, in his tight controlled way, to the kitchen and asked John to confirm my story. Then he hit him on the side of his head so hard that his feet actually lifted off the ground and he crashed onto the floor on the other side of the kitchen. 'Get up!' he shouted. Then he hit him on the other side of the head and he flew across the room again. I had never seen my father lose control, nor hit any of us before. I watched with horror, not knowing how many times it happened, my eyes glued with amazement at John's feet as they left the floor each time.

67

When I first wrote this story in a collective biography workshop I was fascinated by the contradiction between the storyline in which I was being constituted as fragile, as someone whose stomach was too vulnerable to be hit, and the explosive power of my tale-telling that could apparently unleash such a rage in my father, that my little brother, favourite of everyone in the household, could be abused in this way (Davies and Harré, 1992). What interests me now is the fluidity and lack of fixity in what is experienced as power and powerlessness. Though the story, at first, seemed to capture perfectly the moment in which I came to know and embody female powerlessness and fragility, it also made a powerful connection between female fragility and female power, not unlike the connections between self-negation and power that emerged in my stories in Chapter 2. Once again it was my father's words that carried such power. From the perspective of the children, he had uttered what emerged as a sacred rule, something that if broken would lead to a savage retribution. From his point of view, knowing as I do now that he regarded outbursts of uncontrolled anger as signalling lack of character (character being a term he used to define people of the ruling class) the event was one in which he had profoundly failed, revealing his own lack of character. While, in theory, this might have been a moment in which John took up as his own the knowledge of adult male power that he one day would have, it was more likely a critical moment of alienation from male power. He did not like or want the embodiment of masculinity that he perceived in either our father or in Tony. Nor did he see me as fragile, or powerless. The recently declared taboo on punching girls' stomachs probably provided him with what he hoped was powerful knowledge of where my 'Achilles heel' might lie, giving him some chance of winning a fight against me. He has little detailed memory though of that awful event. One thing he does remember is having a series of dreams not long after that time, in which I had male as well as female genitals. We slept in rooms joined by a window, and he would lie in bed, looking past the window into the mirror on the wall opposite the window, trying to catch a glimpse of my naked reflection to make sure it was truly a dream. Thus while beginning to reject for himself the male forms of power that he saw around him, he nevertheless understood male genitals to be associated with power and imagined that my power may have been embodied in that way.

In what ways are we fixed in the female/feminine or the male/masculine and in what ways is our subjectivity fluid and the categories something that we can move in and out of? When does the body dictate meanings and when does it take its shape in response to meanings? The context in which any interaction occurs, the relations that are being played out, intersect with aspects of class and race and gender in ways that make these concepts extraordinarily difficult to pin down. What is evident in reading through the transcripts of the conversations with the various primary school children we worked with, is the ease with which they move in and out of different ways of being, not yet having been pinned down to the narrowness of a unitary or 'complete' self to the extent that adults (adult by virtue of their capacity to be rational and non-contradictory) have learned to be—or at least to believe they should be. At the same time, they are making specific connections, making conscious and unconscious investments of themselves in particular storylines, subject positions and readings of the social world. Such investments may be conscious where they involve 'choice' or active resistance. They may also be made outside of conscious awareness, being part of the obviousness that is not questioned. These investments necessarily shape their subjectivity in ways they are not aware of.

Historically, there appear to be two models through which the categories female/femininity and male/masculinity have been understood. According to Laqueur (1990) the earlier model is the one sex model, where male and female were understood to be essentially the same:

> The notion, so powerful after the eighteenth century, that there was something specific and concrete inside, outside and throughout the body that defined male as opposed to female, and provided the foundation for the attraction of opposites, was absent in the Renaissance ...
>
> To be a man or a woman was to hold a social rank, a place in society, to assume a cultural role, not to be organically one or the other of two incommensurable sexes. Sex before the seventeenth century, in other words, was still a sociological and not an ontological category. (Laqueur, 1990, pp. 133 and 138)

In this earlier model the hierarchy between males and females was not achieved, as it currently is, through an assumption of natural or bodily difference. The interiority of women's genitals (which in all other respects were seen as the same as male genitals) was defined as inferior to the male exteriority. But that physiological difference was seen as mutable: women could become men and men could become 'effeminate' if they spent too much time in the company of women. Physical difference did not therefore provide the central justificatory rhetoric for male superiority. In the one sex model the hierarchy between men and women was based on gender rather than sex. Whereas sex was mutable, gender was seen as fixed, as tied to the cosmic and moral order. Punishments for transgression were extreme, not because people were being 'unnatural', but because they were disrupting the divine, moral order on which civilisation was based.

During the eighteenth-century Enlightenment, however, rationality as a property of *individuals* rather than of God became the source of morality and order. Women's inferior positioning could no longer be based on an externally dictated order. And so the two sex model was created. Biologists, for the first time, began to look for a more detailed set of differences and to define women in terms of their 'natural' oppositeness (and inferiority) to men. Knowledge of sameness was discarded. The knowledge that men could lactate, for example, a knowledge evident in Aristotle's writing, has become startling and almost unbelievable to people who have learned to know maleness and femaleness, and to become male and female, through the two sex model (Laqueur, 1990). The recent research of the feminist biologists has begun to recover some of these discarded knowledges and to undo some of the erroneous research based on the two sex model (Bleier, 1984; Sayers, 1986). The metaphysical nature of the so-called sex differences, the idea of opposite sexes was made unquestionable, not through proving it so, but by making the difference the unexamined conceptual base of the research. Apparently obvious differences thus came to be lodged in the body.

The two sex model has led us to embody ourselves as male and female in a more fixed way than when we understood ourselves in terms of the one sex model. Prior to the Enlightenment there were many more reports of fluid movement between maleness and femaleness: while such movement might be regarded as immoral and punishable, it was not *unthinkable* as it became in the two sex model. Now, when people have sex changes to acquire the 'opposite' set of genitals, governments still refuse to change their passports, believing that their true sex is still somehow *in* their bodies. At the same time, the more and more sophisticated and controversial tests being undertaken in attempting to resolve disputes over the sex of individual competitors in the Olympics, for example, reveal that the simplicity and apparent naturalness of the two sex model can no longer be sustained (Laqueur, 1990).

There are elements of both the one sex and the two sex model in the children's talk. Sameness and difference appear in their talk, are connected in turn to biology and to the larger social and moral order. In either model female inferiority is achieved, in part through the unquestioned assumptions in both models, in part through observations of social rules and structures that discriminate against women, and in part through the boys' positioning of the girls as inferior, as objects of sexual talk and speculation, and as beings with no right of access to male/heroic storylines. This is not to say that both the boys and the girls do not have access to more liberating discourses, nor even that they do not have some considerable commitment to them.

A good example of movement between liberating and oppressive discourses is seen in Mal, an Aboriginal boy at Karobran Public. He is a good looking, charismatic boy, admired and well liked by other boys. The two non-Aboriginal boys in the study group at Karobran were keen to gain his attention and approval. When he talked to Chas about the photos that he had taken of his family and friends, he revealed a world in which Aboriginal women and girls have power which he is very happy to accept. He makes an easy connection between the feminist poststructuralist discourse that Chas has been giving them access to, and the way gender is done in his family and at school. He sees the sharing of power between males and females in terms of an essential sameness between them. He begins with a photo of boys playing basketball with the two Aboriginal girls from the study group, Aleisha and Carolyn:

MAL: The first photo is about boys playing basketball which most people thinks that basketball is a girls' game. Um, I play basketball on the weekends with these girls from my school, Aleisha and Carolyn

CHAS: Do you play on the same team as them?

MAL: Yeah . . . I like playing, I like playing a good game and letting and not taking everything yourself. And giving the girls a go, fair go. Like girls can do, they can do whatever they want. Like they could be just as good as boys . . . We had lunch with the girls today 'cause we had basketball after it. And it helps you know that um somebody is actually good at something . . . At school um we, we play all kinds of sports like touch footie, soccer and basketball and everybody gets a fair go at everything and you usually see um people um people playing like girls playing sports which aren't the type that, people don't think its their type . . . And um when we, when I was on my holidays in Sydney there were all these kids and um we thought they were all boys, me and Jason my friend, and um it turned out that there were three girls in the group that we saw. We thought they were boys 'cause they, 'cause they were doing everything that the boys were doing, like, and sometimes at some things they were even *better*. Um, girls um like in the Olympics, can't run as fast as what the men are but um they're still, I think still training as hard as the men and even *harder* . . .

MAL: I like all my cousins and my relations. And none of them be what they should . . . Like the, they don't follow the discourse like boys and girls should be. They sort of resist it . . . My cousin Nel's a boy

CHAS: What's his name?

MAL: Nel and most people think it's a . . . girl's name

CHAS: What does he do when people tease him about it?

MAL: Oh he just leaves them alone. And he, him and Jimmy they're brothers and they, like Jim likes to, they, Jim likes to do handstands and gymnastics and all that and Nel likes to play hockey and basketball and things like that and doesn't play soccer and football. And Terri my sister, she likes playing touch footie, soccer and also likes rough games. And she's a pretty fast runner. And she, she is a good person. And sometimes me and her have fights, but now we don't have many

(KAROBRAN PUBLIC, MAL'S INTERVIEW)

Mal speaks warmly of his family and friends who disrupt the gender order. Not only are there girls who can be 'just as good' as boys and sometimes 'even better', but there are boys who prefer girls' things and girls who prefer boys' things who are 'good' people. And people who disrupt the gender order by not revealing their sex are a source of surprise but not of disapproval.

But in many of the conversations in the study group Mal positions himself quite differently. He becomes a dominant male, initiating a great deal of talk that undermines the legitimacy of the girls' claims to agentic positionings. What Mal talks *about* in this reflective conversation is a vision of femininity in a world where hierarchy and difference is barely relevant. What he *achieves in his talk* in the study group, when his focus is on his position and status within that group, is unequivocal difference from and dominance over the non-Aboriginal girls. In doing this he achieves sameness with the non-Aboriginal boys and some considerable heroism in their eyes. In contrast to the cooperative, reflective conversation with Chas above, he often uses the study group as a time to display the resistance to adult control that is so fundamental to masculinity. Crawford et al. make this point when discussing the different emotions that male and female children experience when they transgress adult rules. Young men telling stories of their childhood reveal how:

> . . . their transgressions were construed as tests of daring, always with an audience of peers. The transgression was experienced with a sense of excitement, fun, glee. The punishment was 'worth it'. Transgressing adult rules (often the rules of adult women) appeared to be necessary for the construction of masculine identity, particularly when this was in solidarity with other boys. The same pattern appeared in an exaggerated form in some of the young men's danger memories. There was a moral imperative to court danger, to test bravery. (Crawford et al., 1992, p. 187)

Mal's positioning of himself in the following discussions is one that is simultaneously informed by his race, gender and child status. He achieves heroic status by resisting adult authority. He does this in front of and for the boys at the expense of the girls and Chas.[1] At the same time he never specifically attacks the Aboriginal girls, thus partially maintaining the respect for women and girls that he talks about in the conversation alone with Chas.

---

[1]Mal's verbal attacks on the girls upset some readers of this book. They believed I should not have subjected the girls to this abuse. Moreover, I should have made my disapproval of it more visible. It is true that in the pages that follow, much that Mal and the other boys say is offensive. My purpose in displaying it is to work towards an understanding of masculinity in such a way that, as educators, we can begin to see how it might be transformed. Disapproval is not the key to transformation since, as pointed out earlier, disapproval merely confirms for boys that they are successfully attaining their (male) personhood.

Anna's position too, is of particular interest in the conversations that follow. She is much more outspoken and insistent in positioning herself as a boy than is Rosie. She says she has wanted to be a boy since she was about two. She has refused to wear dresses since then. When she is forced to wear them as part of the school uniform, she wears shorts underneath. She plays boys' sports and often sits and talks like a boy. In this discussion between Chas and the Karobran Public study group, they are talking about a film they have recently seen about a heroic woman who sails her ship single-handedly. The discussion very rapidly falls into an argument between Rosie, Carolyn and Chas on the one side, who obviously think women can be heroic, and the boys and Anna on the other who think it cannot be true.

1 CHAS: I really thought she was wonderful in that [film]/

2 CAROLYN: So did I

3 ROSIE: Yeah

4 CHAS: the way she sailed the ship back again and to rescue him/

5 ANNA: That would have been false then . . . because, surely, how old was this person?

6 CHAS: She was a grown woman and she/

7 ANNA: I don't reckon she would have sailed it back by herself/

8 ROSIE: She had to, her husband was missing

9 CHAS: ((to Anna)) Why? What about that girl Cottee that sailed her yacht around the world by herself?

10 BRIAN: No um Chas

11 MAL: No

12 KEN: No, I heard that/ . . .

13 BRIAN: I heard that she picked up someone from a/

14 MAL: Yeah she she picked up a lad from, as soon as she, see she told her boyfriend to swim out and to duck under water and she'd throw a hook down and tap him on the head then he'd come up and then he could sail around the world

15 BRIAN: Probably rammed him on the head

16 CHAS: Oh you're j/- this is that Cottee woman you're talking about?/

17 MAL: Yep

18 CHAS: So you reckon she had someone to help her/

19 BRIAN: Yeah I reckon she had someone to help her

20 CHAS: Why do you think that? Don't you think she could/

21 KEN: Girls are hopeless

22 MAL: Girls are hopeless man

23 CAROLYN: Men just can't do everything, women have got/

24 MAL: They're hopeless

25 CAROLYN: women have got things that they can do

26 ROSIE: Women have got more ability than men

27 BRIAN: How?

28 ANNA: How?

29 CAROLYN: They can have babies

30 BRIAN: So? ((sniggers))

31 ANNA: They are about the same/

32 ROSIE: Women can do a lot more things than men/

33 KEN: Have a baby!

34 ROSIE: They can do almost anything a man can do and they can also do other things that boys can't do

35 ANNA: Men can do a lot of things that women/

36 BRIAN: How come you are sticking up for boys now?

37 ANNA: But I m just saying, men can do a lot of things/

38 BRIAN: ((To Mal)) How come you are pointing at me for?

39 ANNA: and women/

40 MAL: You're her ((Rosie's)) boyfriend

41 ROSIE: ((To Anna)) Name three, name three

42 ANNA: and they can also, and they can also like they can play sports/

43 CAROLYN: Women can play sports

44 ROSIE: So can women

45 KEN: I didn't know, I didn't know a woman could play footie

46 ANNA: And also

47 ROSIE: They can!

48 KEN: They can't

49 ANNA: We can do more things than me[n], we can do different things than men, and/

50 MAL: ((Whispers something to Ken))

51 ANNA: men can do different things to us, that we can't do

52 KEN: Can you play gridiron?

53 ANNA: So its really very even

54 ROSIE: Yeah

55 CHAS: Why do you think that that woman Cottee couldn't sail around the world by herself

56 MAL: Because she's hopeless

57 ANNA: I don't reckon she would have been feeling safe enough
    (KAROBRAN PUBLIC)

In arguing for the validity of the heroic storyline for women, Chas calls on evidence that women can be heroic from a recent news report of a woman who had just sailed single-handed around the world (9). This is dismissed by Anna (5–7) and the boys (10–22). It appears that there already exists a well-known counter story to discredit it (13–15). Rosie and Carolyn argue that while women may not be able to do some of the things that men can do, there are many things women can do that men can't do (23, 25, 26, 32, 34). They give as an example women's ability to have babies (29). In reply this ability is sniggered at (30), girls are repeatedly declared hopeless (15, 21, 22, 24, 56). 'Girls are hopeless man,' Mal says, using the style of black American men he has seen on TV, achieving himself as adult, stylish and black. As well he draws attention to Rosie's sexual status (38, 40), something he sometimes does when the study group meets and which makes Rosie feel really sick. A strong statement is made by Anna and the boys that women cannot do what men can do (37, 42, 45, 51, 52). In particular, the claim is made that women cannot play male sports. It is not clear what is meant by 'can' and 'cannot' here. Is it cannot because they are physically unable, as in the two sex model? Or is it cannot because the rules preclude it as in the one sex model?

The conversation begins with talk about adult *women*. The boys' attack is on *girls* (21, 22, 40). For the remainder of the conversation the terms 'women' and 'men' are used except when Brian asks Anna 'How come you're sticking up for boys now?' Clearly in this conversation the children are not excluding themselves from these adult categories. In (49) and (51) for example, Anna uses 'we' and 'us' in her elaboration of what women can do. So although the girls can and do play boys' sports, the fact that women are excluded from them in the adult games is not just a problem for the future but something that impacts on their idea of who they are now. The rules of adult sport will exclude them. Their sameness now is eroded and undermined by that social fact. *The boys can use that knowledge of social structure to gain ascendancy over the girls and to dismiss the everyday evidence of their competence.* The bodily inscription of femaleness is thus intricately connected to social structure. While Anna is visibly competent in masculine terms, she knows there are things that women (she) cannot do. 'They are about the same. Men can do a lot of things that women [can't], and they can also like they can play sports, and also we can do more things than me[n], we can do different things than men, and men can do different things to us, that we can't do. So it's really very even'. Yet while she comforts herself with the claim that women can do things that men can't do, she prefers maleness/masculinity. And she knows at the same time that she is unsafe, that as female she is precluded from male forms of heroism because women are not safe, alone, out on the high seas (57).

In the following discussion with this same group, Chas had just explained, following a deconstructive reading of *Snow White*, how girls may come to see their victim status, not only as inevitable, but even as desirable. The girls are very interested to explore this idea and its effect on relations of power in the political and social world. The boys cannot resist playing with and enjoying their ascendant male positioning, displaying their capacity to keep girls in their subordinate positions. This is not something the boys invent for themselves in their conversations, but a reiteration and display of the oppositional, hierarchical gender order that they are also attempting to make visible and deconstruct:

CHAS: Can you understand how we might think that you fellows?

MAL: Yep

CHAS: And how you might think that it's a good thing for a girl to be a victim, that it's a sort of normal, natural, desirable thing for them to be?

MAL: Well sometimes it might be a bit stupid but, 'cause they might not get saved

CHAS: So it's only worthwhile being a victim if you're going to get saved?

MAL: Yeah

EN: Yeah

ROSIE: Like Chas in real life women are mainly victims/

MAL: Oh oh I've seen heaps of people

CHAS: Can you let Rosie please

ROSIE: They really are like real victims most of the time because they're victims of rape, they're victims of murder/

MAL: ((whispers)) That's all they are good for

ROSIE: and they're victims of most of the um/

KEN: So are children

. . .

ROSIE: That's why there's only been male prime ministers. 'Cause women think they don't have power

KEN: They don't

BRIAN: Prime Minister, what would they know for them in power?

ROSIE: And men think that women . . . aren't good enough or as good as them to be prime minister and things like that and um they think they should do all the dirty work like just sit down and write everything out/

BRIAN: They don't

ROSIE: They do, most of, if um if you, as working as a secretary there's mainly only women doing that because they do all the writing and the men go round bossing them around/

BRIAN: Do this do that!

CHAS: Could you see how we've perhaps learnt to be like that? Women might have learnt to be like that?

ROSIE: And um my mum's friend um her husband acts like the boss of the house and he's more like her father than her husband because he made this gigantic mess in the kitchen and said 'well you could come and help me clean it up' and she didn't even make it. And he's acting as if he's boss and let her do all the work
(KAROBRAN PUBLIC)

Ken and Rosie both draw parallels between male-female relations and adult-child relations, Ken pointing out that children are victims too, and Rosie describing a husband who treats his wife as if he were her father. They thus make an important connection between victim status and women's lack of access to the forms of agency integral to adulthood.

DESIRING FEMININITY

Some girls have access to a radical feminist discourse that celebrates femininity. They produce this in response to the boys' dismissal of them. As Rosie says in the conversation about the film of the heroic woman, 'Women have got more ability than men' and 'Women can do a lot more things than men' (26, 32). The Eastern Public girls, in particular, waste no time telling the boys to shut up whenever they judge that they don't know what they are talking about. In a discussion on body language, the Eastern Public girls reveal, however, that the celebration of femininity is not just a discourse they can slip in and out of when the situation requires, but necessary for their insertion of themselves into the binary gender order as not-male. In their conversation they talk about the possibility of holding their body in male ways and how they cannot imagine that they could want to do that. They claim that being female entails *wanting* to be so, not just in the way they dress, but in the visible embodiment of that femaleness. To be successfully female, then, is not just a matter of outward appearances, but of inner being, of not only organising one's body as female and not male, but also wanting or desiring it to be that way. It is thus achieved and experienced as ontological, as belonging to, coming from and signifying one's essential self. Its discursive, cultural source becomes invisible. The two sex model is thus achieved and experienced as coming from within rather than imposed from without:

1 CHAS: Now let's get on to body language because body language is really interesting. How one sits can be defined as masculine or feminine. Now if I came and I sat like this, ((legs apart in a masculine, assertive posture)) you know, would that look unusual?
2 ZAC: Yeah
3 STACEY: Yes
4 JAMES: Yes
5 JENNIFER: You'd look, it would look unusual
6 ZAC: It would probably look a bit sloppy
7 JENNIFER: Yeah it would look untidy and that for a girl to be seen like that
8 CHAS: Do you think that it is wrong for a girl to be sitting like that
9 JENNIFER: Nnno
10 STACEY: Well a girl *can* sit like, they probably, most girls probably wouldn't want to
11 CHAS: Why wouldn't they want to?
12 STACEY: I mean 'cause you see boys doing that, I won't say tomboys who want to be like boys
13 PHILO: You'd feel like a boy

14 STACEY: You'd you'd feel, if you wanted to be a girl and you sat like this and you feel really drippy, and you'd feel, I don't know how to explain it

15 CHAS: Wouldn't you want to feel like a boy?

16 STACEY: If you were a girl and really, and you liked being girl, you really would/

17 JENNIFER: You'd want to show that you were girl with body language

18 STACEY: Yeah

19 CHARLOTTE: Without just looking like a girl

20 STACEY: A boy would want to show that he was a boy by sitting like this, by being all drippy 'cause that's the thing that boys have grown into but a girl has to sit up straight and be um polite/

21 JENNIFER: Like all prim

22 STACEY: and not sit like really drippy, but like she's listening and things like that

23 JENNIFER: Guys just hang around the other guys

(EASTERN PUBLIC)

From the point of view of these girls, they *do* have the freedom to be like a boy (9, 10). That is, their not sitting like a boy is not experienced as an external imposition. If they are a girl and like it, they want their bodies to *be* girls' bodies (10, 12, 14, 16, 17) not just to look like girls' bodies (19). Being correctly sexed/gendered, as Laqueur points out, in the two sex model, is an ontological experience. Because male and female are understood as opposite, the embodiment of femaleness must be explicitly not-male. That is, not sloppy, untidy, drippy or generally hanging around. They must be more contained, polite, prim, upright and attentive. The difference to which they draw attention in sitting posture has some similarities to Wex's (1979) observations of women's legs together signalling correct femininity (while signalling weakness in men) and men's legs apart signalling correct masculinity (while signalling sexual accessibility in women). However, these girls constitute their feminine embodiment as simply desirable, rather than as a response to the perceived danger of being constituted as sexually loose. It is thus something which they understand themselves to be 'choosing' rather than something imposed on them. They 'choose' their posture to signal their mode of being with others: they are polite and they listen.

Crawford et al. make a further relevant point in relation to both of these conversations. They claim that both girls and boys strive towards competence and mastery which give them freedom to 'be themselves': 'This was a strong theme in both boys' and girls' memories, though the type of mastery differed. For the boys it entailed a control over the material world, for girls a control of self, of the body' (Crawford et al., 1992, p. 186).

Femaleness and goodness, defined in relational terms, are intricately interwoven with each other. As Crawford et al. point out, girls' sense of agency relates to an understanding of the way the social world works and to their competence in its terms (see also Gilligan, 1982). The Karobran Public study group produced the following list of what adults would think of as a good child:

CHAS: Now let's look at another discourse. The discourse of the good child . . . What sort of appearance should a good child have?

KEN: Neat appearance

BRIAN: Good gentle

ANNA: Caring

ROSIE: Clean

KEN: Brave

BRIAN: Not like you

ANNA: Not a pain like not go up and punch kids and all that. Should be sort of like me . . .

ROSIE: They shouldn't fight with their brothers and sisters

MAL: They shouldn't fight at all

(KAROBRAN PUBLIC)

Although they do not directly point to the fact that this is predominantly a list of feminine characteristics (with the exception of "brave", Mal's statement at the end signals some distance from the category of good child. It is interesting to note that Anna, the tomboy, defines herself as closely fitting this list of characteristics. So while she strongly desires many features of maleness, her subjectivity is not incompatible with (female) goodness.

THE RELEVANCE OF IMAGINED FUTURES

The girls' sureness about themselves and their preference for their own way of being carries over into their projections of themselves into future storylines. The two features that are seen to disrupt their certainty are romantic love and care for babies, both of which they understand as 'natural' and therefore to some extent unavoidable:

CHAS: What about you Jen? You want to be/

JENNIFER: I want to be independent

CHAS: Do you want to have a partner when you grow up?

JENNIFER: I'd like to be independent 'till I go head over heels

JAMES: Go head over heels in love

CHAS: Do you think that you will? Does everybody expect that they might fall head over heels in love?

JENNIFER: Yep

STACEY: Mm

JENNIFER: It's a natural part of life

JAMES: It's part of getting married . . .

JENNIFER: I don't want to rely on my husband or things like that . . . like divorces and everything you see you never know if there's going to be a divorce

ZAC: That's why women are getting out now 'cause the men are always doing the work and getting the money for it

JENNIFER: Yeah, that's why some people aren't marrying because some are useless if you go through all the bank accounts are in joint names and everything and then you get, have the divorce and who gets what

(EASTERN PUBLIC)

One of the solutions the children see to the dilemmas they perceive adults experiencing is to wait until they are older and wiser before they make decisions. Adulthood is seen by the girls as a time when people are less likely to make mistakes. Undermining this view is the view put forward by James that age and wisdom for women is accompanied by ugliness, implying that they cannot in fact wait until they are wise because they will no longer be able to be positioned as desirable within the romantic storyline:

CHAS: So do you think that if people marry it should be for life, would you imagine that you could have one partner for life?

STACEY: I think you should marry when you're about 25 or getting into your 30s and stay like that/

JAMES: You'd be old and wrinkly then

STACEY: When you're wise, when you're wiser you've/

JENNIFER: Yeah you've had more experience with boyfriends and girlfriends and stuff and you'd know if you get, really get interested in some guy you might get hurt and you'll know by then

JAMES: Like in another TV show and (   ) 'cause she's having a divorce

(EASTERN PUBLIC)

The oppositional nature of male and female is not carried over into views about child care. Both male and female children are interested in work and in actively participating in child care. While the boys visibly achieve their masculinity at the girls' expense, they claim that they would not be averse to being the major child carers when they have children. This would appear to be a major shift in discourses about child care which indicates that even while the male–female binary is held tightly in place, some disruptions to it can become imaginable when adults make them visibly practicable:

CHAS: Do you all want to have kids?

ALL: Uh huh

CHAS: You do?

JENNIFER: Well when I get older because you're still doing your career and you've still got a lot ahead of your life and you can't expect to divorce kids when you have them

JAMES: And then you get five kids

STACEY: And you still have to make money if you want to bring the kids up/

JENNIFER: Properly

JAMES: It costs good money to feed us lot

STACEY: properly yeah

JAMES: I wouldn't want, I would only want 2 or 3

CHAS: Charlotte, what sort of relationship do you want with your partner if you get one? If you happen to find one?

JAMES: Chas is stuck for words

CHARLOTTE: So we can tell each other things I don't think it should be for life because a lot of the time people marry and then find out that they're not the person they thought they may have been. And they feel that they should be stuck together and I think they should be able to tell when the other person's sort of, I won't say getting bored with the relationship, it sounds like they're just doing it for something to do. But when they feel it's not right/

CHAS: People change don't they?

CHARLOTTE: Yeah, they change, especially when you get married

CHAS: Right, and if you have kids, are you gonna still do your job if you've got kids?

CHARLOTTE: um

CHAS: You know, if you're a barrister, you get pregnant, you have your baby, what's gonna happen then?

CHARLOTTE: I wouldn't work as much but it doesn't mean that I would stop working all together. I am still going to work a full-time job I am going to try and spend as much of my time at home, in the sense that I like to be with them, not to look after them all the time. My partner, if I found the right person it would probably be someone who would be willing to look after them for the times that I am working

CHAS: Right. James do you want to have kids?

JAMES: Yeah

CHAS: Are you, if your wife wanted to go back to work would you be prepared to stay at home and mind the children

JAMES: Yep

CHAS: You would be?

JAMES: Yeah

CHAS: What about you Zac?

ZAC: Yeah probably

CHAS: What about you Stacey?

STACEY: Well, I, actually I would let the husband do the working because usually the husband earns more pay but sometimes not. But you could always, my aunty's just had a child, a few, well she had it in January and she's taking a 12 months leave and then her husband's going to, then my uncle's going to take another 12 months leave just to bring the child up until the child's ready to go to school, to um/

JAMES: Preschool

STACEY: preschool, whatever

JAMES: Preschool? Oh yeah I started preschool when I was 2

STACEY: Or child sitter's or something

CHARLOTTE: I don't want my child stuck in child care all the time. They get really attached to them and I don't want my kid growing up with that sort of thing, they shouldn't always be looked after by babysitters, I would like to spend as much time with them as I could

(EASTERN PUBLIC)

In the following conversation there is an interesting debate about the relation between the divine order, the gender order and women's nature on the one hand, and concern for the environment on the other. The current discourses on the environment are in conflict with the dominant storyline that women are producers of and carers for children. In the context of talk about the environment, Stacey and Charlotte imagine different alternatives for their futures that do not necessarily involve marriage and bearing children:

CHAS: What about you Jennifer?

JENNIFER: I would prefer to look after my kids. Maybe it's because you've been brought up to, like the women look after the kids, unless you've got a really great job that you really enjoy, good pay and your husband is willing to look after your child I'd always look after my child. Maybe it's the way I've been brought up.

CHAS: Are . . . there ways of living when you've grown up that don't include marriage?

ZAC: Yes

JAMES: Mm

JENNIFER: I don't think so. I mean it's the sort of the way God, not marriage, but the way God meant things to be, like your instinct is to breed, oh I'll use a different term, is to have kids, that's kind of what you were born to do I think. It's not a very nice way to put it but it's your work/

JAMES: It's a blunt way of putting it/

JENNIFER: There's no point, I mean it's bad if you wanted to have lots and lots of kids and over populate the world

JAMES: Five kids

JENNIFER: And but maybe ((pause)) I don't know

CHAS: What about you Stacey?

STACEY: Well

CHAS: Do you think it's inevitable that people that you know, are there alternatives to getting married?

STACEY: Yeah

CHAS: Are there alternative lifestyles that people can/

STACEY: I mean you could always stay single and get a really good job and become rich and not have a need for anybody else in the world or you could of course, there are some people in the world who don't want their children. You could just adopt and raise them up on your own . . . I think you'd probably be rather to be married and have children 'cause then you've got someone to share the 'bundle of joy' as mum puts it, with you

. . .

CHAS: What about you Charlotte? Can you imagine your lifestyle without a partner or without marriage?

CHARLOTTE: Yes I sometimes think of living with a girlfriend and living in a really nice, quite a nice flat maybe or apartment and just like that. She she'd be my partner except we share equal responsibilities

(EASTERN PUBLIC)

GENDER AND CLASS

The St Clement's study group had a radically different discourse on femininity from those of the other two groups. Class is a more salient category for them than either gender or their different cultures of origin, though their elaboration of class differences is often articulated in terms of gender difference. They define males and females from the ruling class as the same except when it comes to sexuality. They do not see being female as excluding them from any male activities. When in the bush or in the world of work, they can do anything a boy or man would do. In the city (if they are country girls) or when they are 'out on the town' they will be feminine in order to attract the right kind of man. It is when it comes to the 'birds and the bees' they say, that men and women are opposite. They do not understand this as a hierarchical opposition, to do with inferiority and superiority, but a desirable choice of physical difference that is imposed on the body for the purposes of sexual attraction.

From the perspective of the St Clement's girls, boys and girls from the State schools display unacceptable and incomprehensible behaviours that are opposite to feminine, or 'being a lady' as they sometimes call it. Their own version of femininity is 'ultra femme' in dress and body management, and while femininity may involve playing at being vulnerable to attract a man, they experience it as a highly agentic condition. In the following conversation they contrast themselves and their femininity with the forms of masculinity they see State school boys adopting. It emerges later in the conversation that ruling class boys are not included in this oppositional category. The subjectivity of these girls is thus not taken up as opposite to all males, but as different from both the non-elite boys and the non-elite girls. The latter they see as being like those boys because they spend so much time with them in their co-ed schools.

Although they are very sure of their own agency and freedom to *choose* to be feminine, they describe their sexual oppositeness in terms of not having freedoms that boys have. They mustn't be big and fat, but boys can be. They must have good skin, but boys can be pimply. They must dress well, but boys can be unkempt. They cannot swear, but boys can swear. Those girls who do not achieve these qualities are ugly, laughable or tough. 'Toughness' is a class as well as a gender category and is interchangeable with 'rough':

TIFFANY: And girls shave their legs and men don't

CHAS: Why do girls . . . shave their legs?

JACQUELINE: To look prettier

TIFFANY: Yeah to/

VICTORIA: To make their legs smooth

TIFFANY: So the hair doesn't grow like mine and yucky and dark

MARCELLA: Yeah yeah my legs look like a hairy (   ) . . .

CHAS: I am interested in this thing about the hairy legs. Why do you think that long hairs on women's legs look/

JACQUELINE: Rough/

TIFFANY: When they are in their cozzies [swimming costumes], 'cause they like to show off when they wear bikinis and all that

VICTORIA: Yeah

TIFFANY: It doesn't look real nice because when you are wearing stockings all the hairs/

MICHELLE & MARCELLA: Yeah, yeah ((laughter))

JACQUELINE: Men don't wear stockings and that's why

VICTORIA: And most of the time you don't see men's legs and stuff

JACQUELINE: Yeah

VICTORIA: And women are always wearing shorts, skirts and everything like so you can see their legs

MARCELLA: And it looks real nice if your legs are shaved/

VICTORIA: Yeah see it doesn't, it doesn't look nice if you walk around with hairy legs like that

CHAS: But men walk round with hairy legs all the time

JACQUELINE: Yeah but they are different

MICHELLE: They wear different, they wear different/

JACQUELINE: Yeah but they are men and we are different and like women have got to look good

MARCELLA: Yeah . . .

JACQUELINE: No hairy legs

VICTORIA: No, no like, not hair everywhere like a man would do, like wearing good/

ALISON: No pimples/

VICTORIA: clothes and like and like doing her hair real nice and like they put their hair up, they put all this make-up on and dangle dangley earrings on/

MICHELLE: And they put lipstick on and everything

VICTORIA: and some girls and the tough girls have all these earrings up to here

JACQUELINE: Yeah

VICTORIA: It looks yuk . . .

CHAS: Tell me what else a girl has to do to look/

TIFFANY: Great/

CHAS: good

JACQUELINE: They have to wear bracelets and rings and stuff like that

VICTORIA: And they have to keep, they have to keep fit and/

TIFFANY: And you are not allowed to, if they get fat, like they have to keep to just the right size

(ST CLEMENT'S)

The feminine is a powerful category for these girls and while they perceive a strict set of rules for looking 'attractive' they regard themselves as inviolable because of their class. As it emerges in a later conversation, they do not think men have power over them. If they find themselves dressing up to attract men and it turns out to be the wrong sort of man (the wrong class) they can dismiss him. They regard themselves as having total freedom to choose to be feminine. Having chosen, there are some strict rules to follow: 'ladies have to look nice'; 'women have got to look good'; 'they have to keep fit'; and 'you are not allowed to get fat'. This involves both dressing like a lady and perhaps displaying yourself as vulnerable:

CHAS: But what about how, do boys think differently to what girls think?

VICTORIA: Most times, sometimes

CHAS: Can you explain how the difference is?

TIFFANY: Well some boys they might think, 'Well I really like that girl over there, I wonder if she likes me' and all this and then he goes, 'I think I'll ask for her phone number' and all this. And then the girl might be thinking, 'I like that boy over there, should I act tough or what, or will I hurt myself and he might feel sorry for me' or something like that, and they are thinking the same but they don't know it

VICTORIA: Yeah

(ST CLEMENT'S)

Positioning themselves as vulnerable in order to display their attraction for a boy is not seen as in any way contradictory with taking up an equal place with men in the public world:

TIFFANY: And the, men and women could have the same jobs sometimes

CHAS: Yeah

MICHELLE: Are we talking about/

VICTORIA: A woman can be a postman or bus driver

CHAS: Or a psychiatrist or a teacher/

MICHELLE: Or, I don t know, nearly anything

(ST CLEMENT'S)

But the more interesting topic for them at this point is the 'birds and the bees' and their differentness from (non-elite) males, which they continue to explore. In the following conversation they begin an imaginary story of their power in relation to these males. Chas then turns the story around to one of vulnerability, woman as a victim being judged for her open sexuality. They listen, obviously recognising the plot, but they reject it outright, calling on the details of their privileged position to defend themselves:

JACQUELINE: Men can look all slobby sometimes and the ladies have to look nice . . .

CHAS: Why do the ladies have to look nice and the men can look slobby?

JACQUELINE So men will get to attract them

. . .

VICTORIA: There might be this girl and she's in the perfect fashion. And then she is walking along and there's a whole lot of drunk boys All drinking there and they walk past her and the girl walks past and they go, 'Oh will you marry me' or 'will you go with me', 'oh you're a chick' and everything ((laughter)) . . . That's that's what the boy says and then the girl, they might say

TIFFANY: The girl might say, 'Oh p off' and then just walk off

VICTORIA: Or the girl might say, 'I think you've got the wrong person here matey'

JACQUELINE: Matey! ((laughter))

TIFFANY: The girl, the girl, what the girl has to do, is the girl walks off and like say she hops off the bus and she has got a really nice hand bag and a mini skirt and she has come home from a party or something at two o'clock at the morning and there is these boys that were that are walking home from another place and they are in all the really good gear and bow tie and they look so cute and that, and she walks off and her bum's wiggling ((laughter)) and they go (whistle) and then she looks back just over her shoulder and she goes, and then a boy goes, 'Come 'ere girl', no

VICTORIA: 'Come 'ere chick'

TIFFANY: Yeah, 'Come 'ere' or something like that and then she goes, like she's not going, 'Yeah' like this.

CHAS: I want to ask you a question. Now you have started the story for me, right there is a young woman, she has got off the bus, it is two o'clock in the morning, she has a short leather mini skirt on

TIFFANY: Yeah, and there is a top that comes to here and her boobs show out . . .

JACQUELINE: Her hair's all nice

VICTORIA: She's nicely built

CHAS: OK she gets off the bus at two o'clock in the morning a car drives by with three hooligans in it/

TIFFANY: Yeah

CHAS: they take that woman, they take her off the street, they abduct her, they rape her

TIFFANY: Mm

CHAS: OK they go to court, they are found out and they go to court, and what they say in court is/

TIFFANY: And she's really scared/

CHAS: wait a minute, and what they say in court is, 'She deserved it because she shouldn't have been on the street at 2 o'clock'/

TIFFANY: mm/

CHAS: and she shouldn't have been wearing the sort of clothes she was wearing. Now what would you say to that? Is that true or false?

JACQUELINE: False . . .

TIFFANY: False

CHAS: Why

TIFFANY: Because like a lady can wear whatever she wants and it like um like because she might, because her parents might not, 'cause say she is about 16 and she hasn't got her [driver's] permit say she is going for her permit the next day or something and like she hasn't really got her licence yet because she couldn't drive home, but if she did have her car I am sure nothing would have happened. But she had to catch a bus and her parents were going to pick her up just up a little bit around the corner and they and the car took off before the parents saw

CHAS: So you think she has every right to wear what she wants to wear?

TIFFANY: Anybody can wear whatever they want

JACQUELINE: Same here

CHAS: What do you think?

JACQUELINE: I reckon that if she was walking on the street with a [swimming] costume on that wouldn't really matter, because if I was wearing naked on the street it wouldn't really matter, because I could wear whatever I want a bra and underpants on the street

(ST CLEMENT'S)

This extreme statement of their right to wear (or not wear) whatever they choose signifies their sense of power, rather than describing what they would actually choose to do. Girls from the State schools, in contrast, choose to behave in ways that the St Clement's girls regard as 'not normal'. Such behaviour is 'not nice', not desirable. Just as the Eastern Public girls take up as their own being female, so these girls take up and embody being ruling class. The behaviour of the girls from the State school, that is, responding positively to non-elite forms of male sexual behaviour, is incomprehensible:

MICHELLE: And see it doesn't look nice when the girl whistles to the boy, 'cause it doesn't look nice

JACQUELINE: 'Cause its not normal

MARCELLA: Yeah it's not normal

. . .

ALISON: I go to German lessons this afternoon and we go to Forest High and we are kind of on the top floor, the second storey and its really high and when you look out the window it is really a long way down. And last lesson, last week when we were there the, um there were four boys just hanging around there being silly/

JACQUELINE: Being idiots/

ALISON: and when we looked out um they whistled out at us and shouted up to us and everything like that

VICTORIA: What did they shout to you?

MICHELLE: (   ) what they shout out to you, they would make this noise 'Ohhhhh I want to make love to you'

CHAS: How did that make you feel?

ALISON: Sort of embarrassed ((laughter)). The other girls, they are all girls in my class, the other girls they are from Riverview Public and they feel/

JACQUELINE: Riverspew/

VICTORIA: They kinda acted strangely to it

TIFFANY: They are probably used to it 'cause they've got boys in their school

ALISON: They were kind of showing off in front of the window, like swinging on chairs and everything like that, like they weren't doing that before . . . I was just sitting in my chair wondering why they were doing all this

(ST CLEMENT'S)

The girls' name for Riverview Public, Riverspew, as Chas pointed out to me, suggests something they imagine ejecting violently from within themselves, something that is physically repulsive, that belongs outside themselves. The term is thus useful for maintaining what might otherwise be experienced as a fluid boundary between the classes. A further reading, suggested by Margaret Somerville, is that spewing is the archetypal behaviour of working class drunken males, whom they perceive the Riverview girls as having become like. It is in the following excerpt from this conversation that the exemption of ruling class males from their descriptions of male as other are most clearly articulated:

CHAS: You said a minute ago that the girls at Riverview Public don't really act like girls

TIFFANY: Oh because like they are around boys and they hear all the boys saying 'Shit' and stuff like that . . . and the girls say swear words, they don't really care how they speak, they might go, 'yep, nup, yep nup'

CHAS: So to act like a proper girl you are not to swear

VICTORIA: And you are not to say 'nup' and 'yep' you are not supposed to say, like 'Nup Mum', for a proper lady you are supposed to go 'Yes Mother'

CHAS: How does a boy act different to the way a girl acts? . . .

TIFFANY: The boy comes up to the teacher and goes 'Please mark that' and just chucks it at the teacher and a girl might come up and say, 'Excuse me Mrs Brown can you please mark my work now'

CHAS: So girls are polite

TIFFANY: Because they have learnt the right way to speak and all that and they know how to

VICTORIA: So do boys

MICHELLE: Boys are good . . .

TIFFANY: Like some boys they might go 'Will you come and dance with me' and like the Anglican Boys' School, and like the ABS boys would go 'Would you like to come and dance with me for this song please' or something like that . . .

VICTORIA: Well um Riverspew, well like a bad school and it is grotty, it hasn't got good behaviour/

TIFFANY: And you don't have to wear school shoes or anything like that/

VICTORIA: so the girls there, seeing they go to a grotty school and everything and all the people there are stupid, the teachers they don't care what they say and everything. Like you go up to a teacher at Riverspew and they go, 'mark me work' . . .

TIFFANY: A boy from Riverspew, I was at his house for the weekend with his sister, 'cause his Mum works at our motel as a cleaner and they invited me out for the weekend and like we were in seeing these lambs and he goes, 'Will you go with me' and I didn't understand what it meant and I go, 'What do you mean' and he goes, 'Like girlfriend and boyfriend' and he didn't go, 'Tiffany would you like' he didn't even address me as my name or anything, so I just said, 'I don't care really' and then I said I'd think about it and then I ended up saying 'No' because he didn't really speak real nice, he just goes, he wears this hat with 'Shithead' on it, and it has this big lump of poo hanging off it.

(ST CLEMENT'S)

From the point of view of the State school study groups, they too see a connection between ruling class behaviour, or being 'a lady', and femininity, but in this case the girls visibly distance themselves from it:

1 CHAS: What other things do girls have to do to be considered feminine?
2 ANNA: Act like a lady
3 CHAS: Act like a lady. How do you act like a lady?
4 ANNA: Being polite and precise
5 KEN: You are not being very precise
6 ROSIE: And you have to dress up in certain way to look decent
7 CHAS: Yes OK you have to look decent. How does a girl look decent?
8 ROSIE: Well
9 KEN: Wear a dress that hasn't got holes in it

10 ROSIE: Well she has to do her hair, she'd do her hair, she'd she um she'd change her clothes every once a week, I s'pose ((laughs)), no she'd change her clothes whenever they got dirty

11 BRIAN: Put on make-up and all that sort of stuff . . . And they wouldn't sit like this in public ((masculine posture with legs apart))

12 MAL: Make sure their room is clean

13 ROSIE: I don't

. . .

14 ANNA: They stick the plum in the mouth all the time when they get on the phone (KAROBRAN PUBLIC)

These girls are not like what they are describing as feminine (5, 13), and when they describe femininity as behaving like a lady the girls use the pronouns 'she' and 'they' rather than 'I' and 'we' in their elaboration of it (10, 14) . Similarly, the boys use 'they' rather than 'you' (11, 12) in elaborating femininity.

To sum up then, the St Clement's girls have access to a form of liberal feminism which interestingly reveals the classed nature of this position. That is, they position themselves as members of an elite who are not different from elite men in any way relevant to the kind of work elite men do. Their right of access to work that men do or freedoms that men take is something they do not question. They thus constitute themselves in terms of sameness to the ruling class boys in their manner of interacting with others and in terms of access to work. Their major difference from males is related to sexuality and is based entirely on the attraction of opposites. This apparent contradiction in the ruling class version of femininity/feminism is not experienced as such by these ruling class girls because their oppositeness is understood not only as a choice but as something external to themselves that they choose to impose on their bodies both for the purposes of sexuality and to signal their difference from non-elite girls.

The Eastern Public girls, and in particular Charlotte, have access to a form of radical feminism. They express intolerance of boys and are not intimidated by them (except for Jennifer, who is afraid of them because she perceives her body as not correctly feminine). These girls celebrate femininity through attention to feminine forms of dress (though not the ultra-femme dress of the St Clement's girls), combined with fitness of their bodies and a belief they can do anything in the public world without compromising the integrity of their relations with the children they might have in the future. Because of their celebration of femininity and their commitment to care for others, they envisage a partial end to their freedom and independence when they 'fall in love'. They talk about getting good jobs so they can fulfill their desire for good spaces to live in without being dependent on a man. Some of them have thought much about divorce and about keeping themselves financially independent.

The Karobran Public girls define themselves in terms of sameness to the boys in terms of what they can do. Their sporting prowess, their speech and their dress are not as markedly different from the boys as either of the other two groups. The girls imaginatively construct heroic and adventurous storylines for themselves without any difficulty. At the same time, they know that women are not given the same access to sport as men are and that in the real world women are victims of male violence. Their agency, fiercely taken up by Anna in particular, is already interrupted by such knowledges.

Femininity thus has multiple meanings. In some of its forms it is only achievable by girls from the ruling classes. And even for them, it is not a consistent achievement. The possibility of being rough or tough is not entirely absent from their talk. Being the same as boys also has many meanings as has difference and opposition. It shifts from one cultural group to another, from one class to another, from one interactive situation to another. All the girls know the victim storyline and some are willing to play it out. They do not necessarily equate this with powerlessness (though it is inevitably disempowering in ways they do not yet recognise). They are very interested in locating ways of thinking both for the present and the future that do not rob them of agency. They have developed strategies for withstanding sexism: these are, for the St Clement's girls, pulling rank or class; for the Eastern and Karobran Public girls, telling the boys they don't know what they are talking about, celebrating femininity, achieving success in the things only boys are supposed to do and, finally, ignoring it. The last of these is perhaps the most dangerous. It allows the boys' talk to go on unheeded, as if it were a normal taken-for-granted, even inevitable, part of the world. I remember vividly the first time a man spoke to me with respect. Suddenly I was aware for the first time that all the previous speakings were disrespectful. Like a clock that stops ticking, you only realise you were hearing the sound of it when it stops.

The powerful visions or images that the girls have of themselves are broken up. Like the wind blowing on the puddle of water, the words they speak involve exclusion, difference, violence. These words and the knowledge of the social structures which discriminate against women break up the powerful images seen so clearly and with such pleasure.

5 (Masculine) Transformations

Everyone calls me a girl
because I wear a bit of pink socks or something.
And I say to them
'my Dad's got a pink dressing gown'
and that makes them think twice

(Mark, aged 9, Follow-up study)

B OYS KNOW in preschool, and probably even before they learn to speak, that the world is divided into male and female, hard and soft, powerful and weak. They know, though not necessarily in a way they can articulate, that they are located in the male half of an oppositional and hierarchical binary. Because maleness is the *unmarked* category, and female the *marked* (Connell, 1987), they may not be able to name the fact that who they are and what they want to be is 'masculine', since masculinity and personhood are experienced as synonymous. They are thus more likely to define themselves as *persons* and as not-girls, rather than as male. These concepts, marked and unmarked, are important for understanding masculinity. Kimmel makes an excellent account of the moment at which he discovered the unmarked or invisible feature of masculinity. He was sitting in on a seminar on feminist theory when he witnessed the following confrontation between a white woman and a black woman. He says:

Their argument centred around the question of whether their similarities as women were greater than their racial differences. The white woman asserted that the fact that they were both women bonded them, despite racial differences. They shared a common oppression as women, and were both 'sisters under the skin'. The black woman disagreed.

'When you wake up in the morning and look in the mirror, what do you see?' she asked.

'I see a woman', replied the white woman hopefully.

'That's precisely the problem', replied the black woman. 'I see a black woman. For me race is visible every minute of the day, because it is how I'm not privileged in this culture. Race is invisible to you which is why our alliance will always feel false and strained to me.'

When I heard this, I was startled. For when I looked in the mirror, I thought I saw a 'human being', a generic person, universally generalizable. What had been concealed—race and gender, and class—was suddenly visible. As a middle-class white man, I was not able to think about the ways in which class and race and gender had shaped my existence. Marginality is visible, and painfully visceral. Privilege is invisible, and painlessly pleasant. (Kimmel, 1990, p. 94)

Maleness/masculinity is thus bracketed. One is a (male) person. The invisibility of masculinity was evident in the way the primary school boys talked about what they did. Toby was one of the boys from the progressive school in the United States in which I collected some data. In response to my description of what I perceived as displays of ultra masculinity on the soccer field, he explains to me that although he does not engage in all of the activities I describe, he and the other (male) soccer players are not doing masculinity, rather they are simply playing soccer:

BRONWYN: One of the things I was noticing about some of the boys in the playground when they are playing soccer they kind of, there's a, kind of, some boys who are, I can't think of a word for it except that they are more into masculinity, like, displaying themselves as strong and tough and sort of spitting and, carrying on like that. Have you noticed, have you noticed boys like that?

TOBY: Yeah I know some who spit

BRONWYN: Yeah, what how do you see yourself in relation to them?

TOBY I see myself as playing soccer, that's the way I see myself I don't see myself as, see myself like strong and tough, I see myself as playing games

BRONWYN: Just enjoying the game

TOBY: Yes

BRONWYN Yeah, yeah, but but, so what are the boys doing who are being, who are into being tough and spitting and so on?

TOBY: I don't know. Some of them when they ( ) fall and you know stuff like that and like one that, when they, when it like, the ball gets kicked into their stomach or something they'll just like keep playing and [holds breath and tenses muscles] go like that, tough and

BRONWYN: Uh huh. So do you, you don't admire them for those ultra displays of masculinity?

TOBY: No, no it's not really that. It's just they kinda hold it in, 'Ouch that hurt! but I can hold it in'

Toby cannot see what I describe as ultra masculinity. 'It's not really that.' It's just the way they are, they can hold the pain in. Even the desirability of behaving in masculine ways can be invisible. It is only the undesirability of behaving in feminine ways that is visible, though even this can be irrelevant for a boy who has perfected his masculinity. In the following conversation with Steve, a tough, charismatic boy from the same school, he explains that anyone can do anything, irrespective of sex gender, though doing something the girls do is not something that ever occurs to him as desirable. Not doing what the girls do is thus constituted as a free choice:

BRONWYN: Do you think that being a boy or being a girl makes any difference to how you are?

STEVE: Not really, I think you could do whatever you want no matter what you are

BRONWYN: Uh huh. But you, would you ever think of doing any things that generally only girls do?

STEVE: I don't really think about that commonly, but I mean?

BRONWYN: But if you, if you, fancied doing something that the girls were doing, would you do it? Like if they were skipping and you thought 'Wow I'd really like to be able to do that', would you do it?

STEVE: I would not

BRONWYN: Why not?

STEVE: I just wouldn't want to

As boys there are powerful subject positions made available to them both in the lived narratives they observe and hear, and in the textual narratives they encounter in books and on screen. Shaping and hardening their bodies and organising their subjectivities to fit these powerful positions is a complex task which few men achieve without some struggle (Jackson, 1990). Learning to 'hold it in', not express pain and emotion, to perhaps not even remember that you were hit; these are essential to its achievement.

Heroic storylines appear to be a central feature of the process of exploring (masculine) subjectivity in imagination and later in action.

I had just written that sentence when my youngest son, Daniel, dropped by. I asked him to tell me his earliest memory, the one he would begin with if he were to write an autobiography. He said he remembered a hole in the wall leading under the house. He would look in and wonder and imagine what might be there—anything could be possible—monsters, other worlds and darkness. He felt awe and thought how brave it would be to go in, though he never did. His other important early memory, he said, is of his Uncle John bending iron bars in the back yard. This impressed him greatly and added to John's 'amazingness'. (And I still remember the pain, watching his feet lift off the ground.)

Rubbing alongside the heroic is the partial requirement of young boys that they be good and obedient children, responding positively to a loving mother, parents or other adults. It is only a partial requirement since being good and even being a child (that is not-adult) are, in some fundamental ways, incompatible with heroism, hardness and male ascendancy. While boys might be required to be and assent to being a child and to being good in some contexts and in some relations, when they do transgress the boundaries of 'goodness' in an exploration of their own lived heroic narratives they experience danger, excitement and intense pleasure. Not to do so would put them at risk of being a 'girl' or a 'sissy'. An adult reprimand is a signal of their correct placement in the heroic storyline that they are playing out (usually) to their audience of peers. Girls, in contrast, tend to experience anger or deep shame if their actions are defined by adults as transgressive (Crawford et al., 1992).

It seems that boys know before they have discovered *how* to harden their own bodies that their own (male) being is equated with a hardness essential to heroism. This can be seen in the follow up interview with Robbie. Robbie was one of the children in *Frogs and Snails* who showed a strong commitment to, and an awareness of, (masculine) personhood. At the same time he was small and thin and suffered from eczema and asthma, so his automatic entry into hegemonic positions was by no means guaranteed. In this conversation he talks about the period of his life, from the time he was four-years-old at preschool until the time of the interview when he was ten-years-old and in fifth class at primary school.

He begins with a description of the games he used to play with transformers in preschool. Transformers are toys which change their form from robots into such things as machines and animals. Their major characteristics, apart from their magic transformability across normal boundaries, are their strength, agency, power, physical domination and aggression:

1 CHAS: Now when you say 'transformers' aren't they those toys that change from one thing into another?
2 ROBBIE: Yep
3 CHAS: And you can get girl ones can you?
4 ROBBIE: Mm we just made that up
5 CHAS: Did you?

6   ROBBIE: Yep

7   CHAS So what sort of games did you play with these transformers, I mean/

8   ROBBIE: We used to *be* the transformers

9   CHAS: Did you

10 ROBBIE: Yes

11 CHAS: Oh I see. So what you'd be an animal and then go into a machine or what?

12 ROBBIE: Yeah. We would sort of, we'd have different sort of weapons like someone would have a knife and he would go around chopping like this and some people would have a gun like that

13 CHAS: Ah ha. Did you have to be rigid like a robot

14 ROBBIE: No

15 CHAS: Or were you allowed to be just 'normal'?

16 ROBBIE: Just normal . . .

17 CHAS So was kindergarten fairly pleasant?

18 ROBBIE: Oh yeah. After a few days I got used to it and when we had drawing times I always used to draw transformers and Voltrons . . .

19 CHAS: Can you remember your favourite stories when you were a really little kid?

20 ROBBIE I used to like writing stories about Voltron . . .

21 CHAS: If you were to think about your life what would be the very happiest memory you could think of?

22 ROBBIE: Um, last year I liked remembering how I beat some of the sixth graders in the tennis championship . . .

23 CHAS: What are the biggest changes that have happened to you, like you remember when you went to preschool and how you are now, what are the biggest things that have changed?

24 ROBBIE: Ah I know I don't like Voltron that much any more and transformers and that I like other things outdoor sports like soccer and stuff . . .

25 CHAS: What do you think about your body?

26 ROBBIE: Um I think, I think it's, I think it's sort of, I think its fairly tough, I mean, it's not, it doesn't cut too easy. 'Cause sometimes when I'm mad, sometimes when I get really cross, I try to do something to m- when I was younger I used to really like putting bandaids on myself. I always wanted to have a bandaid on, so I used to try to cut myself with my finger nail, 'cept it's really tough, and I couldn't cut it

27 CHAS: What do you think about your body now apart from the fact that it is pretty tough, you can't cut it, what else about it?

28 ROBBIE I think, I think I think it's sort of made for running and stuff 'cause it's light and it's and it . . .

29 CHAS: It feels light does it?

30 ROBBIE: Yeah well everyone says I'm really light . . . And it, and it feels, I'm, it's not, so I think I'd rather run than, I'd rather run than do something else because I'm not, I'm not, I'm not bad, and I can sort of, go fairly fast and and my my legs are fairly skinny

(ROBBIE, FOLLOW-UP STUDY)

In the beginning, the fantasy games with transformers actually involved the children becoming a transformer, that is experiencing in their own bodies the power of being a transformer and the imaginary knowledge of their transformability from child into someone powerful (7-16). In preschool Robbie drew transformers and later wrote stories about them (18-20). He thus took up the image of transformers first in his imaginary play and then developed his competence in the symbolic order using these same images and storylines. Another image of toughness and strength that he used was bandaids. Tough men and boys in comic books and in the illustrations in many children's stories have bandaids as a signifier of their toughness.

In Graham's illustration of his character, Crusher, for example, he uses a bandaid along with football boots and a torn guernsey to signify Crusher's toughness. Robbie, in trying to cut himself to gain access to this powerful signifier, discovered that he was in fact quite

From Graham's Crusher is Coming, *1987*

tough, even without the bandaids (26). Eventually the 'real' takes over from the fantasy of early games, the 'real' being expressed in terms of the heroic hardness and competence of his own body being used in combat with others (22, 24). He gives up transformers, since to play with transformers at the age of ten would signify babyishness rather than powerful forms of competence. His exceptional skill at tennis, competing with and even beating people older than himself, gives him his highest moment of happiness. Further, he has found another sport in which he can excel despite, and in part because of, his smaller than usual bodily frame (28, 30). Despite such successes in his transformations of himself into someone who is unequivocally male, there is still a hesitance in his descriptions of his success: 'I think I'd rather run than, I'd rather run than do something else because I'm not, I'm not, I'm not bad'.

Sport is not just a symbolic signifier of male competence but assists in the embodiment of hardness, particularly of external muscular hardness. In male sport there is a competitive pitting of the brute force of one's body against the brute force of others, creating both a carapace for the self and a knowledge of one's own force and bodily competence. To win is to momentarily become the hero whose sureness of body can be taken for granted. To be is to be powerful, and anyone who is not, is flawed. Patrick White, homosexual novelist, calls his autobiography *Flaws in the Glass*.

THE MALE–FEMALE BINARY

Much feminist writing, including my own, has elaborated the binaries through which masculinity and femininity, or maleness and femaleness, are constituted. Wilshire (1989, pp. 95-96), for example, in a study of myth provides the table on the following page.

It is possible to see these binaries being used as metaphors, as adjectives, and as underlying assumptions in the elaboration of the male–female binary in stories, in science and in everyday talk. But when Chas and I first started looking at the data on masculinity we found ourselves in a shifting world where none of these binaries held tight (Davies and Banks, 1991b). We compared masculinity to an Escher drawing in which one enters the house at one level only to find oneself at another, or to a science fiction house which is predictable and square on the outside, but shifting and prism-like on the inside. While male may be equated with mind and female with body, for example, many of the boys that we talked to were obsessed with their bodies and with hardening them and making them powerful.

The Male–Female Binary

kNOWLEDGE (accepted wisdom)	IGNORANCE (the occult and taboo)
higher up	lower down
good, positive	negative, bad
mind (ideas), head, spirit	body (flesh), womb (blood), Nature (Earth)
reason (the rational)	emotions and feelings (the irrational)
cool	hot
order	chaos
control	letting things be, allowing, spontaneity
objective (outside, 'out there')	subjective (inside, immanent)
literal truth, fact	poetic truth, metaphor, art
goals	process
light	darkness
written text, Logos	oral tradition, enactment, Myth
Apollo as sky–sun	Sophia as earth–cave–moon
public sphere	private sphere
seeing, detached	listening, attached
secular	holy and sacred
linear	cyclical
permanence, ideal (fixed) forms	change, fluctuations, evolution
'changeless and immortal'	process, ephemeras, (performance)
hard	soft
independent, individual, isolated	dependent, social, interconnected, shared
dualistic	whole
MALE	FEMALE

Boys' obsession with their bodies appears at first not to fit with the equation of male with mind and female with body. Nor does it appear to fit with the observation that Crawford et al. (1992, p. 186) make that mastery for boys entails a control over the material world in contrast to girls whose mastery is over self and the body. One way of making sense of this that Chas and I developed in our paper on masculinity was to understand the process of transformation of the (male) body as one in which the body is treated like an object, like the transformers. The body, like the toy, is made distant from oneself. The toy, a symbol of masculine hardness, is held away from oneself in play and responds object-like to one's fantasies and commands. The male body, like the transformers, is an object to be manipulated and controlled (even transformed) by the conscious mind. Further the male can be mind rather than body only if he has brought his unruly body under control. The ritual hardening that comes with the extensive practice that excellence in sport requires, consolidates this split between the body as object and the mind as a superior controlling force. We concluded that the hierarchical binary does not work such that male simply equals mind, and female equals body. Rather, the binary is at least in part set up within each male between the superior mind and the inferior body to be dominated and controlled. Once the body is controlled, other forms of hegemonic masculinity become possible, such as domination, exploitation and control of the material world and of the land. Those who never achieve the hegemonic control of the body often opt for control and domination through the power of the intellect. Thus the highly rationalist control of meaning becomes a means for manifesting powerful masculinity just as much as the control of bodies, of women and of the land.

It is in relation to these complex splittings and connections that it makes sense for the female to be viewed as body since she is, like the male body and like the land, an inferior object to be controlled, dominated and exploited (Schaffer, 1988). That she too has 'mind' is necessarily put to one side in the elaboration and maintenance of this particular aspect of the male–female binary.

Deutscher has explored the slippery nature of these binaries through a study of St Augustine's Confessions. She claims that we cannot understand the male–female binary without also understanding the man–god binary: 'in relation to god, man is also humble, submissive, lowly, weak, a child, despised, mere dust and ashes' (Deutscher, 1992, p. 47). What she discovers is that while Augustine asserts that man is rational and woman irrational, man is mind and woman inferior body and so on, man is also irrational, body etc. when thought of in relation to god. God, in this model, is the ideal to which man aspires. He is mind, rational, non-emotional, not-body, all the things man struggles to be and yet can never fully attain because he is not-god. To the extent that he is not-god, he is woman and a child. Woman is thus made to signify the negative, all that man is when he is not like god:

> . . . within Augustine's terms it is impossible that man should coincide with god, for the necessary difference between man and god (upon which god's identity is based, upon which man is parasitic), would then be lost. But in effect this means that the point of pure masculinity which defines man and by which the feminine is 'not-man' is devalued, must be positioned as a point inaccessible to man. Despite the fact that god has been defined as 'not-man', man is only truly masculine insofar as he approximates god. So for all that god is 'not-man', paradoxically it is god who is positioned at the point of pure masculinity. So the recession, while rendering an illusion of masculine identity as mind, or reason, does so by moving toward a point never arrived at. All that is progressively isolated from man and devalued as 'not-man', is displaced onto the feminine. Man

is defined by a term he is nevertheless not, and never at one with, defined by a term which is but a shifting recession to a point it never coincides with. So the feminine, being the extent to which man falls short of god is thereby a term flexible enough to include all that we typically define as masculine: reason, mind, man. (Deutscher, 1992, p. 50)

The masculine and the feminine are thus both the same and yet different. Man, to the extent that he is not-god, is feminine, and the feminine encompasses man. But feminine is also the negative, that which man struggles away from. In this sense masculinity and femininity are not ontological, or essential characteristics of persons, but are processes intricately interconnected with each other. They are also imaginary ideals against which individual success in the world is measured.

The other relevant binary, adult–child, is equally ambivalent. 'The child' is innocent and good. When man is good, in god's eyes, he is innocent like a child. Yet childhood is antithetical to male adulthood and must also be struggled away from in the achievement of (male) personhood. Like the struggle away from femininity, this is always partial and incomplete.

A Christian story written to impress on young boys the goodness, in god's eyes, of being an innocent child is *The Snow Queen*, written in the first half of the nineteenth century but still being reprinted for young children today (Andersen, 1987). In this story little Kay is a sweet, docile boy, who spends all his time in the rose garden with little Gerda, admiring the roses. He is much loved by little Gerda and by each of their good families. The 'Evil One' invents a mirror in which anyone who gazes will see only evil and pettiness. When the mirror smashes, a shard of the glass pierces little Kay's heart and another his eye. He can no longer see the beauty of the roses, of Gerda or his family. As a result he damages the roses, finds no sympathy with Gerda's tears, rejects childish things, argues with and makes fun of his grandmother, develops a love of science and runs off to play with the other boys:

'Why do you cry?' he asked [Gerda], 'you'll only make yourself ugly' . . . he gave the [rose] boxes a kick and tore off two roses . . .

When she came afterwards with a picture book, he said it was only fit for babies, and when his grandmother told them tales, he would be sure to come out with a '*but*—nay' whenever he was able. He would go behind her, put on her spectacles and imitate her talk; it was so exactly like her that people used to laugh when they heard him . . .

His games were now different from what they had been; they were more like grown-up person's amusements. One winter's day, as the snowflakes were whizzing down, he came out with a magnifying glass [to look at the snowflakes] . . . 'Look how lovely it is,' said Kay, 'it is much more interesting than to have to do with real flowers! And there is not a single flaw in them, they are exact. If only they wouldn't melt!'

Shortly afterwards came Kay with big gloves on and his sledge at his back . . .

Down in the square the boldest lads tied their sledges fast to the farmers' carts and thus drove a good distance with them. It was good fun. (Andersen, 1987, pp. 120-122)

This behaviour, which sounds like that of many young boys I've met, puts Kay very much at risk, however. He is, after all, now seeing as the devil wants him to see. He is then whisked off by the Snow Queen who turns the glass shard in his heart into ice. Kay becomes unfeeling and black with cold without knowing it. What saves him are Gerda's profound love and the discovery of Christianity. Through these he is saved from the devil and the Snow Queen. He returns with Gerda to the bosom of his family and discovers he is now an adult (though still a child at heart). Eternity is guaranteed him in this adult but child-like state.

In this version of Christianity, if the boy wants to relate to god then he must be feminine and a child, accepting his own lowly status. While Christianity may have no direct relevance to many children nor to the adults who interact with them, there are other potent cultural forms that have taken its place. Parents and the state have god-like authority over children, insisting on their lack of agency until such time as they define the child as having transcended the condition of being a child. In the meantime, adult behaviours are outlawed for children. As well, there are sporting heroes with whom boys, in particular, are invited to identify. As they watch and become involved with 'their' teams or 'their' particular heroes they imaginatively experience the power and strength of these heroes, knowing at the same time that they cannot *be* these gods. They can only strive in their direction, weaving their images and fantasies about their own strength or the strength of the group they belong to through their heroes.

As well, the heroes of fairy stories and modern super-heroes both display many god-like qualities. The prince in *Sleeping Beauty*, for example, has the breath of life. He is the silent, absent saviour. Like the Christian god who breathed life into Adam, the prince with his kiss can give life to the inert body of woman. Super heroes too have appropriated god-like qualities, such as living forever, in their representation of the masculine ideal.

An early image of my brother Tony. He was forever breaking some part of himself or hurting his body in some awful way as he engaged in yet another extravagant pitting of his body against nature. One day he was out playing in bare feet and trod on a piece of wood with nails sticking up out of it. The nails went right into his foot and he couldn't pull the piece of wood off. He made his way home, screaming with pain, the wood nailed to his foot. The image was clear and stark in my mind. His vulnerability and his heroic strength seemed to come together in this image of the wood nailed to his feet. I see now, consciously, then probably unconsciously, a connection between the nails in Tony's feet and Christ's nails on the cross. Tony's suffering and Christ's suffering coalesced in my mind in that image of nails and holes in the flesh. Christ was up against an unsympathetic world, Tony the same. Both needed to be loved, both were male, both made impossible demands.

The boys in the two public school study groups reveal a striving towards the heroic in much of their talk. Mal, in particular, who is already something of a sporting hero, both in the Aboriginal community and at school, engages in an almost continual display of his (male) personhood:

MAL: I've got, I've got, I've got some photos of the, with the whole Australian team because when I went to Sydney last year we got to meet the whole Australian team and got our photos taken. It was really good

ROSIE: My favourite person, my favourite person in football is captain of the Australian team

BRIAN: Big Mal

ROSIE: Yeah Mal

MAL: Mal!!

ROSIE: He just has to raise his fist to any football player from um/

BRIAN: Great Britain/

ROSIE: from Great Britain and that and they just faint, they die

MAL: What about Wally, Wally just has to stand up like this ((laughter))

BRIAN: Yeah some of those Great Britain fellas!

. . .

ROSIE: What Peter Sterling used to do, Peter Sterling used to pretend he went to school in the morning and he used to go round and climb up through the window and hide under the bed and he used to read books in his bedroom

MAL: Wally, Wally's father when Wally was one day old said that Wally would play lock and Wally played lock for Australia

(KAROBRAN PUBLIC)

THE RELEVANCE OF IMAGINED FUTURES: HEROISM AND MALE SEXUALITY

When the male children in the study groups projected themselves into the future, imagining what they would like to be, the images are of achieving heroic sporting status, or of controlling powerful machines that conquer airways and of heroic storylines in which they have power over others:

CHAS: Right what about you Zac?

ZAC: Oh I'd probably go to Uni and I'd like to be a vet. Um, I'd like to be a vet and I'd probably have a good, I'd like a good tennis career as coaching or international. I'd like to get a good pay and money . . .

CHAS: What about you James?

JAMES I want to get into the airforce and fly A1Os, F14s, F111s, F16s, F18s um um B52s not B52, Boeing (   ) Bramhauffer

ZAC: OK, OK . . .

CHAS: . . . could you fill in a little bit more of the picture for me. How will your life be, what will your life be like?

JAMES: Fast, exciting/

STACEY: Adventurous

JAMES: Yeah, adventurous. I can't think of anything else to describe it

(EASTERN PUBLIC)

CHAS: Anything else you want to tell me? What do you want to do when you get a bit older, when you leave school, what are the things you want to do?

BRIAN: Be a cop

CHAS: Be a policeman?

BRIAN: Yep

CHAS: How come?

BRIAN: They can speed faster

KEN: They can put the foot down

ROSIE: Even policeman can get arrested when they drink and drive

BRIAN: I'm not going to drink. Maybe you do but I'm not

. . .

MAL: I like reading books and playing cricket and athletics and/

BRIAN: He's good at athletics

MAL: I like Maths. When I grow up I want to be a cop

CHAS: You want to be a policeman too. Why do, what is it about being a policeman that really appeals to you Mal?

KEN: Everyone thinks they're tough

ROSIE: I think I know why, he likes to boss everyone around

BRIAN: So do you. You boss your poor old brother around

ROSIE: Poor old brother!

BRIAN: Yeah poor fella

ROSIE: He bashes me up every day

BRIAN: That's the good thing about him

. . .

MAL: And I want to be a policeman so that I can stop all the law breakers in Australia

(KAROBRAN PUBLIC)

Rosie is rather unimpressed by these excessive fantasies of power, pointing out that even policemen can run foul of the law. When she mentions the effects for her of her brother's practising of his (masculine) toughness, 'He bashes me up every day', Brian asserts the virtue of her brother's actions, 'That's the good thing about him'. While Mal sees his future heroism as being one in which he will prevent wrong doing he does not dissent from the claim that the daily assaults on Rosie's body are good. On the contrary, they fit well within the male heroic storyline as the following conversation shows. The transcript begins after the girls have been telling a story about how a gang of boys attack them when they walk near the park:

1   CHAS: Right, why do you think that the boys don't like the girls walking up to the park boys, what reason/
2   KEN: They think they own it
3   CHAS: They think they own it
4   BRIAN: The boys think they're good
5   KEN: Probably got a cubby or a base up there
6   ROSIE: No, they just start it because um/
. . .
7   CAROLYN: No they just start/
8   MAL: They might like you girls
9   KEN: They might like them and just annoy them
10 CAROLYN: When I pick up a really big stick they all run away except for Craig
11 CHAS: But why would they want to hurt them if they like them? That seems/
12 KEN: They might, they might have a base up there
13 CHAS: Yeah
14 KEN: (   ) cubby
15 MAL: Or jealous because they don't like b/
16 KEN: they could have have had a place (   )
17 ROSIE: Katrina and I went past his place before and he had his mates with him and um and he saw them, um we saw them and they said he was going to get the shangeye out and we just ran
    (KAROBRAN PUBLIC)

The boys' first explanation is a territorial one. The gang must have staked out a claim there (2-5). Mal and Ken add a sexual layer to this, suggesting the attack is to do with 'liking', presumably a euphemism for sexual attraction (8-9). Carolyn tells of countering their daring with her own attack (10). Chas asks why 'liking' and hurting are linked (11), but they do not hear the question, or at least they do not hear it as an answerable question. The boys reiterate the territorial element of the explanation (12, 14, 16) adding on jealousy/animosity (15) and Rosie confirms how dangerous these boys in the gang are, her only option being to flee from them (17). The connection between territory, male violence towards females and sexuality is left intact.

Jackson makes a similar connection between the embodiment of oneself as male and learning to connect this to a patriarchial set of beliefs and practices:

> Learning to identify as 'He-Man' masculine . . . was about trying, with difficulty, to embody force. Learning that you were naturally entitled to social, legal and financial power over women was translated into learning to hold power in your body—tautening your muscles, holding yourself firm and upright, striding with a cocky strut, throwing out your chest and walking from the shoulders. (Jackson, 1990, p. 54)

The use of sexual aggression to achieve heroic storylines is also evident in the following transcript. Here Chas and the Karobran study group were attempting to construct a resistive storyline in which they did not fall into patterns dictated by the dominant discourses on masculinity and femininity. Or, more correctly, Chas and Rosie are attempting to do so. The boys are resisting this shift and using the story as an opportunity to assert male power and control over girls/women. While assenting to the fact that there must be a female hero, they find a number of ways to increase their own heroism and the heroism of the males in the story by gaining various forms of ascendancy over the females in the story and over the female story tellers. The group has been discussing what the story is to be about. All want something exciting, to do with danger, murder and mystery. The transcript begins with a struggle on the part of the boys to import rape into the storyline and to connect it to the murder of the rape victim (13). They manage to do this by claiming that they want 'fun' (3) and equality (7-15), that is, there will be both a male and a female victim, so they will be equal/the same. This is a ruse, however, as they are quite clear that the female is to be the 'real' victim (20, 22). Rosie accepts that there must be a victim as she cannot imagine a story without one (17) but she attempts to develop the fun/equality combination by removing the rape (23, 24, 28). She is overruled by the boys and Anna who insist on rape (26, 27, 29):

1 MAL: I've got one, um rape and murder and sex and fun and mystery all together sort of thing, know what I mean? Like there's these people they sort of have sex/

2 BRIAN: Mystery that's boring

3 MAL: it's fun then one of the people want to have sex with a boy so he rapes her and murders her and then it's a mystery to solve it

4 ANNA: Rape, murder, sex and fun . . .

5 KEN: I'd like to do what Mal said . . .

6   CHAS: Now Brian, remember how we're doing a story that completely resists
    all the dominant discourses here and we're going to develop a storyline that
    resists the dominant storylines, we're not going to/
7   KEN: 'cause they are both victims
8   CHAS: Well you'll have to do it in terms of the storyline. Are we going to have
    girl as victim?
9   BRIAN: No
10 ROSIE: No
11 KEN: No
12 CHAS: What are we going to have?
13 BRIAN: Both
14 MAL: Both
15 ROSIE: Both
16 CHAS: Why do we have to have victims anyway?
17 ROSIE: Because otherwise there'd be no story
18 MAL: Because it makes it interesting
19 ANNA: 'Cause that's the mystery part of it
20 MAL: Make it that the girl is the major victim and the guy is just the victim
. . .
21 CHAS: Alright, have you decided you want boy and girl as victim
22 MAL: Yeah, but like the girl is the real victim
23 ROSIE: No . . .
24 ROSIE: They could be having sex and fun and someone comes along and
    murders both of them
. . .
25 CHAS: What are they going to be the victims of?
26 ANNA: Rape and murder
27 MAL: Rape murder
28 ROSIE: No sex and fun because/
29 BRIAN: No rape and murder
    (KAROBRAN PUBLIC)

Thus the boys manage, by assenting to structural equality
between the victims (it is a male and female victim who are to be
murdered, not just a female) to distract attention from their insertion of
the rape into the story, thus guaranteeing at least one moment of male
domination over a female. Mal knows full well that this makes the girl
the 'major victim' (20) or the 'real victim' (22). With the help of Anna, he
manages to overrule Rosie when she tries to change this to a benign
form of sexuality between the two victims (24, 28). Anna's position is
quite different from Mal's and the other boys. As we saw in the last
chapter she knows the world is a dangerous place for girls/women and
does not believe it possible for women on their own to be heroic. She

works at being a tomboy, cultivating herself as male, wanting heroism for herself, not as female but as male. At the same time as she wants a non-sexist world, she works with the boys to hold the male–female binary in place. This is most evident in the next part of the conversation which is a discussion about who is going to be the hero of their story. (They are using the term saviour, following on from their deconstructive reading of *Snow White*.) They start with the idea of using the police but then reject that and finally decide on detectives. Rosie and Chas suggest a female hero (34, 36, 38) but this is rejected by Anna and Ken. Anna wants a male detective (41) and Ken suggests they go for equality again by having a male and a female. This is assented to by Anna on the grounds that the story will not then be sexist. Rosie valiantly tries to continue the story of the female hero who is a friend of the victim, weaving in the male detective as someone she hires (50, 52) but this is regarded as sexist/unequal (53) and so Rosie assents to a male and female couple who are both detectives.

In the following excerpts they discuss first what the female victim, Lisa, will look like and then what the detectives will look like:

30 CHAS: Now, generally in the traditional storylines we have the male saviour, we're resisting that dominant storyline so who are we gonna have or what's gonna happen, who's gonna be the saviour in this?

31 KEN: The police

32 ANNA: Why the saviour?

33 CHAS: Save someone/

34 ROSIE: A policewoman, the girl's best friend, a police woman/

35 ANNA: Can we have something other than that, police this, police that, let's have something different

36 CHAS: Alright, well the girl's best friend?

37 ANNA: The guy's a detective/

38 ROSIE: The girl's best friend found out that she was murdered and she set out to find out who it was so she/

39 ANNA: No

40 KEN: No, no

41 ANNA: A detective

42 CHAS: Alright, it's a private detective but is it going to be a female or a male private detective? 'Cause usually/

43 KEN: Both

44 ANNA: Oh, hopefully male

45 ROSIE: Female

46 ANNA: Have a lady and a man/

47 KEN/MAL: Yeah

48 ANNA: 'cause then it is not um sexist

49 CHAS: Alright, put that down, lady and man

50 ROSIE: But the girl's best friend, she finds she gets a detective/

51 KEN: Yeah, but then it would be sexist

52 ROSIE: to come along and they set out to find out what happened to her

53 ANNA: That'll be sexist if it's only a girl, I reckon there should be two parts, a girl and a boy

54 ROSIE: Actually the two best friends from the man and the woman can set out . . .

55 CHAS: Now we're trying to resist the dominant discourse here. How's Lisa ((the female victim)) going to look, what sort of a girl is she going to be

56 KEN: Sexy

57 CAROLYN: Pretty

58 BRIAN: Scared

59 CHAS: Now look if she's sexy and scared and pretty it's like the dominant discourse revisited. We want something totally different

60 ROSIE: How about this/

61 ANNA: Fat and ugly

62 ROSIE: No

63 BRIAN: Fuckin' ugly!!

64 KEN: Just ordinary

65 CHAS: She could be a bit plump, can't she be a bit plump?

66 ROSIE: Yeah she's chubby

67 ANNA: Abandoned, abandoned with the car . . .

68 BRIAN: ((said very close to the microphone so it couldn't be heard by the others)) Rosie wants to give Mal a root

69 MAL: Brian shut up

70 CHAS: What's Wilfred ((the male detective)) like?

71 ANNA: Dumb, he's big and/

72 ROSIE: No!

73 KEN: No big and sexy

74 BRIAN He's solid

75 KEN: Solid

76 MAL: Solid

77 KEN: Body building

78 BRIAN: Heavy built/

79 CHAS: Alright, solid

80 BRIAN: heavy built

81 ROSIE: He could be a boxer

82 KEN: Like Arnold Schwarzenegger, a body builder

83 CHAS: Now listen you can't have the girl as the wimp then she's got to be just as strong and just as capable as what he is

84 MAL: Big boobs
    (laughter))
85 ROSIE: No she could be sexy looking and very rough
86 BRIAN: That's what you are
    (KAROBRAN PUBLIC)

        In developing the character of Lisa they find it difficult to find an alternative to sexy, pretty and scared. If she cannot be these, she must be fat and ugly (61), even 'fuckin' ugly' (63). This aggressive description from Brian is evocative of an attitude I encountered when counselling an adolescent boy involved in gang rape. He explained to me that girls called 'dogs' are regarded as sexually available to anyone and can be forcefully raped if they do not assent to sex, since they do not belong to anyone. At the same time, my own children explained to me that 'dog' is a common term for ugly girls/women. Brian's whispered statement into the microphone that 'Rosie wants to give Mal a root' (68) follows on from the discussion of the 'fuckin' ugly' victim. It also follows Rosie's attempts to create a solitary female hero. She has put herself at risk by attempting to position herself in her imagination outside the male–female binary and their aggressive sexual talk is letting her know it. The description of the male detective creates no such tension. Apart from Anna's suggestion that he is 'dumb' (71) the group smoothly and collaboratively construct an archetypal powerful male, 'like Arnold Schwarzenegger' (73-82). When Chas asserts that the female detective has to be just as good as the male detective, Mal immediately sexualises her by making her the ultra-female other to Arnold S (84). Rosie assents to the sexuality of the woman, not as sex object, but by asserting that looking sexy is not incompatible with being really rough. This is then turned on her—it is what she is—sexy and rough (86). By association, she is the sexual other to the male hero (Mal/Arnold) and probably at risk of sexual assault.
        Disrupting the binaries is potentially dangerous work. And it is work that is thwarted at every turn. Girls' heroism and power, their claims to an incorporation of masculinity, are made transgressive of their subordinate position to males. Heroism and power are desired and explored by girls, but always undermined, even in the guise of equality. The boys' strategies for undermining the girls are read by the boys as heroic moves against both the girls and the adult women who attempt to control them. Boys' expressions of heroism and power are, in contrast, moves closer towards the male god/adult hero. While they may well be transgressive of childhood and 'goodness', the very adult women who are adult other to their child and who control definitions of goodness, are the very other against whom they can practise their moves towards the god/ideal. Thus Mal and his mates can disrupt Chas's plan to write

a story that undermines the male–female binary with total equanimity. They can do so while appearing to co-operate and to be enthusiastic about the project. Going back to Mal's statement at the beginning of the last chapter, girls can be equal to boys by being like them, and by striving towards the same male god/ideal. But if given the opportunity he will use the girls to achieve displays of (masculine) identity by sexualising them and by undermining the possibility of their achieving heroic positionings. Masculinity is, after all, competitive, and heterosexuality is fundamental to the maintenance of the hierarchical binary.

A DIFFERENT KIND OF TRANSFORMATION

Not all (male) children can achieve the easy, confident dominance that Mal achieves. Nor do all of them want it. In Bird's study of New Zealand primary school children, there was one boy who particularly caught her attention:

> [Sam] constantly disrupted girls' games of elastics, netball and the chase game 'It'. Sam was usually seated away from the other children in the classroom, and would perhaps be called 'hyperactive' by some observers, as he would often call out phrases at inappropriate times, make wrestling poses during class discussion or bring up the off-limits topic of wrestling whenever there was an open discussion of an issue in class. Yet I observed several events that seemed to conflict with my seamless view of Sam as the typical classroom oppressor-of-girls. One day, during writing practice, Sam sat at a table where mostly girls were sitting, hugging a stiff plastic wrestling doll to his chest for the whole lesson . . . On another occasion Sam grabbed a head-band from a girl and then put it on his head across the forehead (Rambo-style, but in lurid pink) to wear for a while. And at a later date, he mentioned a lipstick as an item in a story he was writing . . . I began to wonder if Sam's disruptiveness around the girls' games at lunch times came from an interest in playing games—for example knucklebones—which were off-limits to him because of his gender . . .
>
> . . . For boys, any signs of interest beyond usual male domain of activity can be construed as crossing that barbed wire fence between the genders; of straying from one's real gender to endanger one's proper heterosexual orientation. To take an interest in girls' things is to risk positioning oneself as a girl—to be, in Butler's terminology, boy-as-girl, which in Western culture is synonymous with being a gay male, frequently a reviled social position. How do we react if a boy shows an interest in the touch or feel of a square of satin fabric? Or curiosity about colourful pots of eyeshadow? Or about how a cake is iced? Hush it up! Give that boy a football and pray that he is normal. And if he's a bit rough on his sisters and the girls at school, well boys will be, um, boys, thank goodness. Could it be that homophobic discourses about 'real boys' are

linked with discourses that actually encourage male violence at primary
school, despite competing discourses about fair play and solving conflict
without physical aggression? (Bird, 1992, p. 167)

Sam provides an all too familiar example of the pain that is
involved in squeezing each child into being one and only one of the
oppositional, hierarchical categories male and female. He spills over, is
restrained, becomes desperate. And we are afraid to name what we see.
Children like Sam give us a clue about where the fissures lie, about how
to break open the relentless and apparently intractable polar division of
the social world into male and female. But Sam's struggle is an
inarticulate, perhaps even unconscious one. He does not know what the
problem is, nor how to name what it is he wants. Words like
'hyperactive' and 'gay' are probably all that is available in the discourses
through which the adults in his world speak him into existence. A
discourse through which to speak one's resistance to the male–female
binary and to negotiate one's position in relation to it is rarely made
available to children. If it is made available, as for Mark, one of the boys
in the follow-up study, it makes possible the negotiation of a different
kind of transformation, beyond the male–female binary.

Mark, as a preschool child, was one of only two boys who were
struggling to take themselves up as both masculine and feminine
(Davies, 1989a). He was good at sport and also went to gymnastics and
dance classes. His attempts to incorporate the feminine were not because
he rejected the masculine. Rather, he embraced masculinity whole-
heartedly in many of its forms. In a reading of *The Paper Bag Princess*, for
example, he had said he would like to be like the big male dragon who
was 'after all, the smartest and fiercest dragon in the whole world'. But
he also wanted to be competent in feminine terms, though sometimes he
found the feminine problematic. He was furious once when his father
told me about what he was doing in his dance classes. It embarrassed
him in a way that talk of his prowess in soccer, for example, never did.
He was also very upset when I gave him a feminine gift. Nevertheless,
he had invested himself in a discourse of equity in which each person
should be able to develop in a multitude of ways, unhampered by
having been assigned to one sex or the other.

In the follow-up study I spent a lot of time with him and
discussed a wide range of stories from Corbalis' and Craig's *The
Wrestling Princess* and Williams' *The Practical Princess and other Liberating
Fairy Tales*. One of the predominant themes in these stories is of the king
wanting his daughter to marry and of her finding a way not to, or at
least finding a way to marry a non-hegemonic man of her choice.
Another major theme is that men do not have to be heroic to be likeable
and worthwhile.

Mark was not very taken with stories about men who refused or were incompetent in terms of masculinity. In contrast, he liked *The Wrestling Princess,* Ermyntrude, a tall, assertive and mechanically competent princess. It is the quality of heroism that he likes in any character, with their sex being irrelevant to his positive evaluation of it:

BRONWYN: What do you think of the story so far?

MARK I think that it has been quite funny

BRONWYN: Mmm, in what way?

MARK: Um well it was actually better than the other three stories because it actually had a different character. Like um all the others were um rather stupid males who didn't know much, and this was eh um a strong female um instead of the weak man

BRONWYN: Uh hum . . . So you like her better than you like those three blokes?

MARK: Yes

BRONWYN: And what about her Dad?

MARK: I think that he was a pretty mean bloke [for forcing her to marry]

As the conversation proceeded Mark revealed that he had rejected several constitutive aspects of the male–female binary. He does not perceive male and female as needing to be opposite or different in ways that ensure the dominance of the male. He is quite clear that size and age, for example, are irrelevant in male–female relations. He understands that the world is generally organised to make them so, but he does not assent to this mode of organisation:

BRONWYN: Why do you suppose he did that, measuring the princes ((who were suitors to his daughter))?

MARK: Um because he didn't want um, he didn't want there to be a quite large female and a tiny little male

BRONWYN: Do you think that the woman always has to be shorter than the man?

MARK: No

BRONWYN: So/

MARK: It's the same thing with how old they are. They don't have to be older.

BRONWYN: Right. Does it seem strange to you if the man is shorter than the woman?

MARK: Um, no

Mark's struggle is to establish what Cixous (1981) calls an 'other bisexuality'. Cixous observes that while men are less readily able than women to move beyond maleness/masculinity towards her ideal of an other bisexuality, they nonetheless have the capacity to experience femininity just as women can experience masculinity. Cixous defines other bisexuality, not as the incorporation of two opposite types of being, each defined in terms of their absence of essential qualities that are held in the other, but as the multiplication and inclusion of possibilities in oneself, a multiplication which is possible for those not caught up in the 'false (dualistic) theatre of phallocentrism'. Other bisexuality involves:

> . . . each one's location in self (*reperage en soi*) of the presence—variously manifest and insistent according to each person, male or female—of both sexes, non-exclusion either of the difference or of one sex, and, from this 'self-permission', multiplication of the effects of the inscription of desire, over all parts of my body and the other body. (Cixous, 1981, p. 254)

In moving towards Cixous's other bisexuality, Mark's subjectivity is self-consciously in opposition to the dominant discourse on masculinity. He resists and disrupts the dominant discourse by engaging with and taking on as his own aspects of femininity. To do so he ignores or negates usual signifiers of maleness and femaleness. He experiences himself, not as shaped by his peers, but as following his own commitments and desires, no matter how fraught the consequences might be:

BRONWYN: Don't you think that boys are under a lot of pressure to um prove that they are tough?

MARK: No. Some boys don't want to prove that they're tough. They just want (   ) like me

BRONWYN: Mm. So you don't feel that there's sort of a contradiction. Do you know what contradiction means?

MARK: Na

BRONWYN: Means where

MARK: Absolutely have to

BRONWYN: No, where um one thing's true, seems to be true, but the opposite seems to be true as well. Like you are supposed to be like a boy but you are also supposed not to be aggressive and um a bully and all those things

MARK: Yeah. I'm not aggressive and I'm not a bully

BRONWYN: But if you were too much like a girl would- the other kids would give you a hard time wouldn't they?

MARK: No because I've got this rather large friend

BRONWYN: Yeah

MARK: And um he he just um says 'shut up' and 'be quiet' and they do

BRONWYN: Do they?

MARK: Yep

BRONWYN: So you feel that you are really free to be anything that you want to be?

MARK: Yep

BRONWYN: So, what about, I mean you have to wear clothes like a boy don't you and you have to have your hair like a boy?

MARK: Na not necessarily. Everyone calls me a girl because I've got a rat's tail

BRONWYN: Do they?

MARK: That doesn't mean I'm a girl

BRONWYN: Oh no it doesn't mean that

MARK: And everyone calls me a girl because I wear a bit of pink socks or something. And I say to them 'my Dad's got a pink dressing gown' and that makes them think twice

BRONWYN: Mmm. So are you different from the other boys because your dad is different from other men?

MARK: No

BRONWYN: No. Why do you suppose that you are different?

MARK: I don't know. I don't, I don't want to do the same things as other kids

BRONWYN: Yeah

MARK: I like to try a different approach to things, try and do different things

BRONWYN: But they do pressure you don't they?

MARK: Yep

BRONWYN: They say things like that. And you have just had to develop strategies to cope with that

MARK: Yep

BRONWYN: Does it, does it, is that part of what makes you feel tense?

MARK: Mmm

BRONWYN: It is, yeah

MARK: Sometimes when I get, mostly when I get tense I feel like throwing up

BRONWYN: Yeah. Is that at school or at home or both?

MARK: Both

BRONWYN: And um so that tension comes from that kind of um, conflict between, what you want to be and what the world says you ought to be

MARK: Mmm

BRONWYN: Um, so, now when you go off and play elastics with the girls is that one of the times that you get teased by some of the boys?

MARK: Yep

BRONWYN: 'Cause they think that you are doing it wrong, they don't see that you've got the right to be free like that and do what you want to do

MARK: Yep

BRONWYN: So, so how many boys would there be in your grade who you could say were feminist in that they think that you have the right to do anything that you want to do?

MARK: Quite a few

BRONWYN: Quite a few

MARK: Um, aw then there's this other boy called Damien who is a complete nut

BRONWYN: Uh hm

MARK: He thinks, he thinks um the only way to be is um what he thinks is a boy

BRONWYN: Ah hmm

MARK: And if they're not (   ) he finds something that's funny about them and then just calls them by their name, whenever he sees them

BRONWYN: Oh really

MARK: Actually he calls me 'Ratty' because of the rat tail

BRONWYN: Right, right

MARK: It's really awful

BRONWYN: Uh hm, so how does that make you feel

MARK: Bad

BRONWYN: Why does it worry you, why does it worry you what kids like him think?

MARK: Well I don't really like being teased like that

BRONWYN: Mmm. When you got your hair cut short and the ratty tail down the back what made you decide that?

MARK I um don't know, what I just thought was um, I just wanted to have a haircut like that. Now um there are four or five Grade Fours that have had it shaved off, just got it spikey

BRONWYN: Uh hm with a rats tail or just shaved off?

MARK: They've just got it spikey here

BRONWYN: Right, right so in a way short at the top like a traditional boy and long at the back like a traditional girl?

MARK: Yeah

BRONWYN: Like a, an amazing combination

MARK I mi- I might even try and get it long here

BRONWYN: Yeah

MARK: And then no one will be able to call me anything

BRONWYN: Right because you'll be both

MARK: Yeah

BRONWYN: Would you like that?

MARK: (   ) I'm trying to get this rats tail to grow a bit longer

Mark somewhat heroically refuses to take up the masculine as it is defined in the dominant gender discourses, that is, as excluding the feminine. He relies on his Sancho Panza-like friend to defend him from the worst excesses of the category maintenance work that is directed at him. For him, masculinity has become highly visible, in part through his marginal status created by his refusal of the dualistic, hierarchical definition of maleness. 'Marginality is visible and painfully visceral' (Kimmel, 1990, p. 94): 'Mostly when I get tense I feel like throwing up'. It has also been made visible through the discourse he shares with his parents about what it means to be a person not trapped inside the gender order. While Mark does not negate masculinity, he includes signifiers of femininity. It is this inclusion that leads others to position him as one who is marginal. While he can call on his father's authority (as the wearer of the pink dressing gown) to aid in the legitimation of his transgressive position, it is nonetheless made transgressive in Damien's talk. Damien with his nickname 'Ratty', and the boys who call him a girl, position him in such a way that he cannot simply be part of the crowd. From this marginal position he struggles to take himself up within the terms of the commitments or investments he has made in a non-hegemonic discourse. Just as it is dangerous for girls to transgress, so too is it difficult for boys. It creates a sickening bodily tension for Mark even though there are 'quite a few' feminist boys in his class who do not position him as marginal. Though it is a struggle, Mark does successfully combine the masculine and the feminine, not as opposites arranged hierarchically against each other, but as a multitude of pleasurable possibilities that he has access to.

In the next chapter I will further elaborate the part that sexuality, and in particular images of sexuality, plays in maintaining the male–female binary.

6 Sexuality

CHAS: *Did you say a slut?*
KEN: *Yep*
CHAS: *Why do you think she's a slut?*
BRIAN: *Oh well she/*
ROSIE: *She's not. She hasn't even been out with a boy*
BRIAN: *So!*
MAL: *Yeah Brian*
ANNA: *She's not a gutter snipe*
BRIAN: *You are though*

TO WRITE of sexuality, with myself in the text, is somehow to ask more and differently of myself than in the previous chapters. Until now I have been writing myself in as a way of connecting with the otherness of the children of the various studies, and of gaining access to what they say through writing of my own subjectification. But sexual knowledge is more unconscious than conscious. The unconscious, Weber says, in his essays on Lacan, is constituted through discourse, though not in the same way as the conscious. It is the 'traces' of discourse, the limits and possibilities it provides, its scene setting properties and its storylines that impact on the unconscious:

As a concept the unconscious is thus 'forged on the trace of what works to constitute the subject'. (Weber, 1991, p. 10, quoting and translating Lacan's *Ecrits*)

> . . . if discourse can be said to set the stage, the unconscious marks the eccentricity of its enabling limits. There is the unconscious, not as an object of perception or intuition, not as a clinical object, but as a theatrical scene that in turn is inscribed in an ongoing scenario. (Weber, 1991 , pp. 10-11)

The unconscious provides the individual sexual subject, then, with enabling limits, with images or theatrical scenes and storylines or scenarios through and in terms of which we constitute our sexual selves. Sexual knowledge also belongs in the Imaginary, the preverbal; it is inscribed in the body.[1] To write of one's own sexual subjectification and to write that of others is to write more from the body, to submerge oneself in the intangible, the unsayable, and to allow it to surface. It is an attempt to think beyond and outside the inadequate available discourses on sexuality.

Cixous' ideal is that we should always write this way:

> . . . 'to write *of* always slips into 'to write *on*', which puts the writing subject in the position of mastery. Cixous wants to write as often as possible *of* or *with* a body, a thing, that exists in an instant never arrested, fixed, but leading to the next instance of presence, essence. Not the tomb, the mummification. The other remains distant in her proximity, forever other, not to be appropriated, repressed, forgotten. Women are more open to otherness because of their cultural position and because of their relation to the child, a relation thought of as the effect of *jouissance*, of pleasure, rather than on the level of the organ. They know how to *s'eautrer* (to become other in birth water) as *mer-mere* (sea-mother) and to communicate preverbally from unconscious to unconscious. To write *with*, derived from the expression *to be with child*, insists less on a presence, a perception, than on a *process* of gestation and birth, away from irreversible genealogy . . . (Conley, 1991, p. 100)

---

[1]The Imaginary, according to Cixous 'is both a chronological stage in individual maturation that is dominated by the perceptual and the later survival of sense making patterns marked by these preverbal, pre-Oedipal forms of understanding (1986, p. 165). The 'unconscious' is used in various ways by different authors. In its most usual Freudian sense it is part of an oppositional hierarchical binary with consciousness being the ascendant binary opposite of the unconscious. The conscious–unconscious binary has many features in common with the male–female binary, woman and the unconscious both being the dark and mysterious continent to be controlled and dominated. I do not use the term unconscious as part of such a binary. The fluid movement between conscious and unconscious aspects of mind precludes such a binary division. I use the term unconscious to refer to all that we know except that which is conscious at any particular moment. As such it includes the Imaginary as well as later acquired verbal and perceptual knowledges. What we know consciously can slip into the unconscious and vice versa. Unconscious knowledge informs and is informed by conscious knowledge. It can be highly restricting and it can also be a creative and liberating force. While unconscious knowledge is in some ways more fluid than conscious knowledge, being less constrained by rational forms of thought and more able to make connections through metaphor and image, it can also be more intractable because it is less accessible to straightforward examination.

In writing this chapter, then, I have tried to write with the children, giving birth to myselves from the *sea-mother* of my own unconscious, enabling me to relate to them as other, both distant from myself, yet coming to know each 'I' as my own, multiplying the positions from which I can write and speak.[2]

The part that stories play in shaping the unconscious, the traces and the enabling limits is difficult to capture. What slides into, informing and shaping the unconscious is, by definition, not open to inspection. It surfaces through dreams, in tranquil meditative moments, in poetry and other forms of creative writing and in powerful, inexplicable emotions. It can also provide the storylines through which we organise our talk and our relations with others without any conscious recognition on our part that we are doing so. Although we cannot know precisely how the unconscious functions, we can nevertheless observe some of its effects.

An example of unconscious storylines structuring talk took place in a conversation that I observed between a primary school teacher and his students on their first day back at school. Consciously they were having a light-hearted friendly chat about the holidays. Consciously the teacher regarded the boys and girls as both learning to be 'well adjusted' and at the same time learning to be agents of change. Unconsciously he evoked the (hetero)sexual storyline in which the boy he was talking to was a solitary adventurer while his sister was a fragile child needing to be cared for, or alternatively someone who would grow up to become an attractive woman who would make male adventures all the more exciting:

1 MR GOOD: ((Looking at John)) Tell us about your trip to Sydney, mate
2 JOHN: Um, we went down to Sydney with Aunty Sue on the plane, and came back on the plane by ourselves
3 MR GOOD: Was that a thrill! Was that the first time you'd been on an aircraft?
4 JOHN: It's the first time I'd been on one by myself, ah back by ourselves
5 MR GOOD: And Deb! Deb, . . . how did you like it on the aircraft?
6 DEB: Really good
7 MR GOOD: Hostesses look after you well? Were they good lookin'? Pretty? ((Mr Good raises his eyebrows and rolls his eyes upwards and smiles. The students laugh. He looks back in John's direction.)) Pretty hostess makes a flight very nice doesn't it?

Mr Good constitutes John as his mate and interprets his trip as a solitary thrilling adventure. In (1) and (3) 'your' and 'you' can be heard in the singular. Though John indicates in (2) that Deb was there too, he

---

[2]In doing so I have found myself speaking/writing my way into a number of highly controversial positions in relation to childhood sexuality. I hope that what I write here opens up dialogue on some of these issues rather than further entrenching the barriers between the existing 'camps'.

slips in (4) into the same storyline as Mr Good, but then corrects himself. At this point, Mr Good, not having heard the earlier plural reference, expresses some surprise (5) as he remembers that Deb was on the trip. He turns to Deb, but constitutes her experience as quite different from John's. The images relevant to the male heroic narrative are maintained with Deb positioned as the fragile female (who can be looked after or presumably saved) or as the sexy woman who can make the adventure more exciting. The subject position of hero, who goes out adventuring, was not made available to her in making meaning of her experience. John and Deb and the other children in the class can join in the talk and make sense of what Mr Good says because they know these positions and this narrative without having to consciously attend to it. (See Davies, 1990c, for a more detailed analysis.)

And so it is with the interpretation of stories we read. We know how to hear them because of what we already 'know' and our 'knowing' is further informed in the hearing. When we hear a story, such as *Little Red Riding Hood*, for example, we almost certainly do not consciously hear it as a story setting the limits on adult–child sexuality. It is a story about a girl and her grandmother and a bad wolf. On hearing the story we know that it is not relevant to ask *why* Little Red Riding Hood is dressed as she is. The image of her in her little red hood, carrying her little covered basket is, rather, taken on as a visual image necessary for the imaginative construction of the story about her vulnerability in a dangerous world. But it is an image easily connected in the unconscious with the flower-like hooded clitoris, the wing-like labia and the vagina holding good but hidden things. The conscious mind might balk at such a connection, since it has learned the adult–child binary, the innocent asexual nature of childhood, and to construct its knowing in rational linear terms. The unconscious need not so balk, since image and metaphor, the unnameable, can readily be accommodated there.

Little Red Riding Hood is a little girl, her pink face hidden by a red hood and the red wings of her cape flowing out behind, protecting her. She is entreated by her mother not to stray from the known path, rather to do exactly as she is told by her mother. Blinkered, she must not look into, nor stray towards the forest, the unknown. But she does stray from the known path, thus failing to constitute herself correctly as (obedient, cautious, female) child. The danger that her mother had warned her against, without ever naming it, was rapacious men, the wolves who would 'devour' her (and even her grandmother). The little girl is sexually vulnerable without that fact ever having been named. Moreover she is responsible for her vulnerability because she did not properly constitute herself as girl/child, as obedient to the instructions which would have kept her properly innocent.

From Zipes, 1986, p. 245

If such a reading is taken on unconsciously, the little girl knows, without being able to speak it, both the wrongness of her own sexuality and her guilt should she be sexually molested. Thus at the same time as the girl child is constituted as one who is ignorant of sexuality, a complex unconscious knowing is made available that 'sets the enabling limits' of her experience. When constituted as a sexual being she may well be trapped into a combination of horror and an inability to speak her resistance. Virginia Woolf's description of her molestation at the hands of her older step-brother illustrates this dynamic perfectly:

> There was a small looking glass in the hall at Talland House. It had, I remember, a ledge with a brush on it. By standing on tiptoe I could see my face in the glass. But I only did this if I was sure that I was alone. I was ashamed of it. A strong feeling of guilt seemed naturally attached to it . . . [I experienced] ecstasies and raptures spontaneously and intensely and without any shame or the least sense of guilt, so long as they were

disconnected with my own body. Another memory, also of the hall, may help to explain this. There was a slab outside the dining room door for standing dishes upon. Once when I was very small Gerald Duckworth lifted me onto this, and as I sat there he began to explore my body. I can remember the feel of his hand going under my clothes; going firmly and steadily lower and lower. I remember how I hoped that he would stop; how I stiffened and wriggled as his hand approached my private parts. But it did not stop. His hand explored my private parts too. I remember resenting, disliking it—what is the word for so dumb and mixed a feeling? It must have been strong as I still recall it. (Woolf, 1976, pp. 78, 79-80)

The feeling is 'dumb and mixed', unspeakable, not clear, but very powerful. It is clearly informed by the unconscious, since it is nothing she can speak, but something she feels strongly, knows in her body and emotions. I will return to this story again, later in the chapter, as well as in subsequent chapters.

Sexuality informs children's conscious and unconscious minds long before they are actively sexual. And as became evident in the last chapter, there is a slippage between adulthood and childhood in children's subjectivities. Stories constitutive of the girls and their lives often included the terms woman and lady, and the boys slipped between constituting themselves as boys and as men. Children's striving towards agency or adult forms of knowledge and control over their lives (such as in their managing of the perv, Mr Molner) co-exists with their placement in the category of (non-sexual) child whose life is controlled by adults.

In the following conversation about the film *Pretty Woman*, the St Clement's girls display this co-existence perfectly. They are clearly involved in the identity of the central (adult) female character, enjoying her sexiness and her relaxed and humorous control over the use of condoms. As well, they experience her upset at being robbed of agency when she is sexually molested, positioned against her will as prostitute or slut, available to any male for the taking. The fabric of the conversation itself contains the same slippage between knowledgeable control in relation to sexuality and fear of being positioned as children without agency, as beings who can be punished for their sexual knowledge:

CHAS: Tell me why you like it, what makes it a good story as far as you're concerned?

TIFFANY: Well *Pretty Woman*, its interesting and its got sexy women in it ((laughter)) and she goes 'what colour condom, pink one, purple one, blue one', there's really funny parts in it and it's just really/

VICTORIA: Oh that was sad at the end. How you know the man who the other man works with, the tall man, you know, the short man how he goes, 'If I just mm! you' then they (   )/

TIFFANY: No, you can say it, Chas is not gonna get angry

VICTORIA: Will you tell anyone?

CHAS: No

VICTORIA: Promise not my parents?

CHAS: Cross my heart, spit my death

VICTORIA: And he's going like this 'If I just screw you'/

ELIZABETH: If I what?

TIFFANY: Screw you, root whatever

VICTORIA: Yeah and then he goes, 'Screw you' And then he gets on top and she goes 'Get off me get off me!'

CHAS: Oh that was horrible/

VICTORIA: I know

CHAS: I hated him

MARCELLA: Did you see that?

CHAS: Yes

MARCELLA: Oh, that was the best movie

(ST CLEMENT'S)

At first, Victoria manages the two worlds by telling her story, but omitting the crucial sexual word that displays her knowledge ('If I just mm! you'). Tiffany intervenes, defining Chas as the sort of adult who will not be angry if they display sexual knowledge. Guarantees are then extracted from Chas that she will not betray them to other adults. She gives her word, slipping back into childhood culture with the words 'cross my heart, spit my death'. Having gained this guarantee that they will not be positioned as powerless children, the conversation becomes one among women, Chas's talk and the girls' talk flowing together as they share their horror at the way in which the female hero was robbed of her agency.

Nowhere is this slippage between agency/control and 'being a child' more evident than when sexual relations are either being discussed or played out. Where boundaries are potentially least clear, there we can expect the strongest taboos, the intended function of which is to keep the boundaries intact. Taboos may be enshrined in law or religion or in parental maxims. They may also be encoded in storylines, in metaphors and images that are apprehended not so much by the conscious mind as by the unconscious. They are taken on as one's own, they form the substance through which one knows and feels, they are experienced as coming from within, an expression of the 'real self'. The taboos that we eventually come to experience as 'natural', what anyone would want and feel, are arguably those where a great deal of work has been done to establish the boundary in the first place. The boundaries between adult and child, between male and female and between (acceptable) heterosexuality and (unacceptable) homosexuality are three of the boundaries that become relevant in this chapter.

Ignorance/innocence in relation to sexuality or lack of interest in it has long been one of the primary defining features of childhood, in particular of female childhood. This has not always been so. The original version of *Little Red Riding Hood*, as Zipes shows, was one in which the girl both knew about sexuality and had agency in relation to it:

There was a woman who had made some bread. She said to her daughter:

'Go carry this hot loaf and bottle of milk to your granny.'

So the little girl departed. At the crossway she met *bzou*, the werewolf, who said to her:

'Where are you going?'

'I'm taking this hot loaf and a bottle of milk to my granny.'

'What path are you taking,' said the werewolf, 'the path of needles or the path of pins?'

'The path of needles,' the little girl said.

'All right, then I'll take the path of pins.'

The little girl entertained herself by gathering needles. Meanwhile, the werewolf arrived at the grandmother's house, killed her, put some of her meat in the cupboard and a bottle of her blood on the shelf. The little girl arrived and knocked at the door.

'Push the door,' said the werewolf, 'It's barred by a piece of wet straw.'

'Good day, Granny. I've brought you a hot loaf of bread and a bottle of milk.'

'Put it in the cupboard my child. Take some of the meat which is inside and the bottle of wine on the shelf.'

After she had eaten there was a little cat which said: 'Phooey! . . . A slut is she who eats the flesh and drinks the blood of her granny.'

'Undress yourself, my child,' the werewolf said, 'and come lie down beside me.'

'Where should I put my apron?'

'Throw it into the fire my child, you won't be needing it anymore.'

And each time she asked where she should put all her other clothes, the bodice, the dress, the petticoat, and the long stockings, the wolf responded:

'Throw them into the fire my child, you won't be needing them anymore.'

When she laid herself down on the bed, the little girl said:

'Oh Granny, how hairy you are!'

'The better to keep myself warm, my child!'

'Oh Granny, what big nails you have!'

'The better to scratch me with, my child!'

'Oh Granny, what big shoulders you have!'

'The better to carry the firewood, my child!'

'Oh Granny, what big ears you have!'

'The better to hear you with, my child!'

'Oh Granny, what big nostrils you have!'

'The better to snuff my tobacco with, my child!'

'Oh Granny, what a big mouth you have!'

'The better to eat you with, my child!'

'Oh Granny I've got to go badly. Let me go outside.'

'Do it in bed, my child!'

'Oh no, Granny, I want to go outside.'

'All right, but make it quick.'

The werewolf attached a woollen rope to her foot and let her go outside.

When the little girl was outside, she tied the end of the rope to a plum tree in the courtyard. The werewolf became impatient and said: 'Are you making a load out there? Are you making a load?'

When he realised that nobody was answering him, he jumped out of bed and saw that the little girl had escaped. He followed her but arrived at her house just at the moment she entered. (Zipes, 1986, pp. 228-229)

When explicit sexuality was removed from such stories it was encoded in the images (such as dress) and in the storylines in such a way that the information was still there but not in a readily consciously apprehendable form. And as Zipes points out, that submerged sexual storyline shifted dramatically away from the competent girl who can manage to look after herself in the face of male sexuality towards an ignorant and incompetent girl/child who is a victim at the mercy of rapacious wolves and totally dependent on kindly men to save her. The storylines and images which inform the unconscious then, are historically and culturally specific. But because of the way gendered identity is constructed as ontological, we come to experience the storylines and images as natural, timeless and our own.

As became evident in the previous chapters both male and female children strive to have agency. But agency, and in particular sexual agency, is made problematic for girls in a number of ways. As the modern Red Riding Hood story shows, or as Rosie experienced in her attempts to tell a story with a female hero, agency puts girls at risk, not just with adults but with boys their own age. Even to be named as having sexual interests can be dangerous since that is constituted as *inviting* sex from boys/men. Heterosexuality is continually constructed in the children's talk as they separate and heighten the difference between themselves as male and female. So pervasive is this construction that even the most simple initiative on a girl's part, such as asking a boy for a pencil, can be overlaid with compromising (hetero) sexual meanings. The boys, in contrast, are not compromised by (hetero)sexuality. Mal's constant linking of Rosie and Brian in the last chapter sickened Rosie, but elevated Brian. In the following transcript, Philo displays an easeful shrugging off of unwanted sexual positioning in marked contrast with the girls:

JENNIFER: . . . yesterday I considered that I went as low as to actually ask a boy if I could borrow a pencil 'cause we were doing those um drawings . . .

STACEY: You really wouldn't want to ask them, um, people would tease you and you wouldn't, it's not very nice to be teased about something when you are just asking for a pencil, and somebody, and people get the wrong idea

CHAS: What idea do they get?

STACEY: Like you really like them . . .

CHARLOTTE: Like um, if you are just talking to a boy like in clay work, me and Tania were talking to the boys in front of us and Jill kept on calling us 'flirters' just 'cause we are talking to them

JENNIFER: Yeah

STACEY: Mrs Brown, Mrs Brown sometimes says 'I'll move the boys'

JENNIFER: Which she doesn't . . .

CHAS: So will you boys not talk to girls because you are afraid that people will think that you fancy them? Is that the case with you boys too?

BOYS: No not really

JENNIFER: Philo hasn't said nothing just about

CHAS: Philo is over there in deep thought. There are going to be pearls of wisdom drop out of that mouth before we know it ((laughter)). Are you worried about talking to girls Philo?

PHILO: No

ZAC: Especially not when it's his girlfriend

PHILO: I just, say if I went up and asked Judy for a pair of scissors or something, she goes (   ) or something, and if she hangs around with me in the playground you just say 'Oh go away'/

JAMES: Yep/

PHILO: Then she doesn't bug you any more

(EASTERN PUBLIC)

Only those who are in committed (or admitted) relationships can talk to each other without fear of being teased. But even Stacey, who is in a love relationship with Jake, has to be careful about the boundaries of the relationship. At her age, she says, she must confine the relationship to contacts at school, or else run the risk of being 'one of these tarty and floozy sort of girls':

CHAS: Do you see each other out of school time ever at all?

STACEY: No

. . .

CHAS: Oh, so really it's a relationship that's very much centred around the school/

STACEY: mmm/

CHAS: being at school

STACEY: 'Cause ah well, I'm not, I've probably got parents who are a bit stricter than others, mm probably, not strict but want me to grow up to be a nice girl not one of these tarty and floozy sort of girls

CHAS: Mm right, so are you saying that they're not the sort of parents that'd really let you go out with a boyfriend at this age?

STACEY: Not at this age. They probably thought it's fine to have a boyfriend at school but not anywhere else

. . .

CHAS: I see, so would you say in fact that you felt love for Jake? ((nods)) You do, you love him? Do you think that he loves you?

STACEY: I hope so.

CHAS: Well do you think he does?

STACEY: He wrote a letter to me saying so

CHAS: He did did he?

STACEY: Yep

CHAS: Right, right, so it's more than, as far as you're concerned it's more than just a sort of little school romance, you actually feel love for this person. Right, have you fantasised about for example you know marrying him when you're older and/

STACEY: Yeah, I have actually, I was thinking about things and what will it be like and wonder what happens when I get married and he always comes in the picture as my husband

CHAS: Does he?

STACEY: 'Cause I can't imagine anyone else sort of thing

CHAS: Right

STACEY: Even if I do have someone else he probably wouldn't be much different

(EASTERN PUBLIC—CONVERSATION WITH STACEY)

Even prior to the striking up of actively (hetero)sexual relationships, then, there are prototype relationships. Being in one of these is safer than not being in one in many ways. Stacey and Philo, who each have admitted relationships, are free from the kind of teasing that Rosie, for example, was subjected to by Mal. The other safe path is to avoid any contact at all, to heighten the difference between male and female so that contact becomes irrelevant and undesirable. The patterns of femininity and masculinity traced in the last two chapters are exaggerated in this process. The boys' heroism and god-like status in relation to the girl's otherness, her fragility and sexual availability, is made more central. The experience of sameness and of shared competencies is lost (at least in the boys' eyes) in this heightening of difference.

In the following conversation about why boys and girls do not play together, James and Zac describe male–female differences that profoundly contradict the obvious similarities in the study group. This is followed by a strong refusal, by the girls, of these claims of difference. In reply, James uses a metaphor from *Sleeping Beauty* thus drawing on knowledge of story to articulate the difference. While there may actually be no observable differences, and while the girls might say they do not want to be cast as fragile and vulnerable, according to James, their *desire* is informed by such storylines, they 'really' want to prick their fingers and become like Sleeping Beauty.

The conversation begins just after Chas has asked James whether he has any friends who are girls, to which he replies that he has not:

CHAS: Why is that I wonder? Why do you think that might be James?

JAMES: 'Cause it's not interesting probably, I don't know

STACEY: It is probably because girls don't see, they might look at each other and say 'Oh yuk I don't like this person 'cause of all the things they do and the way they'/

JENNIFER: Yeah, the way they don't have any female friends! Apart from his dog

CHAS: Zac do you have female friends?

ZAC: Nup 'cept for my sister

CHAS: Do you Philo?

PHILO: Yes

STACEY: Yes

JENNIFER: Yes ((Laughter))

CHAS: You do have female friends?

CHARLOTTE: Girls are inclined to say, besides having a boyfriend, it's yukky to sit next to a boy or to socialise but I think/

CHAS: Do you think there is a lot of friction and conflict between the boys and girls at school?

ALL: Yeah yeah

STACEY: No, no, no

CHAS: Zac why do you think that there is friction and conflict?

ZAC: Well for a start boys and girls are never playing the same games with each other ((Laughter))

JENNIFER: Want a bet? ((tone of voice heavily loaded with sexual innuendo)) . . .

ZAC: And um boys stick to their games and girls stick to theirs 'cause girls play their games

CHAS: What are the girls' games?

ZAC: Um games/

JAMES: That aren't rough . . . And don't require much, and don't require much strength and energy/

JENNIFER: Energy!

JAMES: like they'll sit down and talk

ZAC: (They play) netball

JAMES: Yeah, netball but they don't do stuff like swing a really heavy bat or anything like that and they just go around passing the ball/

JENNIFER: Ohh !!!

JAMES: with netball

CHARLOTTE: Some people, some people who are really skilled in netball, I would like to see you get up and play some of the champion netballers

JENNIFER: I doubt very much you could be runner up in your um/

CHARLOTTE: It is very hard, its really, I don't/

CHAS: Do you think there is a lot of competition goes on between boys and girls? Like I hear you saying, 'girls can't do this' and I hear the girls saying 'Oh yes they can'. Does this sort of thing go on in schools a lot?

ALL: Yes

STACEY: Yes, boys tend to put girls down as lazy and not active, but some girls are just ((sniggering from boys))/

CHAS: That's all right this is what I want to hear about

STACEY: well some girls are just really active, and like Charlotte likes doing gymnastics and is really good at it and she is quite active all the time and I like doing swimming and tennis and running and I I am active a lot and sometimes I just can't keep still, like I have to get up and do something . . .

CHARLOTTE: I think it is getting back to what the differences are in what they do because boys, I think, it may not be true, but I think boys tend to go back to that sort of thing of saying, 'Girls are supposed to like pink and they are supposed to do the cooking, and they are not supposed to do this', but things have changed and they do do more . . .

CHAS: Well do you fellows think you think differently to girls?

JAMES: Yeah 'cause girls rather prefer pricking themselves with a needle than doing something like agriculture

CHAS: Do you agree with that?

CHAR STACEY, JENNIFER: No, no no definitely not

CHARLOTTE: I'd love to do agriculture, I think it would be interesting with all the sort/

STACEY: There are some girls who *might* want to do things like pricking their finger/

CHARLOTTE: Nowdays it is even less um common that boys and girls are different, but I think um from way back when they *had* to be different and they had to do separate things is only just sort of growing out. Like um boys *still* think that, you know, 'Oh I have to be a boy so I have to do this and this' and you know I have, they sort of don't like these colours and like to do this and think this way and so it is just coming less common but it is still there

(EASTERN PUBLIC)

The girls are readily able to argue that the boys are wrong, that girls cannot be constituted as opposite to boys in the way that they are doing. These girls are not vulnerable and fragile (lacking in strength and energy). Not only are they observably active and competent but they can see that the champion netballers far exceed these boys in strength and energy. But they are also aware of the same storylines the boys are drawing on. They concede that some girls might want to be traditionally feminine ('There are some girls who *might* want to do things like pricking their finger'). But Charlotte argues that while the boys might push the girls and themselves into being opposite and different, that this is really a left over from the past and no longer appropriate.

But the separation nevertheless takes place. And, at the same time, that separateness and difference is eroticised. The investment in difference which leads to the separation comes to be read as sexually exciting. As the following conversation with Jennifer shows, she doesn't know where this knowledge comes from, nor does she find it easy to put into words:

CHAS: Would you like to go to a private school?

JENNIFER: No

CHAS: Why not?

JENNIFER: No boys . . . Because boys sort of you know, just like a friend, like boys have a different side of them and everything and it's more interesting than just having the sort of girls' view. They'll probably swear a bit more and everything but it's more interesting, it's more fun to hang around with a boy

CHAS: But you give the boys such a hard time

JENNIFER: I know, well they give us a hard time

CHAS: I don't understand, explain this to me, when/

JENNIFER: Oh we give the boys a hard time 'cause, 'cause they're boys. I mean because sometimes you hate them swearing and sort of hanging around all tough and spastic like that but then again you sort of want, you want them to do that

CHAS: Why do you want them to do it?

JENNIFER: ((laughs)) I don't know. Oh because you want a different relationship, you know, you had a girl relationship all through your life and then the boys are so different and you want something different, you don't want to live all your life you know hanging around with the girls 'cause, all this about you know what I've just said, that's something I've never thought about before. I've never ever thought about that. It's weird

CHAS: That's great it's/

JENNIFER It's you. It's you, I'm telling you it's you, you made me say something I've never thought about before. That's why I'm having difficulty saying it

(EASTERN PUBLIC—CONVERSATION WITH JENNIFER)

Just as Jennifer struggles to say how it is that these awful boys can be attractive, even desirable, so I have wondered how I made the transition from the gentle, sensuous, easy affection I experienced with my girlfriends to an almost intractable heterosexuality, so often debilitating, unpleasant and destructive. It seems from the children's talk that the process is one of refusing to be marginalised, of struggling to name oneself and be named as acceptable, as being located correctly within the dominant discourses on sexuality. Those who escape the imposition of the inevitability of heterosexuality must either resign themselves to being marginal in some way, or find a group in which the dominant form of heterosexuality is not spoken into existence as inevitable.

Mark, from the Follow-up study, talked about the way in which boys heighten their masculinity in order to be popular. In a more recent conversation with him at the age of eleven, he says he doesn't do that because he wants to be himself, which is a 'bit like a girl'. For this he is often teased and marginalised by these boys, but he has learned to take it, to go along with them: 'If they say I'm dumb, I just say, oh yes I'm dumb'. Occasionally, he thinks of lines that put an end to their teasing:

MARK: A lot of the more masculine people tease people about being gay. Paul Redden, who's very masculine called me a poofter. I said 'If I am is it any of your business?'

BRONWYN: Did that shut him up?

MARK: Yes

In the following transcript Tiffany is clearly seizing an opportunity to display her sexual knowledge/competence. Her knowledge includes details of homosexuality. She works quite hard to position herself, however, as one who has this knowledge but is nevertheless heterosexual. She engages in category maintenance work on the others as a partial display of this knowledge and as a way of maintaining her own position as heterosexual. At the same time Elizabeth's lack of knowledge is painfully evident. Imagining this conversation from Elizabeth's point of view, in awe of the unknown words and the detailed knowledges of others, it is possible to see how vulnerable one is in not sharing the obviousnesses talked into existence by others. Knowing them, making them your own, is an essential prerequisite to membership of the social group:

TIFFANY: I know what I was gonna say. Can I say it before I forget it again? Well if a boy wanted to read a girls' book he'd be a poofter/

VICTORIA: He would not. If he wanted to read a girls' book he could read a girls' book!

TIFFANY: Cut straight through me again why don't ya

CHAS: Why do you think that? Why do you think that if a boy wants/

TIFFANY: Because boys don't normally read girls' books unless they're a poofter or something is wrong with them, and then if girls sort of like read boys' books, she's sort of like a tomboy

. . .

MARCELLA: A boy isn't going to put perfume on to read a girls' book!

CHAS: Why not?

TIFFANY: Well there's something weird with him

CHAS: Why isn't there, tell me Marcella

MARCELLA: You know how girls like pink and boys like blue and green well my brother likes pink

TIFFANY: So. Oh my brother likes pink

MARCELLA: And I like blue and green. They're my favourite colours

TIFFANY: It doesn't matter, I'm not talking about the colours

MARCELLA: Well I can read a boys' book if I want, it doesn't make me a lesbian/

TIFFANY: Errh!

MARCELLA: or whatever

CHAS: So you don't like lesbians either?

TIFFANY: No. My mum used to be a lesbian

CHAS: Well what's wrong with lesbians?

TIFFANY: I don't like my mum

MARCELLA: I'm just saying it doesn't make you a lesbian

ELIZABETH: What is a lesbian?

CHAS: A lesbian is a woman/

TIFFANY: If two girls have sex or like they finger each other/

MARCELLA: And they go to, and they go, and they hang around with each other

VICTORIA: Like boys who do it together are gay and girls who do it/

CHAS: Two women that love each other is what it is generally/

TIFFANY: Like finger each other and/

CHAS: Well men and women do that to one another it's/

TIFFANY: I know but a lesbian is that, two girls. I almost got fingered the other day but I didn't

VICTORIA: Who by?

TIFFANY: Not telling, oh well it was on New Year's Eve anyway

(ST CLEMENT'S)

Following Tiffany's displays of knowledge of the male–female binary and her expression of disgust at Marcella (Errh!) for even mentioning the word lesbian, Alison, in the next conversation, opens up the possibility that some same sex sexuality is acceptable, on the grounds that it is 'natural'.[3] Significantly, she draws the line at lesbian parenting following some form of artificial insemination, both because it is not natural, and because you can't choose the father, since the sperm would come from 'some old one' that you didn't know or choose.

What emerges in this conversation, then, is the fact that these children have gained access to a discourse which constitutes homosexuality as 'natural' and therefore acceptable in the same way that their heterosexuality is, but which also establishes and maintains a

---

[3]Use of the term 'natural' to mean acceptable and inevitable is a constant feature of the children's talk. The natural is, in their talk, biological, scientific, and belongs to the unequivocally real.

binary division between homo- and heterosexuality. In other words, each person is understood to be naturally one and not the other. Signs of one's sexuality will be interpreted as coming from one's inner essence. The conversations among these children in which 'signs' of homosexuality are assiduously searched for, and used to accuse and marginalise the perpetrator, indicate the extent to which the hegemonic discourses about the unacceptable nature of homosexuality are still active. These, combined with the fearful possibility that one might be naturally so, make the new discourse on homosexuality a perfect tool for maintaining the male–female binary. Like palimpsest, the new discourse is written over the old, but does not erase it. The children can thus talk about homosexuality as natural, but they do not want to experience that naturalness as their own:

ALISON: I don't think that being a lesbian or a gay person is that bad. Like sure you can rather a woman to a man and go around with each other but this idea about having sperm bank, really it's not natural

VICTORIA: What do you mean by sperm bank?

TIFFANY: Sperm bank, if a lady wants to get pregnant, she goes to the sperm bank and then inserts it and then she's pregnant without having sex with a man

VICTORIA: Oh that's dumb

((Overlapping conversations))

ALISON: You don't have to be married

TIFFANY: I know

MARCELLA: And you want a child instead

ELIZABETH: I was a sperm

CHAS: You weren't a sperm, you were an ovum and a sperm that connected together

ELIZABETH: 'Cause my mum had no (   )

CHAS: That's right. Then why don't you think it's a good thing, then you're saying so it's not a good idea for women to be able to have babies without a man involved, is that what you're saying?

ALISON: Yeah, because sure they hang around with each other and finger each other and do whatever they want, do anything that comes naturally to them but don't get artificially inseminated. I don't think that it's/

TIFFANY: Because it's not natural

MARCELLA: It's not natural

ALISON: Like sure, like if a man and a lady go together like it is natural but/

VICTORIA: If they just get some old one/
(ST CLEMENT'S)

As with the St Clement's girls, the Karobran study group also have access to a discourse that constitutes homosexuality as hypothetically all right, yet they do not want if for themselves and still see being 'queer' as having 'something wrong' with you if it is lodged in the familiar romantic storyline:

CHAS: What do you kids think about homosexuality generally? . . .

ANNA: As long as they don't do it on people that don't want to/

ALL: Yeah/

ANNA: sort of thing/

CHAS: But you do think it is all right for men to love men if they choose to/

ANNA: But only if the/

BRIAN: Only if the other man loves them/

ANNA: To be, to love the other man and the other man wants to love you

ROSIE: Yes

CHAS: You don't see anything morally wrong with it?

ROSIE: No

BRIAN: No

KEN: No

MAL: Nup

ANNA: As long as the other don't take it out on other people and make other people suffer that don't want to suffer . . .

CHAS: What about lesbianism do you think that it is all right for women to love women?

ROSIE: Only if it is the same?

ANNA: Only if they are the same yes . . .

CHAS: how come you call her ((Anna)) names? This is what I don't understand.

BRIAN: (   )

CHAS: Can you explain it to me a little bit

MAL: Go for it

ROSIE: No

ANNA: Ask Kenneth he can (   ) we are always fighting aren't we?

CHAS: Ken why is it? Do you think that being a tomboy is all right?

KEN: Yeah I s'pose so

ROSIE: Most people think there is something wrong with tomboys, and they like

ANNA: Like we are not queer or anything

(KAROBRAN PUBLIC)

Ken's grudging 'Yeah I s'pose so' reveals his access to a discourse which claims that a refusal to heighten male–female difference is acceptable. But clearly he doesn't like it. His relentless strategy is to suggest that Anna is unacceptable, marking her transgressions and positioning her as marginal.

At St Clement's the girls do not seem to rule out boyish behaviour. There is no need to do so because they regard agentic behaviour as appropriate in terms of their class position, *and* they actively (and without coercion from boys) heighten their own femininity in anticipation of future sexual encounters. Their freedom to be agents and to maintain free access to boyish things is undermined, however, by their policing of the heterosexual/homosexual boundary. In the next conversation Tiffany imaginatively constitutes herself as agent. She imaginatively constructs a different lived storyline which would give her independence from family and husband. The others instantly accuse her of being a lesbian, just as she accused Marcella in the earlier conversation. In the face of this category maintenance work, Tiffany shifts back to a less radical storyline of living together with a boyfriend before marriage. It seems that there is a constant tension between agentic positionings outside traditional storylines followed by a rapid pulling back into old patterns. The power of naming others as transgressive seems to be a means of positioning yourself as knowledgeable/acceptable in contrast to others whom you position as marginal. Those who do not resist, either by admitting they are in a love relationship or, like Mark, finding no problem with being called a poofter, are no use in this game:

CHAS: Right, can you girls imagine yourselves not getting married when you're bigger and what would you do?

MARCELLA: I would I would

TIFFANY: I want to live with my best friend/

ALISON: I want to live with my mum and dad/

TIFFANY: When I'm 16 I'm leaving home/

MARCELLA: I wanna, I wanna/

TIFFANY: When I'm 16 I'm leaving home

ALISON: Chas, Chas can I just say something

CHAS: No wait a minute I want to hear what Tiffany's got to say. When you are 16 you are going to leave home

TIFFANY: Yeah. And I'm gonna live with my best friend/

ELIZABETH: What if you don't have a best friend

TIFFANY: down in Sydney/

ALISON: Well what if she's not your best friend by then?

TIFFANY: She *is*/

ALISON: Well now when you are 10 or 11/

MARCELLA: You won t be able to find her

TIFFANY: Yeah, I know where she lives. And we're gonna live in a house together and we're gonna like, we're probably like we are gonna rent it/

JACQUELINE: Be lesos

TIFFANY: Yeah, yeah I really want to be a lesbian ((sarcastic))

VICTORIA: ((joking)) Are you going to be a lesbian ha ha . . .

TIFFANY: And I'm gonna have a boyfriend and like I won't get married straight away, like we're all gonna share a house and boyfriend and that, and we're just gonna, we're sort of gonna live together for a while and then probably get married when we're about 21 or something/

(ST CLEMENT'S)

SEXUALITY AND CLASS DIFFERENCE

Speaking and thinking as usual is a powerful force in the maintenance of difference. As Cixous says:

> But we must make no mistake: men and women are caught up in a web of age-old cultural determinations that are almost unanalyzable in their complexity. One can no more speak of 'woman' than of 'man' without being trapped in an ideological theater where the proliferation of representations, images, reflections, myths, identifications transform, deform, constantly change everyone's Imaginary and invalidate in advance any conceptualization. (Cixous, 1986, p. 83)

So fundamental is the oppositional, hierarchical nature of sex difference to heterosexuality as it is constituted within the binary discourses available to these children that when observing class differences they interpret these as sexual transgressions. This elision between class and gender occurs, for example, when the St Clement's girls are discussing an article that Chas has brought in about a woman called Toots. She is a big, grease covered truck driver who is a mother and grandmother. Her dirtiness is taken by them as a sign that she is gay:

TIFFANY: And maybe she has got something wrong with her that she has to do a man's job or something

MARCELLA: Or she's like a gay or something . . .

ALISON: When she's maybe when she's all clean and her nails aren't yuk and all her body's clean and she got clothes/

TIFFANY: Probably scrubs up all right/

(ST CLEMENT'S)

Key signifiers of sex difference are located not just in dress, then, but in the cleanness and neatness of that dress. Boys, for example, must dress sloppily to be opposite to girls' neatness. Distance is also central. From the boys' point of view in particular, the greater the distance, the more desirable and the more object like is the other. These two points are illustrated in the discussion around one of the stories that Chas used with the study groups. *Princess Smartypants* is a story about a princess who does not want to marry, preferring a life of leisure with her monstrous pets. Her parents insist that she marry and she finally agrees to set tasks for the various suitors, saying she will marry anyone who can do them. The tasks are impossible and the suitors leave. Then Prince Swashbuckle turns up and is able to carry out any task that Smartypants sets him. She kisses him, seeming to capitulate to her fate, but instead she turns him into a warty toad who flees from the castle in his little red sportscar. Smartypants returns to her life of leisure. In this discussion of the story, sexual terms of abuse are used by the Karobran Public boys to describe Smartypants on the grounds that she is a woman who doesn't like or desire men. *Snob* (upper class) is made to equal *slut* (sexually available woman).

 1 BRIAN: [Smartypants] is a snob
 2 CHAS: So you think she's a snob Brian?
 3 BRIAN: Yep and a slut
 4 CHAS: Why do you think that? A snob and a what?/
 5 BRIAN: No, I won't/
 6 CHAS: Did you say a slut?
 7 KEN: Yep
 8 CHAS: Why do you think she's a slut?
 9 BRIAN: Oh well she/
10 ROSIE: She's not. She hasn't even been out with a boy
11 BRIAN : So!
12 MAL: Yeah Brian
13 ANNA: She's not a gutter snipe
14 BRIAN: You are though
15 CHAS: When you say the word 'slut' you're like me, I think, that it means someone who has really loose sexual sort of morals/
16 ANNA: Like with everybody
17 CHAS: Who does it with everybody and anyone/
18 ANNA: And gets money for it
19 CHAS: But Brian, when you say slut what do you mean?
20 BRIAN: Ah um
21 MAL: A whore
22 CHAS: No, wait a minute, what sort of person do you mean?
23 BRIAN: She doesn't like very many people like/
24 MAL: Yeah, like Samantha (   )
25 KEN: Posh
26 BRIAN: Yeah man, she's got the voice of a man
27 ANNA: Who?
28 BRIAN: Samantha
29 ANNA: No she hasn't
30 BRIAN: Yes she has
31 ANNA: No she hasn't
32 KEN: Well she's very posh
33 CAROLYN: And people with their socks up, and people at ABS school well they think that they're really posh

34 CHAS: Oh do they?

35 ROSIE: 'Cause that's what it seems like, everyone folds their socks down

36 BRIAN: Everyone calls ABS fellas poofters. Just because they put their socks up

37 MAL: My dad works at ABS and I don't call him 'a jolly', I don't call any of those guys a jolly, they smoke [and] . . . they had a party there one night and they smashed windows and all

(KAROBRAN PUBLIC)

The claim that Smartypants is a slut is resisted by the girls, 'She's not. She hasn't even been out with a boy' and 'She's not a gutter snipe' (10, 13). In response the boys abuse them, 'You are though' (14) . Smartypants is compared to a girl they know who they claim is posh and has a voice like a man, suggesting she is sexually transgressive (22-28). Again the girls resist. They then elaborate the term posh, by talking about the boys from The Anglican Boys' School who are called 'jollies' and presumed to be gay, unless they can provide proofs of masculinity such as smoking or other disruptive (adult) behaviour. A significant connection in this conversation is that for women and girls class difference combined with social distance (not liking (male) people) leads to a definition of that person being sexually available to anyone—a whore (21-23). In other words, if a girl/woman doesn't behave as if she is attracted to men in the way men think she should, she can be taken by force, made to know her correct heterosexual position. This starkly reveals the compulsion lying behind the teasing of girls who do not correctly achieve their (hetero)sexual femininity. It also suggests a compulsion behind the St Clement's girls ultra femme behaviour that they are not yet aware of.

Like Smartypants, Anna cannot refuse femininity in the way she does (in speech and dress) as well as the dominant storyline on love and marriage without continually having to assert that she is not a 'lemon' (lesbian):

CHAS: What do you want to do for the future Brian?

BRIAN: Nothin'

ANNA: I'm gonna work hard and earn my dough, earn me dough

CHAS: Yeah

ANNA: I'm gonna be a big he-man, a old greasy old mechanic. I'm going into business with my friend and then we're gonna, we're not lemons, we're gonna live together probably, in a flat. Different rooms though. And I'm gonna, in my spare time, I'm gonna write comics, I'm gonna sell comics, do comics whatever you want to say comics and I'm gonna go fishing and own my own big, build a fisher cat or whatever they call them and um . . .

CHAS: Are you gonna have a partner when you grow up?

ANNA: What do you mean by partner?

CHAS: Well a partner, you know someone that you share your life with

ANNA: Well, probably, my parents. Or do you mean someone not in the family?

CHAS: Someone not in your family probably . . .

ANNA: No not a boy, a girl. I don't want to have a boyfriend . . . I'm not a lemon it's just that I'm going into business with another girl 'cause men they, they're stupid. They're unreal, incredible, irritates.

KAROBRAN PUBLIC)

Thus the establishment of 'correct' (hetero)sexual positioning in children takes place partially through taboo and ignorance and partly through the discourses and storylines through which they position themselves and are positioned within the male–female binary. Despite the girls' active pursuit of agentic positionings and of physical competencies, the boys are able to position themselves as powerful and as opposite in this power to girls. Moreover, as the girls revealed in the conversations in Chapter 4, their desire is to correctly constitute themselves as girls.

SEXUALITY AND POWER

Our storylines are not, however, as simple as male equals power and female equals powerless. Children inhabit a world where there are many powerful women though their power is generally different from male power:

> [Cixous] distinguishes between two economies, one *masculine* . . . : centralized, short, reappropriating, cutting, an alternation of attraction-repulsion; one *feminine:* continuous, overabundant, overflowing. These economies produce differences in inscription on the textual level, but they do not refer to one or the other of the sexes in exclusive fashion. They are, at all times, to be found in varying degrees *in both* men and women. Yet because of cultural repressions, an economy said to be feminine may more often be found in women. (Conley, 1991, p. 98)

The control of female libidinal energy, of *jouissance,* takes place through a containing of female power. The boys are relentless in this, attacking and undermining girls who do not know how to correctly position themselves as female, as passive and vulnerable. The idealised female sexual form in fairy tales is passive, inert, without power. She lies asleep for a hundred years, or in her coffin as if she were dead. She becomes so, in the fairy tales, often from the actions of powerful/evil women/witches such as the Queen in *Snow White* or the wicked fairy in *Sleeping Beauty*. Virtue is passive, evil is active. The virtuous/passive/

asexual women are given life in these stories only through the power of the prince's (or the woodchopper's) heroism/sexuality. In contrast, male libidinal energy is focused, driving, conquering. It is highly prized in men and only occasionally tolerated in women. If women have competitive, individualistic, conquering male libidinal energy it is always of negative value. Girls who position themselves as tomboys, such as Anna, are making a claim for this different kind of energy. While she was admired for those boyish skills so highly prized by all the children, she was constantly undermined and marginalised. The radical potential of her desired way of being was defused/diffused through her subjection within the terms of the hetero–homosexual binarism.

The follow-up interviews with Penny, the tomboy in *Frogs and Snails*, showed how the position of tomboy is made nonviable when (hetero)sexual discourse becomes the predominant discourse through which subjectivities are constituted. Penny was committed to gaining access to masculine forms of power from a very early age. She learned about masculinity through reading books about gangs. She created her own violent gang and wore a necklace with 'War and Death' on it, having located these as the key signifiers of masculinity:

PENNY: . . . when I was a little kid I used to want to be called Peter instead of Penny. And um I s'pose I grew up thinking that I was a boy. I liked doing boy's things better. Like I liked football and I liked soccer and things like that. I liked skate boards which was a bit not normal for a girl . . . I was physically stronger than most other girls and even some of the boys. And I felt pretty stable . . . [Girls] want to be more like, play with dolls usually. But I was never really attracted by Barbie dolls or anything . . . I was deeply into gangs in primary school and I read lots, lots about that sort of thing. Like about gangs that roamed Sydney and things like that . . . And things like *Gangs and War* that's a book with three stories about gangs in it and things like that. There weren't many books about them but which ones there were I read . . . I was a little violent thing in in Year 5, maybe, maybe I s'pose . . . I was into war and things I, I found it quite, really interesting. War and violence and things like that. And I just thought I'll go along with it and I'll be violent myself, so it was like that . . . I was even more violent than the boys I s'pose . . . like the way I talked I s'pose and the way I sort of acted to people 'cause I acted sort of like I was a big macho person. And I was really into wars and I even wore a necklace saying 'War and Death'. I made it myself out of cardboard . . . I made up a gang and went around bashing up little kids but that was about the furthest we ever went really . . . I used to live in Clay St and there were a few kids there that I played with. They were sort of rough kids mainly. And we used to go and bash up this little kid. One of my friend's little brothers

. . .

Towards the end of primary school, however, Penny began to relinquish her masculinity. The boys began to forcefully constitute girls as potential objects of their sexual interest. Penny fell short because she was 'butch'. She had not achieved herself as opposite, female, conquerable. She could no longer be one of the boys and she hated them for sexualising her. To escape her marginal status as butch (homosexual) she became a member of a girls' group in which she could begin to discuss life from a girl's point of view. In doing so, she learned to like the boys, not as one of them, but as opposite to them. Her heterosexuality was thus established in the absence of any romantic interest in boys. It was more to do with refusing to be placed in the margins:

PENNY: I started changing at the end of sixth grade. So I sort of went more gradually to be more feminine, and then go into year seven and become more feminine so people wouldn't tease me any more I s'pose . . . I suppose it was because I was becoming more attracted to boys, yeah . . . I started hating boys . . . generally just hating boys and um, so I just thought, I went out to get female friends because I thought they would be more sensitive I s'pose and different to boys in lots of ways that I liked . . . 'Cause like the boys (were) the main ones who would tease me and I just felt pretty bad about that, so I didn't like them for a while and they are pretty nasty in year 7 . . . they started calling me 'butch' and stuff like that . . . Like the boys in Year 8 they used to say things, they used to be really sarcastic towards girls and it used to really upset lots of the girls. They'd say horrible things about them. They were giving them scores and stuff like that . . . Looks and your hair, your hair was the main one, blonde was the good one but it was mainly yeah your body, it didn't have anything to do with your personality. It was pretty horrible. It just happened a few weeks ago actually. But I bashed him up, I slapped him . . . With boys you just tend to play sports with each other and sort of play (   ) you never talk or anything. With girls you don't do that because, I don't know why, but you don't play hand ball or anything, you just have more time to talk and share secrets and stuff.

Despite the radical potential in Penny's early refusal of her place in the male–female binary, she nevertheless finds her position unworkable and so makes substantial in her body the relevant ways of desiring and being for a girl. She does draw the line at the total commodification of her body, though, bashing the boy up who presumed to give her a 'score'. But even in telling of this bashing, it is modified into 'slapping', a recognisably feminine form of aggression towards men: 'I bashed him up, I slapped him'.

And thus transgressions are brought back inside known storylines. Male and female are maintained as opposite, heterosexuality as normal: the male–female binary is held in place. Homosexuality is either made into an intolerably marginal position, or normalised in terms of heterosexual storylines.

THE ADULT–CHILD BINARY

The adult–child binary is slippery and quite difficult to hold in place. It is not just children who slip from one to the other in their talk, but adults who blur this boundary. When it comes to sexuality, female children must learn to distinguish between rapacious wolves and trusted woodchoppers. And often the critical information they need for making such distinctions is not available. As Patrick White says:

> One of the frustrating aspects of childhood is not being able to peel off the webs of mystery which cling to certain events and your own haphazard presence in them. The Headmaster had a fiery face and a globular figure. I can't remember his appearing in the classroom, but he supervised our cricket games, sometimes taking part in them, when he thwacked the ball so hard that even I was impressed. When not performing he sat among the boys in his white flannels, glaring at the game, smelling of men. One alarming evening he stood in the centre of his study, fiercer of face, the smell of man more pronounced as he held me against his stomach instead of using the cane as a junior master had recommended. When I realised I was forgiven I dissolved in a mingling of gratitude and anti-climax. He disappeared from our lives soon after, without adequate explanation. (White, 1981, p. 18)

Adan tells another story where lack of conscious knowledge about sexuality features large in the girl's inability to protect herself. Daphne was repeatedly sexually molested by a disturbed older boy whom her parents had placed in her care. She was terrified of his attacks and yet only resisted them passively, desperate, but finding no way to stop him until one day he crossed a boundary that unleashed from an unconscious source an active fury and resistance:

> Glen . . . was suddenly in the shed behind her, pulling off her tennis shorts and underwear and letting them fall down around her ankles like a hobble . . . Daphne had no knowledge of sexuality, and when she suddenly felt Glen's penis and some liquid touch her skin, she did not conclude that Glen had been masturbating but instead that he had urinated: 'I was just hysterical . . . I thought he urinated on me . . . I was in a state of shock and hysteria and everything all at once and I turned around and I shoved him down and I yelled at him, said things. You know. I called him a pig, and I told him never to come near me again . . . um—I'll never forget the emotional, the intensity of the emotions that day. I just felt—like an explosion. It was, I knew right then that was the last time that was ever going to happen—how you could go from one extreme to the other that quickly, I don't understand. It was like—I thought he had urinated on me and that was the most offensive thing I had ever heard of in my life. It nauseated me'. (Adan, 1991, p. 205)

Her resistance comes from something she doesn't understand. Her lack of conscious knowledge of sexuality is accompanied by some other knowledge of a boundary constituting herself as not-sexual female child, a boundary that cannot be crossed, a boundary that defines what

Glen does as revolting, nauseating, unspeakable. It is a boundary constituted through stories, through multiple layers of metaphor and through those intangibles which are known without conscious apprehension.

A current powerful discourse on childhood sexuality, which Daphne's story in particular emphasises, is the child sexual abuse discourse. In the more innocent 1970s and early 1980s, when my children were small, our focus was quite different. We talked not about abuse, but about not teaching children the inhibitions that we had begun to unlearn in our own minds and bodies. It was not unusual to sit chatting over coffee while children stripped off and played sexual games in a corner of the room. Parents were amused and indulgent, and perhaps a little uncomfortable. We wanted our children not to be inhibited in the ways that we still were.

In my own childhood sexuality was unspoken. We learned about sex through secret explorations, through silences and innuendo, and the occasional whispered exchange of (mis)information. ('Babies are born out of your navel' my friend across the road told me. But how could something so big come out of a hole so small? I wanted to explore the taboo area between my legs to see if there was a larger hole, but good girls didn't touch themselves there.) Some of us learned about sex as we heard our mothers' cry out with pain through the thin bedroom walls, when our fathers came home drunk. I learned from the resigned expression of distaste on my mother's face when she dropped the sheets from her bed into the wash. But I also learned from my Uncle Llewellyn a joy and a rapture and a laughter when he chased us up the hall into bed at night and bounced us up and down until our teeth rattled, when he invited us, wickedly, to play 'touch tongues', and when he threw back his head and laughed with his mouth wide open, a joyful unconstrained belly laugh.

But in the last decade the horror of child sexual abuse has relentlessly emerged through the telling of one grotesque story after another. We needed the freedoms of the 1970s and 1980s to begin to imagine how to find the words to speak of that darkness and to experience our outrage. We began to tell and to discover the damage that the silences covered. Our plundered bodies and our mute terror and guilt fuelled much of the radical feminist rage. The re-constitution of women's sexuality as powerful and good, begun in the 1970s, was shaken by these stories to its foundations.[4]

---

[4]According to Cocks, 'when we look at the turn body politics has taken, we will see that an original Yes to the female body by a female slave struggling to snatch power and pleasure for herself has been drowned out by a No a refusal of power and pleasure to the female body for the sake of protecting it from victimization'. (1991, p. 154)

In stark contrast to the child sexual abuse discourse, the emergent discourse on female sexuality celebrates sexuality and its multiple and varied expressions. It rejects hegemonic, male definitions of sex. In place of the hydraulic, genitally focused definition in which 'penetration' equals 'sex', we have begun to talk about the whole body, about foreplay being not 'fore' play at all, but sex itself. Male patriarchal sex is re-constituted through this discourse as hopelessly limited, as having lost the oceanic, whole body, multiple experience that women are capable of and want. In terms of the child sexual abuse discourse it is essential to know where the boundary lies between acceptable sensuality and unacceptable sexuality. In terms of the emergent feminist discourse, there is no such boundary except that created through one discourse or another. Children's first oceanic experience is probably at the breast. My own first remembered oceanic experience is of suckling my first child.

An event that brought these two discourses into sharp focus for me took place at a lunch party being held in a friend's back yard, during the mid-1980s. It was a beautiful sunny day and the children were running around naked. Their nakedness made me uncomfortable. It assumed, I thought, that adults had no sexual interest in children, and that the children were safe, even from being looked at with sexual interest. The emergence of the child sexual abuse discourse had disrupted the innocence, for me, of such an occasion. After lunch I was sitting on the grass with a group of friends chatting. One of the children, aged three or four, came and sat on my lap, snuggling comfortably into my arms. I absent-mindedly stroked her tummy while concentrating on the talk. My (innocent) sensual stroking was interrupted when she asked me in a dreamy and relaxed voice to tickle her 'fanny'.[5] I abruptly stopped stroking and suggested she go and play.

This incident bothered me for some time and for a number of reasons. I had inadvertently broken a taboo on child–adult sexuality. Worse, I had, instead of naming the taboo in explanation of my refusal, placed an absence and a silence around her fanny and its touchability, thus perpetuating an inhibition central to female sexuality. Even more difficult to deal with, was the realisation that, in retrospect, I was sexually 'turned on' at the thought of the child's uninhibited sexuality. I wanted to be able to experience sex so simply, as a child, without shame and embarrassment, without silences and inhibitions, to say without shame what I wanted. I was, at the same time, alarmed at how much she was at risk with any unscrupulous adult who might take advantage of such uninhibited sensuality.

---

[5]Australian and British slang for female genitals.

Some time later I read an excellent thesis on inter-generational sex (Leahey, 1991). On the basis of interviews with willing participants in intergenerational sex, Leahey concluded that such sex could be a positive experience for children. Many of them talked of it as a situation in which they had agency, in which they were treated with the kind of respect usually only accorded to adults, in which they felt in control of the situation. I was largely convinced by his argument and by his evidence, and glad to find something to counter-balance some of the heavy negativity of the child sexual abuse discourse. The sense of agency is, for me, quite central to sexual pleasure. Imagining oneself as a child whose body has not been negatively inscribed and with the right to name what one wants is a powerful aphrodisiac. But agency is far too problematic in relation to children for this to be any simple 'answer' to what might make childhood sexuality acceptable. My own experience of being sexually molested as a child makes me acutely aware of this.

As De Salvo (1991) reveals in her book on Virginia Woolf, the terrible bind for children who suffer sexual molestation from adults is that they are dependent on those adults for the care that, as children, they genuinely need. They are also savagely at risk if they incur the wrath of those adults. In Woolf's case, her older step-sister, Laura, was permanently locked away in the far reaches of the house, inaccessible to the family, for incurring her father's wrath. Laura did not read well, and when her father raged at her and punished her, she became angry and violent in return. It was Laura's refusal to take her punishment willingly that led to her being locked away. Woolf thus had her own 'mad woman in the attic' as proof of what would happen to her should she actively and angrily refuse the repeated sexual attentions of her older half-brothers. As a child, Woolf referred to Laura as 'Her Ladyship of the Lake'. As De Salvo argues, Woolf's alienation from her own body and her eventual death by drowning are not unconnected to her suffering of molestation at the hands of her brothers and her image of Laura, the one who dared to defy male control, as submerged in the lake.

TRANSGRESSING THE BOUNDARIES

Female sexuality is constituted for women as a passivity which can only be overcome at considerable risk. The discovery of feminist writing on sexuality which names the unnameable, and which taps the possibility of sexual pleasure without fear and inhibition was, for me, like being washed clean in the sea, a return to the mother, to love of women, of myself, of my body. At the same time it provided the faltering first steps to both confirming and unlearning the feminine (Irigaray, 1985; Greer, 1986; Cixous, 1990).

I first understood what Cixous meant by the abundant flowing through oneself of the female libidinal economy when I went to the seaside alone, not long after my father's death. I was reading *The Body and the Text*, and, at the same time, had begun to listen to Pavarotti. In *The Body and the Text* Cixous says:

> The body is linked to the unconscious. It is not separated from the soul. It is dreamed and spoken . . . When one speaks, or writes, or sings, one does so from the body. The body feels and expresses joy, anxiety, suffering and sexual pleasure. Sexual pleasure is the least constrained, the least bridled manifestation of the body. 'Feminine' sexual pleasure (*la jouissance feminine*) is overflowing, undecided, decentralised and not caught up in the masculine castration scene, and is not threatened by impotency. The body lets desire pass through . . . Feminine desire is flowing, so we often find images of the spring, of liquid, of water. (1990, p. 39)

Though the 'feminine' is available to anyone there is always a struggle to separate possible ways of being from the named/sexed body. Elsewhere Cixous says, in trying to love and write about the Other independent of their gender:

> I should also say that in order to know it [this love for *personne*][6] better inside, I close my eyes, I avoid looking her straight in the face because it is not impossible that at first sight [this person] may look a little like one of these men who are not at all feminine, but who are capable of this slow inner dance, who have a loving, elastic rapport with the earth and are thus a bit f . . . thus in short a bit m . . . and thus . . . And then I feel [this person] so clearly and again I know without any doubt how lightly powerful [this person] is like a man who is lightly powerful like a woman who is powerfully light like a man who is gently powerfully powerful like a woman of powerful tenderness . . . (Sellers, 1988, p. 41)

I felt during that week at the seaside, when I listened to Pavarotti sing, and reading Cixous' words, that I was hearing the overflowing abundance of feminine *jouissance*, that his powerful body could allow a liquid flowing through that expressed an abundance of joy, of love, of uncontainable beauty. In his singing he erased masculine and feminine as oppositional hierarchically organised terms (or, as Cixous says, the m . . . and the f . . .). In listening to him I experienced that erasure, becoming powerfully gentle and gently powerful, I felt flowing through my body the sound he created.

---

[6]Cixous uses the word personne here, meaning someone and no one, and which in French is a feminine word. The female pronoun that follows refers to *personne* and at the same time breaks up the assumption of heterosexuality.

During that week I wept, not just for my father and the absences between us, but for all the pain of my life. There were so many tears to weep into the sand and the wind and the sea (*ma mere*).

Pavarotti releases a 'feminine' love in his audiences that is tangible when he sings (Pavarotti with Wright, 1981). He creates, as well, an 'animal excitement', particularly when he transgresses the male–female boundaries and sings 'unnaturally' high notes. Rather than celebrate this transgression as a profound disruption of the male–female binary, however, Pavarotti uses the metaphor of the matador to re-cast what he does inside the male heroic storyline:

> The whole business of top notes for a tenor is sad and a little ridiculous. You can sing badly all evening, but come in strong with your high C and the public will forgive you everything. On the contrary, you can sing like an angel for three hours, but one cracked top note will ruin the whole evening. Somebody said, 'An evening never recovers from a cracked high note.' It is exactly like a bull fight. You are not allowed one mistake.
>
> I don't know how the opera public became this way. I suppose there is something undeniably exciting about a grown man singing full out those difficult, unnatural high Cs. It creates a wild, almost animal excitement. Then too, there is the excitement of the matador danger, the closeness of sudden death. (Pavarotti with Wright, 1981, p. 133)

But then, transgression of the boundaries is dangerous and it is heroic. And it is also intensely exciting as Penny found in her primary school years. While the children often took steps towards the transgressive, they rarely had the words to legitimate what they were doing. Further they did not know precisely how it was that what they were doing, and what they found themselves desiring, undercut and negated the different storylines that they occasionally tried to construct for themselves. Mark was one exception to this. In a conversation with him when he was eleven, I asked him whether there were any similarities between him and the hero, a conscientious objector, in the film *Boy Soldiers*. He said, 'I think there might be one. We're slightly more girlish than most other people, or boys, and sometimes we're afraid to be like that and sometimes not'. But, he said, unlike the hero of the film, he was not heroic because he did not think that he could change the world. We have to learn to live with violence, he said. This lack of a sense of himself as powerful agent is at first sight problematic. But it indicates a relinquishing of the male-god connection which may be a significant first step to writing new stories for himself that do not always come back to the inevitability of male power.

An exciting new field of research is opening up looking at the connections between music, gender and sexuality. Much of classical music and the accepted interpretations of it are both sexist and heterosexist in nature. But there are subtleties and contradictions in this music urgently in need of study. As McClary points out, for example, the appearance of mad women in opera is not simply because women are seen as given to madness but because they provide a chance for composers to break the bonds of musical rules and thus to write their most exciting music:

> If we review the portraits of famous madwomen in music, we find that the signs of their madness are usually among the favourite techniques of the avant-garde: strategies that for each style hover at the extremes, strategies that most successfully exceed the verbal component of dramatic music and that transgress conventions of 'normal' procedure. These same techniques are used without comment in our most complex, most intellectually virtuoso instrumental music .
> . . . the very qualities regarded as evidence of superior imagination—even of genius—[for] each period of music are, when enacted on stage, often projected onto madwomen. (McClary, 1991, p. 101)

It is obvious then, that we need to imaginatively move beyond existing discursive, interactional and structural constraints and to construct new storylines and new ways of relating to our bodies, if we are to escape the relentless impositions of binary definitions dividing male from female, heterosexual from homosexual, limiting our selves and our sexuality.

> Let us imagine a real liberation of sexuality, that is to say, a transformation of each one's relationship to his or her body (and to the other body), an approximation to the vast, material, organic, sensuous universe that we are. This cannot be accomplished, of course, without political transformations that are equally radical. (Imagine!) Then 'femininity' and 'masculinity' would inscribe quite differently their effects of difference, their economy, their relationship to expenditure, to lack, to the gift. What today appears to be 'feminine' or 'masculine' would no longer amount to the same thing. No longer would the common logic of difference be organised with the opposition that remains dominant. Difference would be a bunch of new differences. (Cixous, 1986, p. 83)

In the last two chapters of this book I will explore the possibilities of new ways of reading and the possibilities that open up in the writing of stories. The connections we have made in the unconscious and inscribed in our bodies and emotions and that can profoundly limit us, can also be the source of liberation, of exciting transgressions, of new ways of being, outside the confines of the male–female binary. Although the children's talk reveals them as very much trapped in the masculine and the feminine, there are many powerful points of resistance, and many possible alternative storylines that they already have access to. These can be used as the basis for working with them towards more liberating possibilities, to an understanding of how it is that they get trapped and how they might extract themselves and each other from what appear at the moment to be a set of depressing inevitabilities.

In the following chapters I will look at deconstructive reading and at fictional writing as strategies for unpacking some of those inevitabilities.

7 Poststructuralist Theory and the Study of Gendered Childhoods

CHARLOTTE: *It is amazing. All the things you ever thought, you ever think about*

JENNIFER: *Yeah*

CHARLOTTE: *I mean you get taught this and this and this but you never get taught all the different perspectives and all the different ways of looking at it, like discourses, all the different things it could mean*

JENNIFER: *My Mum used to put me in all these pretty frilly lovely dresses that she thought I should wear and all I wanted to wear was shorts*

CHARLOTTE: *I didn't want to wear anything when I was little. I used to always take m' clothes off. Always. I would never hardly ever have clothes on*

JENNIFER: *Typical me*

—Eastern Public

ONE OF my favourite fairy stories, in my early primary school years, was *The Fairy Who Wouldn't Fly*. This was a story about a fairy who didn't want to do the things that other fairies did and so refused to fly. She was sent to a frightening dark place called the Woodn't where those who wouldn't do what they were supposed to do were sent. There she met other beings like the glow worm who wouldn't glow and the bat who wouldn't fly by night and a little lost boy who was crying for his mother. They huddled together in a dark cave at night

151

frightened and lonely. The fairy realises that if only these other beings would do what they should, things wouldn't be so bad. If the glow worm glowed, for example, they would have some light. She persuades them to try to overcome their fear of doing what they should, and they each try and succeed, each experiencing great pleasure that they can do these things after all. During the night when all the others are asleep she climbs alone onto the top of a jagged purple mountain, unfolds her beautiful wings for the first time and with fear and trepidation leaps off the mountain. When she discovers she can fly she is filled with joy. The next day she sets off back to Fairyland with her newfound friends. The Fairy Queen sends a beautiful carriage pulled by butterflies to pick them all up and take them home. The last picture is of a domestic scene with baby hammocks slung between beautiful blossoming trees and mother fairies singing lullabies. That final scene with blossoms and babies and lullabies 'sang peace into my breast'.

This is a phrase from a poem that I loved in adolescence by W.B. Yeats called *The Stolen Child*. It had a refrain that went:

> Come away, O human child!
> To the waters and the wild
> With a faery, hand in hand
> For the world's more full of weeping than you can understand.

The child goes to faery land, seduced by these faery songs and then the poem tells all the things he will never hear or see any more, like the kettle on the hob that will no longer 'sing peace into his breast'. There was the same tension in this poem as in *The Fairy Who Wouldn't Fly*, between the seductive wild unknown and the secure domestic scene, between being good and thus securing a place in that domestic scene, and refusing that scene. These are as much tensions in my life now as they were then. Morrison points out that the tension between domesticity and adventure is not experienced by black women, domestic security and adventure not being defined as alternatives:

> It seems to me there's an enormous difference in the writing of black and white women. Aggression is not as new to black women as it is to white women. Black women seem able to combine the nest and the adventure. They don't see conflict in certain areas as do white women. They are both safe harbour and ship; they are both inn and trail. We, black women, do both. We don't find these places, these roles, mutually exclusive. That's one of the differences. White women often find that if they leave their husbands and go out into the world, it's an extraordinary event. If they've settled for the benefits of housewifery that preclude a career, then it's marriage or a career for them, not both, not and. (Morrison, 1983, p. 122)

Yet for me the fairy who wouldn't fly was unequivocally both. She didn't unreflectingly do what she was told. She resisted given patterns and structures and worked out for herself how to be an adventurer. And, moreover, she was also womanly and belonged within the family scene. Now, I find the story quite difficult to see as an acceptable story since the author's intentions appear to be about the importance of learning to conform and about the virtues and rewards attached to this. If my father had read this story (which I'm sure he didn't, though his nickname for me was 'fairy') he would no doubt have approved the moral that he would have perceived, namely, that there is no point ignoring what your parents tell you, since you will only discover through painful mistakes that they were right after all. In a rare outburst, not many years ago, he told me that the reason my life was a failure (in his perception) was that I always had to discover things for myself and would never listen to what I was told. My resistance to the upper middle class domestic scene that he envisaged for me was something he never accepted.

What is important here is not to ask which is the true reading of the story, since there are always multiple possible readings of any text. More important is to ask how it is that our lived fictions and the fictions in texts intersect and (in)form each other. The multiple layers of writing can be compared to the multiple layers of lived experience. In reading the texts of our lives, or in reading written text on a page, we have learned to divide, the 'real' from the 'fictional', imposing yet again the limitations of binary thought. We divide the world thus as if there really were linear, singular truths separable from the multiple layers of possible readings of events, of emotions, of texts. The interplay between lived and textual narratives can probably best be understood through the metaphor of palimpsest. Du Plessis writes of palimpsest in the context of H.D.'s writing:

> But her enacted tactics and certain statements show the force moving in and by means of overlays of languages. H.D. has used a term from ancient scribal habits, palimpsest, to define this overwritten text. Such a text, made of at least two kinds of scribble at different times yet on the same parchment, is split between its wholeness as object or ground and its veering multiplicity as figure. It also takes a different tack (tact) towards time, suggesting a psychoanalytic sense of the persistence of earlier configurations, and residues which are volcanic, irruptive. Palimpsest is a surface erased, but imperfectly erased, with old words visible, perhaps readable and interpretable under the new ones. (And/Or perhaps old words just confusing the new.) Palimpsest, scratchings, incisions of memory and event, little tracings and fleetings which may recede or may suddenly rear up as if the darkest letter. Palimpsest indicates the desire to manifest, by some verbal or textual gesture, the sense of presence, simultaneity, multiple

pressures of one moment, yet at the same time the disjunct, the absolutely parallel and different, the obverse sensations of consciousness in reality. (du Plessis, 1990, p. 111)

In this chapter I want to explore that interweaving of life and textual fictions. I also want to explore the ways in which children can become aware of that process and turn their critical, reflexive gaze on the usually invisible process of subjectification via text. Central to this process is the acquisition of new analytic concepts as well as new storylines, new ways of telling the world.

RE-COGNISING GENDER

Like many other young feminist women I made a decision in the early 1980s to stop reading novels by men. For years I hungrily read (and still read) feminist stories and novels and autobiographies by women. They made a different living and telling of my life possible. They provided the minute lived detail of a new consciousness of life lived as a woman, not as an object of the male gaze, or as an accessory to male lines of action. No theory can fill out this detail of feminist consciousness, feminist embodiment, feminist life, in the way that fictional and life stories do. While feminist theories provide an essential discourse for grasping the new life, for appreciating the new stories, for articulating the reasons for abandoning the old stories, for making sense of the hold that the old stories have, feminist stories breathe life into feminism, making it more readily livable. But even when self-consciously making such a decision to read work by women, the knowledge gained was a palimpsest of conscious and unconscious layers of meanings, of emotions, of bodily awareness, of new possibilities.

Generally discourses and their attendant storylines are taken up as one's own in a way that is not visible, since discourse is understood as the transparent medium through which we see real worlds. Just as we disattend the pane of glass in order to look at the view out the window, so we generally disattend discourse. (It is not until the glass fractures or breaks, for example, that we focus differently.) When discourse is understood as transparent, then any text that mobilises that discourse is taken to describe a real and *recognisable* world. One understands oneself, in reading, to be *re-cognising* that which the author of the text cognised. A reading that is thus achieved is experienced as a true, even authoritative reading of the text. This aspect of understanding text has been made a central feature of much of the current reading practice taught in schools, most notably reader response theory. Reader response theory asks readers to assume that there are real characters in literature and that the students' task is to use their own experience of being a 'real person' to come to know what the literature is 'really about'. By inserting themselves into the text and by drawing from their own experience of life they can achieve true readings of the text. Although I would see this as one necessary dimension of reading, I also regard it as a dangerous form of reading if it is the whole rather than one part. If students can import unreflective sexism or racism, or other oppressive and limited forms of thought into the text and then see that as an authoritative reading of that text, texts can only confirm the legitimacy of the oppressive world they live in.

Patterson points out that the importation of self into text in reader response classrooms takes place invisibly. The connections the students make are regarded as an obviousness not needing to be examined. She describes a group of English students 'responding' to a poem. They import storylines with heavy moral judgments into their reading of the characters in the text without realising that they are doing so. In one particular exercise the students were asked to underline the scant textual references from which they had derived their information about the characters:

> The students began to re-state their readings, prefacing many of their comments with such phrases as, 'It's obvious that . . . '; 'You can see that she would . . . '; 'It's typical of bored, rich women to . . . ' and so on. When pressed further to account for the production of such detailed readings from so little textual information they offered general explanations such as 'expectations formed by other similar stories'; 'from experience of life'; 'personal experience' and 'reading between the lines' and even, in a confident denial of the validity of readings other than their own, 'it's obvious from the clues that are given'. The students, it seemed, had learned a reading practice that promotes a particular formation of character by encouraging the filling of textual gaps so completely that they are both unaware of them and of their own operation as readers. They have learnt to feel that they are finding a meaning that is there in the text, while also bringing to the reading their own personal experience. (Patterson, 1992, p. 16)

The children in the follow-up study, aged eight and nine, displayed a very similar pattern in interacting with stories in text. Just as one makes sense of everyday life through gathering a great deal from the small details (they're gay because they've got their socks up) so it is with story. Using their own history of living in the world and the interpretive work necessary for survival in that world, and presuming that the obviousnesses of the everyday world apply in the worlds in texts that authors write about, the children bring a wealth of general, cultural and specific, personal knowledge to bear on the task of interpreting text and of making a coherent reading of that text. Just as they have learned not to attend to the interpretive work they do to make the everyday world coherent (which is constituted as real rather than a fiction), so with text. The fictional world of the text is made real in the same way.

One of the most popular stories among the children in the follow-up study was *Princess Smartypants*. If you remember from the last chapter this is a story about a princess who does not want to get married. She likes to live alone with all her monstrous pets. Her parents insist that she marry. She finally agrees to marry anyone who can carry out the impossible tasks she sets them (all of which she can do, including riding powerful motorbikes). None of the princes succeed and so they all leave. Then Prince Swashbuckle turns up and to Smartypants' dismay, he carries out all the tasks she sets him. So she kisses him. But it is a magic kiss and the unwanted Swashbuckle turns into a toad. He flees in his little red sports car and Smartypants takes up her life where the story began.

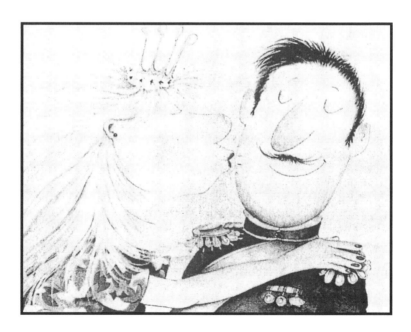

From Cole's Princess Smartypants, *1986*

In order to read this as a feminist story in which the female hero resists the apparently inevitable press of social structure, of parental authority and of the expectations of others, it is necessary to have access to the storyline that women are often unjustifiably oppressed and that marriage is one of the institutions through which that oppression can take place. It is also necessary to have access to the idea that not all authority is benevolent. It is also important to be able to position yourself as Smartypants and to experience the story from her point of view.

Joanne was interviewed in the follow-up study. She appeared in *Frogs and Snails* many times as one who was very interested in disruptions to the male–female binary. She knew that she had to be identifiable as a girl and so wore her hair in a girlish top knot, but otherwise she was intent on gaining access to all of the powerful and exciting things that were generally the prerogative of the dominant gang of boys. Her mother was particularly supportive of this, having experienced the same desires when she was young. Tony was often torn between his membership of the gang and his friendship with Joanne and was often given a hard time by the gang for spending time with Joanne (because she was a girl). They had remained buddies, however, since preschool, and came to the follow-up interview together. They had no trouble in hearing *Princess Smartypants* as a feminist story, in which Smartypants' exceptional skills are to be celebrated and in which marriage is a highly problematic institution for women:

CHAS: What sort of a wife do you think Swashbuckle would want Smartypants to be?

TONY: Probably one that's like a slave sort of one

CHAS: Like a slave sort of one

JOANNE: Yeah making dinner every time he comes home from work or whatever he does

TONY: He probably sits in a luxurious chair

JOANNE: Yeah

When asked whether she thought Smartypants behaved correctly Joanne says:

JOANNE: I think that it was right because he thought aw he's just going to go in there and he's going to marry her and get rich and stuff and he's gotta, and she's going to have to sit down just being a queen when she wanted to go out doing stuff. And he just, aw he was just going to go in and take over charge of everything

(FOLLOW-UP STUDY)

Smartypants' breaking of her contract and using her magic to escape the awfulness of marriage are understandable and justifiable behaviours as far as Joanne and Tony are concerned. Their access to the idea of legitimate challenge to parental authority and to the story of marriage as an oppressive institution are central in their capacity to do a feminist reading of the text.

In marked contrast to this are Sebastian and Catherine. Sebastian was a small, shy boy who appeared in *Frogs and Snails* as the one who managed to see Prince Ronald as heroic even when the dragon flew off with him, holding him upside down by the seat of his pants: 'I'm glad he held onto his tennis racquet so hard,' he said. 'When you've done that, well, you just have to hold onto your racquet tight and the dragon holds you up.' As well, in a reading of *Oliver Button is a Sissy*, Sebastian explained that Oliver should have done what his Dad told him so that he could be a 'proper boy', no matter what his personal desires might have been. Central stories in Sebastian's interpretive repertoire, then, were that parental authority is benevolent and that fathers teach their male children how to become (male) heroes. In the follow-up study, after reading *Princess Smartypants*, Chas asked Sebastian, 'do you think it was fair that Smartypants turned him into a toad?' Sebastian revealed no sympathy for Smartypants. His interest was in reinstating Swashbuckle as a hero: 'Well in my opinion um, from the part we know, I reckon when she kissed him that if they kissed at the same time she would turn into a frog as well.' As far as Sebastian can see Swashbuckle had power to equal Smartypants. He just didn't exercise it. His power, like much male power, remains invisible, implicit, unquestionable. But Smartypants has levelled a considerable challenge to Swashbuckle's power and Sebastian feels somewhat affronted by this. When Chas asked him what he would do in Swashbuckle's place if Smartypants were to turn him into a toad, he positions himself as Swashbuckle without hesitation and takes his revenge on Smartypants:

SEBASTIAN: I would, I'd stay in the palace

CHAS: Would you?

SEBASTIAN: Yes, because I've completed all the tasks that she wants and because of that, that means that she can marry exactly who she wants because he can, he can do all these tasks for her

CHAS: Brilliant. So would she still have to marry him then even though he was a toad?

SEBASTIAN: Yes, probably her mother and father would make her because she um he's tough and they all think that he's the exact kind of person that she wanted because if she didn't then she wouldn't have given him all of the tasks, she would have given him different tasks. And I would just stay in the palace

(FOLLOW-UP STUDY)

Smartypants is to be held to her contract and the parents will insist with Swashbuckle on the rightness of this. As in *The Frog Prince*, the girl is perceived as petty and selfish and in need of parental reprimand. As a result of her stupidity she will have to accommodate the toad in her bed. The authority of parents is unquestionable, and their requirement that she marry in the first place is not defined by Sebastian as unreasonable. It is interesting to reflect on the fact that Sebastian lives in an egalitarian household, his father being very involved in child care and household matters and where parental authority is exercised in a very reasoned and caring manner. It would seem that non-sexism, or absence of sexism, does not provide storylines powerful enough to counteract or disrupt more traditional storylines in which the male–female binary is put in place and maintained in place. Many experts in the area of children's literature do not believe feminist stories are necessary and advocate instead the use of 'non-sexist stories', by which they mean stories in which sexism is absent. These stories, like non-sexist households, do provide an alternative to the sexist world we live in, but it may be that they are not powerful enough to disrupt that sexist world. Precisely because non-sexism is an absence rather than a presence, it provides no arguments or analytic tools to counter or disrupt the dominant sexist discourses which are ever present in children's lives and children's texts.

Catherine lived in a household not unlike Sebastian's with parents benevolent and caring in their control of their children. In *Frogs and Snails* Catherine was one of the home corner girls. On one dramatic occasion she put on a male waistcoat in order to act forcefully and get her dolly back from George who had stolen it. Once back in the home corner with her dolly, she shed the waistcoat and put on several dress-up skirts to re-gain her femininity. Her mother, who worried about Catherine's dependence and lack of social competence was nevertheless horrified when I told her what I'd observed. She did not mind if Catherine was 'assertive' but she must not be 'aggressive' (presumably since that was to be like a boy). Like Sebastian, Catherine believed that all authority was benevolent and that Smartypants was in the wrong. She should have done what her parents said (or did). Unlike Sebastian, however, she thinks of the story from Smartypants' point of view. But when she tries to imagine acting like Smartypants, she cannot, because within the storylines available to her only exceptional or 'smart' girls can constitute themselves independent of parental authority:

CATHERINE: She looks happy. She doesn't, she can't marry the prince

CHAS: Can you understand, what do you think about the way Princess Smartypants behaved?

CATHERINE: Naughty

CHAS: You think she was naughty?

CATHERINE: Yeah, to make all the princes do those things

CHAS: Mm. What would she have done if she, if she'd been a good princess?

CATHERINE: She would have married a prince, and done the things that her mother and father did

CHAS: Right. So you think she should have obeyed what her mother and father told her to do?

CATHERINE: Yes 'cause most princes and princesses do what their Mum tells them to

CHAS: If you had've been Smartypants/

CATHERINE: Mm

CHAS: would you have behaved like that?

CATHERINE: Well if I was smart I would but if I was like me and I was Smartypants I would have obeyed my Mum and Dad

(FOLLOW-UP STUDY)

LEARNING TO SEE THE CONSTITUTIVE FORCE OF TEXT

It is not enough, then, to simply expose children to feminist texts, nor is it enough to ask them to interpret those texts on the basis of their experience, if we want them to be able to 'read against the grain' or to grasp feminist storylines and use them to deconstruct and call into question the sexist texts that make up so much of the everyday world. They need as well to discover themselves in the act of sense making, of importing their own knowledges into the text (and of importing ideas and images from text into their lived storylines) in order to examine the complex relations between lived experience and text. They need to discover the ways in which their category memberships (as male or female, as white or black) lead them to interpret differently and to be positioned differently in the text. They need to discover the way in which the cultural patterns constantly repeated in stories are taken up as their own, becoming the thread with which life is woven and desire is shaped. They need to see the author as a person with intentions and ways of understanding that are expressed through shared cultural symbols, assumptions, connections, images, metaphors and storylines. They need to see that while on the one hand, authors cannot guarantee meanings because of the active way in which their texts are read, their intentions may nevertheless be discernible and might be called in question.

In other words the authority of the author needs to be troubled, and the author reconstituted as one like any other who draws on what is known to fashion something that is both able to be imagined and yet new. Children need to find the silences and gaps in texts, and to question what it is the author understood as obvious and therefore not in need of saying. They need to understand the power of those silences to reinforce the obviousness of what does not need to be said. And, they need to find authors and texts who break the silences, who begin to say the unsayable. They need to become writers themselves, creating texts that disrupt certainties and open up new possibilities.

The processes of reading and writing are essentially inseparable. Where they are taught separately in schools a false division is created. I have partially recreated it here, by dividing the chapters in this way. I did so because there seemed too much to put into one chapter—and old patterns die hard. The two chapters need to be read very much together. Deconstructive reading and writing go hand in hand.

The principles that Chas used with the study groups were:

- any authoritative message that they find in texts is both culturally and historically specific;
- lived storylines are fictional and the gendered nature of these is examinable;
- discourses of resistance are legitimate disruptions to unwanted and oppressive impositions.

There was always the possibility that the children did not want to hear what Chas had to say and that they would fall into traditional classroom relations where nothing productive occurred. On several occasions, however, the right balance did occur, traditional authority relations were disrupted and the children became very excited about what they had begun to understand:

CHARLOTTE: It is amazing. All the things you ever thought you ever think about

JENNIFER: Yeah

CHARLOTTE: I mean, you get taught this and this and this but you never get taught all the different perspectives and all the different ways of looking at it, like discourses, all the different things it could mean

(EASTERN PUBLIC)

In the study group session that ended with this excited talk, Chas and the children made their own life stories and the stories they encountered in text and on screen relevant in their talk as they made their way together through this complex new way of interacting with text. In what follows, there are two excerpts from the conversations in which these concepts were introduced and made relevant by the children in their talk. On this particular occasion Chas had chosen the discourse about a 'good child' to illustrate the concepts of power, powerlessness and of positioning. It was chosen as something the children could make sense of in relation to their own experience as well as something that could be seen to change over time and across cultures. It was a discourse that they could thus stand inside of and at the same time stand back from.

1   CHAS: Now, the discourse in the olden times about a good child was, a good child should be seen and not heard, that was the discourse about a good child/

2   JENNIFER: Children should be seen and not heard

3   CHAS: Now the person speaking that, that puts adults in a very powerful position doesn't it? But it puts kids in a very powerless position, I mean if you can be seen but not heard you don't have very much power in life do you?

4   STACEY: And you don't have very much um *position* you know/

5   CHAS/JENNIFER: Status

6   CHAS: Status right, so you see how that discourse positions adults as powerful and it positions kids as power*less*. Can you think of any other discourses that put you in a powerful position or put you in a powerless position?

7   JAMES: There was a movie on the other night that had a woman who adopted a couple of child[ren] her kid M/

8   JENNIFER: Oh 'Mommy Dearest'

9   JAMES: And she had, she was/

10 JENNIFER: Joan Crawford

11 JAMES: Yeah, she wasn't/

12 JENNIFER: A novel written by an actor

13 JAMES: she was doing that and she had a race then she gave her daughter a race and she won the first time and then she gave her a head start and then she beat her and then she almost beat her, and then she got into trouble. Then the kid got into trouble a couple of times and she's locking her up and that/

14 JENNIFER: Yeah it was really horrible

15 CHAS: So what was her discourse about, what was Joan Crawford's discourse about a good child?

16 JAMES: A child that does what it's told

17 JENNIFER: Yeah told that you know/

18 JAMES: Because the kid was in there and she had a brush and she said 'oh yes' and was acting like her mother/

19 JENNIFER: And then her mother saw her/

20 JAMES: And she got into trouble, and then her mother got the scissors and cut all her hair off

21 ZAC: Yeah, like assault, um parents can harm their kids

22 JENNIFER: Yeah, assault

23 STACEY: And there's nothing that you can do about it, they, like nowadays if somebody does something that you don't want done to you then you have the right to speak out

24 CHAS: Right, so you're in a powerful position if you've got these new discourses of resistance haven't you about child abuse? Great, you understand/

25 JAMES: My mother hit me and hit the cane on me

26 CHAS: Who did?

27 JAMES: My mum, we were having, me and my brother were having a fight and, every morning almost, and mum was going to hit me with the cane and she, dad yelled out and said and mum let go of the cane and said 'Don't yell at him, just hit him with the cane' and I'd already taken off with the cane

(EASTERN PUBLIC)

Chas starts with the discourses used in 'olden times' on what it meant to be a good child and invites the children to stand back from that discourse and examine it in terms of how it positioned children as people without power (1-3). Stacey tries to use the term position to talk about the children's powerlessness (4) and Chas takes up what she says and does the kind of talk Stacey was trying to achieve, showing how the concepts of power and positioning can be used together to talk about adult–child relations. She invites them to think of other discourses that function in this way. James and Jennifer enthusiastically tell about a movie they have just seen about a child who is abused by her (adoptive) mother (6-14). Chas asks them to clarify the way in which this is an extension of the earlier talk (15), which is followed by further elaboration of the abusive nature of the parental behaviour. Zac and Jennifer comment that parents are capable of assaulting their children (21-22) and Stacey shifts back into the present in which child powerlessness is changed because of children's right to 'speak out' against abusive adult authority. Chas links this talk about having the right to speak out to 'discourses of resistance' in relation to child abuse (24) and James tells of an escapade in which he resisted abusive adult power. Interestingly, the resistance he talks of involves actions rather than words. By using the text of a movie and later a life story, the children generate a discussion which makes possible the use of the ideas and concepts that Chas has introduced into the talk. They make their own immersion in these storylines relevant to their understanding. At the same time they stand back and judge as unacceptable the discourse that makes children powerless, and in contrast discourses of resistance are judged to be a modern day right.

In the following discussion, Chas uses the concept of positioning to talk about the way each person locates themselves in a story when they read it. Her purpose is to explore the link between positioning, gender, power, storyline and desire:

1 CHAS: OK, so you understand this idea that when we read a story it's something that we do very actively. And we position ourselves and insert ourselves into the story as one of the characters. Now, usually what happens is boys position themselves with the male characters and girls position themselves as the female characters. It's very very rare that you'll get a swapping over

2 STACEY: I read a book just recently and there was this girl called Lara in it

3 JAMES: Lara Higgin?

4 STACEY: No and she sometimes, she was out in the bush and all this and she had her favourite dog and I just positioned myself, me as herself as her and for days on end I kept on thinking I was her and I was always going to be like her

5 CHAS: That's very interesting. Yes. That's very interesting indeed. So in fairy tales boys are always positioned as the heroic rescuers/

6   JENNIFER: Muscular/

7   CHAS: and girls generally are positioned as the ones to be rescued, the victims/

8   JAMES: Damsels/

9   CHAS: of the treacherous parents, aren't they, in fairy tales?

10 ZAC: The dragons/

11 STACEY: The ones that can't defend themselves but have to be defended by
     others

12 CHAS: Right, so in fairy tales you're positioned powerfully if you're a boy . . . and if
     you're a girl you're positioned powerlessly as the victim usually, can you see that?

13 SEVERAL AT ONCE: Yeah

14 JENNIFER: Like what you said before, like the older is always the more
     powerful and the younger is powerless so you're sort of saying that if you
     were a girl sometimes you are really quite powerless

15 CHAS: That's right

16 CHARLOTTE: Sometimes I wouldn't like to be the one that's the victim, like
     just sometimes I think about watching Ninja movies, I'd like to kill for the CIA
     or something like that and/

17 ZAC: Yeah, your mind plays tricks on you, if you see a really gross movie

18 JAMES: See a movie like *Nightmare on Mainstreet*

19 ZAC: And you don't like the thought of going to bed on that/

20 JAMES: But I'm not/

21 CHAS: It does too, your mind does play/

22 ZAC: You feel like you're gonna/

23 STACEY: Yeah me too

24 CHAS: OK, so the important thing is that we position ourselves . . . according
     to gender, don't we, that's the first thing we must remember, OK so what it
     means is that boys when they read this story, this is the thing I want to get
     across to you, when boys read this story, their hearing of the story is very
     different to when girls read it because they position themselves differently.
     OK, and the messages that they get from the story are going to be very
     different. The messages that girls get/

25 STACEY: It's like when you're first read that story to you and the child is old
     enough, well nearly old enough to know what it needs they see 'oh well I have to
     be the princess or the queen' and the boys think 'oh I have to be the prince and
     live up to what the prince means' and that's how we've got our sort of/

26 JENNIFER: Yeah, another influence

27 CHAS: That's right, that's what I'm trying to get across to you

28 STACEY: It's another influence

29 CHAS: Yeah, it's another influence, exactly . . . We take those stories and we
     put them into our head and they become our stories

30 STACEY: Or actually our lives

31 CHAS: Yes

32 STACEY: Influence what we do

33 CHAS: Yes, that's right/

34 JENNIFER: And what we say

35 CHAS: Right, and because of the gender differentiation, that's one of the ways that we maintain that gender difference is through stories. OK, great so fairy tales in a way offer sort of guidance don't they to the way we should live our lives

36 STACEY: That's just one of the whole discourses of being a man and a woman

(EASTERN PUBLIC)

Chas links active reading with the idea of positioning or inserting oneself into the story and reading the story from the point of the character of the same sex (1). Stacey instantly recalls reading a book in which she positioned herself as a girl called Lara, not only reading the story from her point of view, but imagining being in the world both now and in the future as Lara (2, 4). Chas explains the way in which the subject positions in stories are so often the male hero who has power, and the female victim who is powerless (5, 7, 9, 12). Throughout her explanation the children offer words and phrases such as 'muscular' and 'damsels' showing that they know what she is talking about and thus contributing to the explanation (6, 8, 10, 11). Stacey then makes a link between the imbalance of power in gender relations and the earlier discussion on adult–child relations (14). Charlotte then returns to the point Chas made at the outset about readers imaginatively positioning themselves as the same sex character. She offers an example of positioning herself as the male aggressor (16). The others pick up, not on the cross-gender aspect of Charlotte's point, but on the uncharacteristic emotions that one can experience watching a violent movie (18-23). Probably without conscious intention the link that they make negates and undermines Charlotte's imagining of herself stepping out of her gendered positioning since they construe it as her mind 'playing tricks' on her. Chas re-states her original point (24). The children then make a number of significant connections with the influence on young children's thinking about how to be male and female from the stories that are read to them (25-29), and how these stories become lived stories (30-34). Chas picks up and reiterates their point (35) and Stacey links the discussion to the concept of discourse (36).

These are profoundly important discussions for these children. They have started to see discourse as visible and as powerfully constitutive of their lives. Their active involvement in the conversation, drawing on their own immediate experience and building on the words and meanings they already have access to means that they are able to position Chas not as authoritative adult/teacher who closes down discussion, but as someone from whom they can gain new and important concepts and with whom they can open up discussion on ways of using those concepts to make sense of their own lived experience.

Following these discussions, the group read together two children's stories, *Snow White* and *Princess Smartypants*. These were chosen, rather than stories more appropriate to their age group, for the highly practical reason that their length made it possible to both read and discuss them in one session, and because they readily lend themselves to deconstructive readings.

SNOW WHITE AND THE SEVEN DWARVES

 1 PHILO: It's dumb
 2 CHAS: Why is it dumb?
 3 JENNIFER: Cause it's ah/ . . .
 4 CHARLOTTE: It's just/
 5 PHILO: Old
 6 JENNIFER: Very sexist
 7 ZAK: When you hear it that many times it's dumb
 8 JENNIFER: It's stupid
 9 CHARLOTTE: It's just
10 PHILO: I reckon it's sexist because/
11 JAMES: Yeah, it's sexist it's always the woman that gets into trouble/
12 JENNIFER: You shut up James, keep your mouth shut for once
13 JAMES: Isn't it Chas, it's always the woman that gets into trouble
14 PHILO: Yeah, and how come there's seven dwarves, they're all men and um/
15 JENNIFER: Oh shut up Philo
16 CHAS: No, just let him say this
17 PHILO: Make me
18 CHAS: No, go on Philo, how come there's/
19 PHILO: Um, because there's seven dwarves/
20 JAMES: and there's no females/
21 PHILO: and they're all men and why can't there be a woman dwarf?
22 CHAS: Yeah, that's one good point
23 CHARLOTTE: And there's always/
24 JAMES: Yeah it's/
25 PHILO: Is it because they all mine?
26 JAMES: Yeah, but the woman/
27 CHARLOTTE: The lady is the victim
28 JAMES: Yeah, but the woman dwarf could come out and they could forage/
29 CHARLOTTE: Kids like to hear that sort of thing they like/
30 JAMES: And also why couldn't it be the bloke that's in trouble and the woman comes and saves him?

31 CHAS: Well I don't know. Charlotte, what were you saying, the woman's the victim? . . . Yeah, go on, and why were you saying little kids like to hear that sort of thing?

32 CHARLOTTE: I don't know/ . . .

33 CHARLOTTE: they just like that sort of set up, I don't know why they just like the man being strong 'cause um people know that men after a certain age are naturally stronger so they have to, they have a sense of playing a role of the stronger person who's obviously put in the position to rescue somebody (EASTERN PUBLIC)

The first reaction is to reject the story. It is too familiar (1-8). It is also sexist (6). Philo and James launch into an analysis of the story's sexism in terms of storyline: 'it's always the woman that gets into trouble' (11-13) and all the dwarves are men for no reason given in the text (14, 19-21) except perhaps that they are miners (25). The girls see the boys' analysis as out of place (12, 15). When Chas confirms the validity of what the boys are saying (22), Charlotte acknowledges the point about women being victims (23, 27) but claims that it is the way it is because that is what kids want—a realistic depiction of the way the world is in terms of gender, the naturally greater strength of men making heroic roles appropriate (29, 33). Overlapping with this point of Charlotte's is James' pursuit of his and Philo's earlier points—why are there no female dwarves and why not position the woman as saviour (28, 30)?

34 CHAS: Right, well what sort of a person's Snow White?

35 STACEY: She's a beautiful fair/

36 JAMES: ((very softly)) Ugly

37 PHILO: A person like/

38 STACEY: And it has/

39 PHILO: Thoughtful, kind

40 STACEY And it follows the line that the woman's naturally

41 PHILO: Naturally perfect

42 JAMES: A prefect

43 STACEY: In all fairy tales/

44 JAMES: A tart/

45 STACEY: you have all the perfect people

46 JENNIFER: Qualities of life huh?

47 CHAS: Yeah

48 JAMES: She's a tart

49 CHARLOTTE: She's got all the—Oh James!

50 JAMES: How can they know that she couldn't, why don't they write about ugly?

51 CHARLOTTE: Why do you always be critical of everything?

52 CHAS: Well/

53 STACEY: Why do you always not do/

54 JAMES: Because people/

55 STACEY: what everybody says?

56 PHILO: Because people are ugly um you know, they're nor/ they're normally, 'cause people tease them about being ugly they're normally/

57 JAMES: Ugly!!

58 CHAS: No let him finish, he's making a really good point here

59 PHILO: They're normally um they normally tease them back but if people are pretty no one teases them. Everyone helps them!

60 CHAS: Yeah that's right

61 JAMES: For all we know there might be a really ugly old hag that might help them

62 CHARLOTTE: Oh you are so critical of everything you love criticising people and what they are saying

63 JENNIFER: Shut up James!!

64 JAMES: ((softly)) I'm not criticising anyone/

65 JENNIFER: Oh no, not by half/

66 JAMES: I am just asking why didn't they write it for an ugly old person

67 CHAS: Well I'll tell you why they didn't write it for an ugly old person, because if it was an ugly old person/

68 JAMES: No one would care/

69 CHAS: we wouldn't identify, we wouldn't want to identify and position ourselves as an ugly old person, we want to position ourselves/

70 CHARLOTTE: You couldn't/

71 JENNIFER: James would/

72 CHARLOTTE: make the story work as well/

73 JAMES: Yeah but/

74 PHILO: An ugly old person is probably prettier than James is/

75 JAMES: (   )/

76 CHARLOTTE: because like the man wouldn't um want to rescue her if she's ugly

77 JENNIFER: Anyone would be/

78 JAMES: I'll shut up for a while anyway/
        (EASTERN PUBLIC)

Chas asks them about the character of Snow White (34) and they discuss the way in which women in fairy tales are presented as naturally perfect and concerned about quality of life issues (35-46). James runs a subversive line, claiming that Snow White is really ugly and a tart (36, 44) and, again, the others do not hear his offering as acceptable. They define it as an attempt to disrupt the conversation (49, 51). Charlotte and Stacey focus on James' disruptiveness, what they claim is his tendency always to criticise (49-55, 62). James persists with his idea that characters ought not to be automatically beautiful (50, 61) and Philo attempts to explain, in answer to James' question, that ugly people are treated differently, they are teased and so can't be the person who gets saved (56, 59).

Up to this point all the children, except for James, are seeing the story as a realistic portrayal of fundamental truths about the social world. They are looking for those truths in the text and seeing James' requests for a different kind of text as out of place. They are experiencing the text from inside itself, and finding James' position outside the text a nuisance. But Chas takes up James' point and draws attention to the author and the use of beautiful people to draw the reader in, to position themselves with the character, while ugliness would be an authorial device to distance the reader from the character (67, 69). Charlotte picks up this point, seeing that the story needs Snow White's beauty as a device to make the prince desire her and save her (70-76). At the same time Jennifer and Philo answer Chas's point, saying that James is ugly (74) and would position himself with an ugly person (71) whereupon James says he is retiring from the conversation (78). When he does so Charlotte takes up the issue he has been raising, arguing that the prince's character needs to be called in question if he only saves Snow White because of her looks.

79 CHARLOTTE: But that's another thing of the man's personality, that we might not know what he's really like although he rescued her, she was really good looking but imagine if it was someone who was really ugly 'cause it said, at first he fell in love with her so that might be the only reason why he rescued her

80 CHAS: Well what sort of a person was the prince?

81 JENNIFER: A mean um ((Charlotte laughs))

82 STACEY: Handsome

83 JAMES: A fe- a male

84 CHARLOTTE: Handsome

85 CHAS: Yes

86 PHILO: Brave

87 CHAS: Brave

88 PHILO: Sensible

89 CHARLOTTE: Rich/

90 PHILO: Not like the dwarves. He just knocked/

91 CHARLOTTE: Rich

92 PHILO: the apple out of her throat

93 CHAS: Sensible, *rich,* he was rich/

94 JAMES: He was rich/

95 CHAS: Yeah. What else?

96 JENNIFER: He was a typical man. He married her because she was beautiful/

97 ZAK: Ohhhh!

98 CHAS: And not because of any other quality that she might have had

99   CHARLOTTE: It doesn't say that in/
100 JAMES: And he was rich/
101 CHARLOTTE: It doesn't say that in the story it just says he straight away fell in love with her which indicates probably because we all know that/
102 JAMES: She's good lookin/
103 JENNIFER: she was beautiful that was only because she was (   )
104 CHAS: Right, so it was her physical appearance that was the most important thing
105 PHILO: This is what Mum sometimes says, she says 'first you sink into his arms then you have your arms in the sink'
106 CHAS: That's true, I used to have that above my sink for years. It's the truth! (EASTERN PUBLIC)

Chas takes up Charlotte's point and they turn their attention to the character of the prince (80). It is at this point that the nature of the conflict between James and the girls becomes clear. It is not so much that the girls cannot see the value of James' critique, but that a critique of Snow White as central female character is actually perceived as an intended attack on them. Now the prince's character is to be looked at they can jokingly retaliate and attack the boys by attacking the prince. Jennifer thus says the prince is mean, and Charlotte laughs (81). They then go back to the text and list the characteristics that the story gives him (82-94), but when Chas asks what else (95) and Jennifer returns to the attack: 'He was a typical man. He married her because she was beautiful' (96). Zac expostulates, 'Ohhhh!' (97). Charlotte observes that this is a silence in the text, something that can be filled in with 'what we all know' about men and romantic love (101). Philo confirms this by quoting his mother's saying about romantic love, 'first you sink into his arms then you have your arms in the sink'.

106 contd. CHAS: OK, well from this what sort of message do we get about, what's considered from the perspective of this story, what's a girl's most valuable asset then?
107 STACEY: Beauty
108 CHAS: Beauty. That's right, that's the message we get/
109 JAMES: Jewellery/
110 CHAS: That's right/
111 PHILO: And money.
112 JAMES: Or clothing or jewels
113 STACEY: Yes, because um also that um the witch, the wicked witch could have been a man and he could have, well she/
114 JAMES: The wicked man!/
115 STACEY: well she only married the man 'cause he was rich
116 CHAS: Right
117 STACEY: Just for power

118 CHAS: And from the storyline remember how we talked about storyline here we've got the young girl, she's the victim of her treacherous parents/

119 CHARLOTTE: Yeah/

120 CHAS: and what happens then she's saved by a male saviour, the woodcutter saves her or the servant or however we're gonna call it. Then she goes into domesticity. Right, and then there's the treacherous parent again and then there's the male saviour again and that's like the storyline isn't it?

121 STACEY: Like we did the other day

122 CHAS: OK so what we understand from that is that girls, that a beautiful girl, she's oppressed at first but ultimately in the end she's saved by the handsome heroic prince. Isn't that what/

123 JENNIFER: Though the story doesn't show how much, show much how the woman actually feels about all this

124 CHAS: No that's right/

125 JENNIFER: like she might be getting really lonely just living with the seven dwarves, she might that might not have worked out/

126 JAMES: She might be greedy/

127 JENNIFER: she might have other feelings towards things that happened

128 ZAK: They did, they said she was happy living there

129 CHARLOTTE: Yeah but still!

130 CHAS: So from this story what's beauty usually associated with, is it/

131 ZAK: Princesses

132 STACEY: Women

133 PHILO: Power, rich, money

134 CHAS: Right, yep and what's ugliness generally associated with?

135 PHILO: Being poor

136 CHARLOTTE: Being cruel

137 STACEY: Witch, cruel

138 CHAS: Being a witch, yeah that's right

139 CHARLOTTE: I watched a thing about these witches and they had a black hat and sort of wore black clothes because she was a widow and they had to find out if she was a witch and they did things like pinching her on a certain place on her neck/

140 JAMES: A vampire/

141 CHARLOTTE: and the final thing that they had to do was put them in the water and if she sank then she was/

142 JAMES: A witch

143 CHARLOTTE: not a witch but then she died and if she was a witch she probably would have lived

144 CHAS: Right, but she died anyway

145 CHARLOTTE: And she, so she wasn't a witch seeing she died
(EASTERN PUBLIC)

Chas asks them to think about the message in the story about girls' most valuable assets (106). Jennifer says 'beauty', but the boys go on the attack again and talk about jewellery and possessions and, by implication, girls' materialistic greed (109-112).

Stacey opens up a possibility of changing the sex of the witch (113) but Chas draws the discussion back to an examination of the way in which the storyline is one that is repeated through many fairytales (120-122). Jennifer then notices another silence in the text—it doesn't tell us 'how the woman actually feels about all this' (123). She might have wanted to get away from the dwarves (125) or, as James points out, she might just have been greedy, presumably marrying the prince for his money (126).

They then look at what beauty and ugliness are linked to in stories (130) and they link these not just to good and evil but also to wealth and poverty (131-137). As well, through witches and their treatment, they make a connection with the unfair treatment that is sometimes meted out to people who are positioned in the negative pole of these binaries (139-145).

What is of particular interest here is the movement in and out of the text, revealing both the extent to which the children emotionally position themselves with the same sex characters, such that criticisms of those characters are received as criticisms of themselves, and the ability to use the concepts they have been gaining access to to see the storyline as oppressive and the images and assumptions, the gaps and silences, as highly problematic. In the discussion that follows about *Princess Smartypants* there is again the same warfare between the male and female characters/children, this time with the clear exception of James who sees and appreciates the story from Smartypants' point of view, defending her action in terms of the oppressive nature of parental authority and gender relations. Zac and Philo carry the flag for Swashbuckle. In doing so they not only find themselves negating the validity of Smartypants' resistance but also denying the oppressiveness of gender relations, while, at the same time, engaging in oppressive talk in relation to the character of Smartypants (and thus also of the girls).

PRINCESS SMARTYPANTS

1   PHILO: That was a hopeless story
2   CHAS: Alright. Why was it hopeless, tell me why you thought it was hopeless
3   JAMES: It was exactly the opposite
4   PHILO: I don't know, you just thought, you just knew what was going to happen
5   JAMES: That's probably because you had a look at it

6 STACEY: That one was a good story because it showed that/
7 JAMES: She was resisting
8 STACEY: She yeah she's resisting the female discourse/
9 JAMES: Yes/
10 STACEY: She was doing what she pleased and not/
11 PHILO: (she was) riding motor bikes
12 JAMES: Not what her parents wanted her to do /
13 STACEY: Not just/
14 JAMES: Get a handsome/
15 STACEY: She was just riding motor bikes, roller skating, not doing things that Princesses do/
16 JENNIFER I like roller skating
17 STACEY: would do
18 JAMES: I can't
19 STACEY: And raise pets and/
20 JAMES: I don't have any things/
21 STACEY: and and she still has some of those really magic in fairy tales like a 'magic ring and a magic kiss and all those things like that but she's but she's not a tomboy but she's resisting the female discourse
22 CHAS: Right, the dominant female discourse. What sort of person do you think she was?
23 JENNIFER: Not a snob
24 CHAS: She wasn't a snob
25 CHARLOTTE: Independent ((*very softly*))
26 ZAK: She was a snob
27 CHAS: She was a snob?
28 JAMES: Snob's totally different/
29 CHAS: Tell me Zak why you thought she was
30 JENNIFER: Zak doesn't know what a snob is
31 PHILO: He should he's looking at one/ ((softly referring to Jennifer))
32 ZAK: Well she um wanted them to think of her
33 CHARLOTTE: He keeps looking at Jennifer
34 JAMES: That's not snobbish
35 CHAS: No, can you let him finish and then we'll/
36 ZAK: She wanted him to feed her pets and she wanted them to um to do things that um/
37 PHILO: Were virtually impossible
38 ZAK: Yeah
39 JAMES: That's not snobbish, that's the male discourse. They have they do things that are literally/
40 ZAK: Yeah, but none of them accomplished it except one
41 CHARLOTTE: She was independent

42 CHAS: Ah ha. What do you think Philo. What sort of person do you think she was? You don't have to like her. I mean you know there's no, I want you to honestly say what you think. What sort of person do you/

43 PHILO: I think she'd be best for a doormat

44 CHAS: Why do you think that?

45 PHILO: Oh because you know if she set all the Princes on one task and go and do it then it, um like they'd have to travel away and all that and that'd be heaps heaps better like most fairy tales but that one was just totally different and *stupid*

46 CHARLOTTE: That means you're being sexist though 'cause/

47 JENNIFER: You just said you like the story

48 CHARLOTTE: Yeah you said that/

49 PHILO: No
    ((interruption))

50 STACEY: What happens is that you think that what happens is the female should be the helpless one and the male should be the ones to prove her wrong but she ended up winning in the end. Not the male. That's why/

51 ZAK: Philo just doesn't like the story

52 CHARLOTTE: Well that means you're being sexist, saying that about the doormat/

53 ZAK: We've all got different opinions/

54 CHARLOTTE: Um, then that means that you think that she should just *have* to do exactly what her mother says and have to follow that um discourse that her parents have set that she has to go out and marry a man and live happily ever after

55 ZAK: Well we've all got different opinions

56 CHARLOTTE: Yeah I know, and I put that opinion about his opinion, I can still say that

57 CHAS: Ah ha. What sort of opinion do you think that Smartypants had of herself?

58 JAMES AND STACEY: She thought she was good

59 CHAS: She thought she was pretty good

60 PHILO: She thought she was the best because no one could carry out what she could do

61 JAMES: No one could carry out her deeds

62 JENNIFER: But she could carry out what she'd set down. So it must mean you know for once that she's not going to be the helpless one

63 CHARLOTTE: It doesn't mean that she was/

64 JAMES: Yeah, it is going to be the men that are the helpless one, the women with strength

65 JENNIFER: Yeah, it's about time something happened like that
    (EASTERN PUBLIC)

Philo rejects the story on the grounds that it was a simple reversal of roles and therefore too predictable (1-4). When Stacey and James start elaborating the virtues of Smartypants as one who resisted the 'female discourse' (6-10) he only briefly contributes to the description of who she is (11). Stacey notes with enthusiasm the use of elements of the old stories, such as the magic kiss, combined with a discourse of resistance (21). A series of attacks and counter attacks then breaks out with claims that Smartypants is a snob from Zak (26), with claims from Jennifer that Zac doesn't know what a snob is (30) and Philo claiming that Jennifer is a snob (31). This is a sexually loaded attack if 'snob' is being used in the same way here as it was in the conversations analysed in the last chapter. Zac and Philo say that Smartypants' tasks were impossible and James points out that it is part of the male discourse to have to carry out impossible tasks, so has nothing to do with Smartypants being a snob. Charlotte tries twice to get a different line of discussion going around Smartypants' independence but this is not taken up (25, 41). Chas asks Philo to elaborate his attitude to Smartypants and he states that the best thing for her was to be a 'doormat' (43)—presumably her heroic actions warranting putting her down completely. There is confusion at this point over Philo's attitude to the story and to where he stands, but it is pointed out to him by the girls that his attitude is sexist, his rejection of the story being because of his investment in adult authority and in the imposition of their oppressive discourses on womanhood (46, 50). Zac comes in saying one can like or dislike stories without these political implications, but his argument doesn't convince anyone (51-56). (From the point of view of reader response theory however, his view would have been confirmed and his reading regarded as unproblematic.)

Chas then turns the talk to Smartypants' view of herself and they say that she not only thought she was good, she *was* good—she could carry out all the tasks she set and for once there was a woman who wasn't going to be helpless (57-64). 'It's about time something happened like that' says Jennifer, her imagination caught by the strength and competence of Smartypants, her magic and her ability to resist oppressive social structures (65).

THE FORCE OF FICTIONAL WORLDS

What emerges in these conversations is the impressive power of traditional storylines to assert oppressive gender relations as natural and correct. As readers position themselves as characters in the text, finding themselves being able to *read* the characters from their own experience (the girls wanting to be beautiful and perfect, the boys wanting to be strong and heroic), they understand the text as telling a fiction; but it is a fiction of what they experience as the real world. In imaginatively bringing the characters to life they bring the detail, the threads, the emotions of their own experience to bear on the words on the page and so make the characters live. The text then seems real, the repeated storylines are the storylines of life—the way life is. The battle between the characters in the stories and the characters reading the story are impossible to unthread from each other.

It might be argued on the basis of the sexism of some of the boys that the girls would be better off without them when doing this kind of work. The St Clement's girls did not, however, achieve the kinds of insights displayed here. They imported oppressive male perspectives into their discussions without having to have the boys present to do so. In the mixed sex group the sexism is more visible and therefore able to be analysed and rejected. This is not to say that there are not occasions in which girls can profit from being together without boys, but that even when they are present in a sexist way, this is not necessarily an argument for separating them off. The more important consideration is the development of the analytic/deconstructive skill in both sexes to see and begin to shift oppressive patterns in the texts of their everyday lives and in the written texts they encounter.

The ability to read against the grain requires knowledge of 'real world' critiques of the apparent inevitability of the gender order. It also requires imaginative constructions of desirable alternatives, and the conceptual tools to make the text visible as something constructed from a particular vantage point and with constitutive force and with political implications. The excitement of being able to do this is captured in the conversation at the beginning of the chapter. Charlotte sees what they have done as very different from usual learning. Into the opening created through the conversations they have just had, Charlotte and Jennifer present new possible readings of themselves as resisters of oppression from the outset. Jennifer, who thought she should 'sit down and shut up' like her mother told her, and who feared the naming of herself by others because she would believe them, now finds a new story about herself as one who resisted the imposition of femininity even as a small child. And Charlotte finds a vision of herself as able from the outset to throw off all constraint.

Fundamental to the deconstruction of the written and lived texts that constitute a sexist world is the ability to imaginatively create alternatives, to imaginatively know ways of being which might replace the existing ones. Writing plays an important part in the imaginative construction of those different ways of being. In the final chapter I will look at the process of writing, at the writing of feminist stories and at some of the stories written by the study group children.

8 Writing Beyond the Male–Female Binary

> How far is it from a star to a self, O what inconceivable proximity between one species and another, between an adult and a child, between an author and a character what an unfathomable distance, from one heart to another what secret proximity.
>
> —Cixous (1988, p. 35)

THREADED THROUGH this book are a number of my own stories and the stories of others. These have been arrived at as ways of writing our lives by any number of different routes. The collective biography workshops, for example, which produced the bath-tub story and the story of my little brother, were part of an exercise in finding the cultural threads, the discourses, out of which individual lives are woven. We met to tell our own stories. We wrote them down. We examined the words and images and ways of telling. We peeled back the layers of explanation and rationalisation and made new tellings, tellings which satisfied us all. Although the specific detail of each story still belonged to the one who first told it, from whose specific memory it came, it was recognised as made up of the cultural, discursive threads that we also came to see as the stuff out of which our own lives were woven.

My autobiographical stories are also attempts to find those same threads. In listening to and reading the children's words and in seeking to understand them, I used my own experience of being a child to position myself inside the spoken and written texts they produced and to see the world through them. Instead of leaving that imaginative construction invisible as it most often is in academic writing, I chose to make it visible. I did so because I wanted to disrupt my own authority as invisible author, to reveal in more detail the processes by which I had come to see in certain ways, not just through the data but through the lens of my experience of being in the same world. I wanted, too, to use the opportunity of writing about children to know myself as child better, to know my own history of being in the world not just as a being with specificity but also as one who is produced out of the storylines and ideas of my culture and time.

The collective biography stories and the autobiographical stories are not written as idiosyncratic stories, then, but as evidence of the cultural detail through which we are each spoken/written into existence. It is, as du Plessis says, 'Writing not as personality, [but] writing as praxis. For writing is a practice—a practice in which the author disappears into a process, into a community, into discontinuities, into a desire for discovery' (1990, p. 172). At the same time writing one's stories is intensely personal and there is an immense pleasure in engaging in the process of telling and writing. That which may not previously have been spoken or written or even remembered is retrieved, achieved, recognised, as simultaneously one's own, a telling of one's own specificity, and also as a moment in which one was threaded into the culture; made a speaking subject; subjected.

There are so many possible ways of telling any one story, so much detail that might be included. A story might seem flat and dull, or obscure, or apparently trivial, or incomprehensible, yet strongly felt. We may not have any way of explaining why we felt a particular way at any one time, or even why we remember it, or what value it has in the telling. Then, discussing it with others, seeing it in the context of others' lives, as part of the process of subjectification, of becoming gendered, writing it down, we can find the mutual, cultural discursive threads, discover ourselves and others being spoken into existence in parallel ways: what we *experience* as specificity, that which we refer to as 'I', 'my' experience, is created out of the same discourses and practices as other 'I's.

Such writing is, in a sense, travelling backwards in order to travel forwards. I discover that 'I' is not the private and personal possession I had learned to see it as, that the choices that 'I' have made speak as much of my context and time and cultural location as they do of any separate identifiable individual. In this process I appear to be losing myself, losing the particular nature of my own existence. But in that loss I also discover the strength of my connection with other subjects. I discover how it is we can communicate, how we can understand each others' feelings and experiences to the extraordinary extent that we do, despite our separate embodiment and the specificity of each of our life histories. I discover how and why we can join together in common causes. I also realise that if we have been spoken into existence through systems of binary thought, that we can equally find new ways of speaking, thinking and writing ourselves that partially write over and rub out old limited and limiting thought systems.

The process of retrieving one's own stories, of making them tellable through autobiography or through fiction, or through collective biography workshops, is partly a process of retrieving the detail of one's specific personal history, one's memories, necessarily using currently available discourses to (re)tell them in the terms that those current discourses make possible. At the same time it also involves a movement back inside the body, a movement back in time to another context, another way of feeling and thinking than the present one. It is a movement back and within that makes it possible to experience again through the body the taste and touch and feel, the sensation and emotion of the original experience that is being (re)told. The current discourses and the original experience are in creative tension with each other, each lending meaning and energy to the other, opening up the possibility of new ways of feeling and new ways of saying (Davies, 2000a).

This creative tension is visible in Virginia Woolf's successive tellings of her molestation at the hands of her half-brother, Gerald Duckworth. De Salvo (1991) has assembled these successive tellings from Woolf's writing, beginning with a novel written in her childhood and ending with the explicit telling quoted in Chapter 6 (p. 118). In that final telling Woolf mentions the shame she feels when looking in the mirror in the hall at Talland House. Connected to that shame is the experience of being placed on a high ledge outside the dining room door, in that same hall, by her half-brother and of being sexually molested by him. It is highly probable, according to de Salvo (1991), that Woolf did not actually remember the exact experience until this final telling in her memoirs.

The earlier tellings are of the bodily and emotional experience of shame and embarrassment, of isolation and fear and helplessness, of a sense of terrible disorder. Each of these successive tellings, prior to the telling in the memoirs, reveals the struggle to write/know the unknowable, unsayable. They show how story and autobiography can be used to express the intense particularity of one's own experience in words that both express and remove the isolation. What is expressed in the early tellings is very much a writing from the body, a telling that accesses the bodily sensations, the emotions, the context. At the same time it is a telling which moves it from the specific to the cultural, since in the act of speaking/writing it, the experience becomes that which everyone knows, that which anyone else can then begin to speak.

The first telling is from Woolf's childhood novel *The Experiences of a Pater-familias*. On this occasion the scene is one in which a young woman finds herself stranded high on a chair in the dining room. The dining table is tipped over, plates and food are scattered everywhere. She wants to get away but is unable to move:

> . . . she was left standing on her chair looking at the wreck before her. Soon she remembered that there were gentlemen present and that she was not in a very dignified position but she could not move for as the table tumbled she had not remembered to pull her skirt up after her and so the table tumbled onto her train and she was left sticking onto the chair not wanting to stay there and not knowing how to get down. (de Salvo, 1991, pp. 157-158)

In the holographs of the early versions of Woolf's published novels de Salvo found more of this image, each time deleted from the final version, as if it could not yet publicly be told. Of the early version of *To the Lighthouse* de Salvo says:

> But the most terrifying image . . . which shatters the possibility for 'harmony and completeness,' is related to the boar's head that scares Cam. It is a reflection of 'a pig's snout' in a mirror which 'broke the mirror' . . . It must have been significant, for it is reworked many, many times in her various draft versions. In one version, the snout in the mirror thrusting itself up meant death, and starvation, pain, it was difficult to abolish its significance, and to continue. In another, Woolf writes, 'how could I forget that ugly snout'.
>
> In the longest and most fully worked version, the appearance of the snout in the mirror is the event which unleashes a storm of chaos and inappropriate matings:
>
>> . . . that black snout—that purple foaming stain—had so gravely damaged the composition of the picture that they had fled. They had gone in despair. They had dashed the mirror, to the ground. They saw nothing more. They stumbled and strove now, blindly, pulling their feet out of the mud and stamping them further in. Let the wind blow, let the poppy seed itself, and the carnation mate with the cabbage. Let the swallow build in the drawing room, and the thistle thrust up the tiles . . . Let all civilisation be like broken china to be tangled over with blackberries and grass.
>
> The tremendous autobiographic significance of the boar's head is apparent in the early version of the novel, for Virginia Woolf habitually called the Duckworth brothers 'pigs' and the thing which scares Cam is the boar's head. The event that shatters the possibility of order, initiating, among other things, a period of unnatural cohabitations (the carnation mating with the cabbage) is the appearance of the pig's snout in the mirror, just as the . . . experience of sexual molestation, which she probably saw in the mirror in the dining room passage. (de Salvo, 1991, pp. 177-178)

Later, in 1937, Woolf began to take notes on her 'ups and downs' in order to discover some pattern or meaning to them, to discover why she fell into such terrible depressions, depressions which finally led to her taking her own life. De Salvo points out the detailed similarity between the bodily emotions Woolf describes herself experiencing when she is depressed and the original experience of molestation. Woolf wrote:

> I wish I could write out my sensations at this moment . . . A physical feeling as if I were drumming slightly in the veins: very cold: impotent: & terrified. As if I were exposed on a high ledge in full light. Very lonely . . . Very useless. No atmosphere round me. No words. Very apprehensive. As if something cold & horrible—a roar of laughter at my expense were about to happen. And I am powerless to ward it off: I have no protection. And this anxiety & nothingness surround me with a vacuum. It affects the thighs chiefly. And I want to burst into tears, but have nothing to cry for. Then a great restlessness seizes me . . . [;] the exposed moments are terrifying. I looked at my eyes in the glass once & saw them positively terrified. (de Salvo, 1991, p. 110)

It is not until the end of her life, in her memoirs, that Woolf finally, explicitly writes the passage in which she names Gerald Duckworth and the details of the molestation. De Salvo's guess is that only then did she remember those specific details. Yet while not able to remember that precise origin of her horror of powerlessness, of isolation and unnatural chaos, of shame, and fear of the roar of laughter at her expense, she nonetheless felt them and was seriously disturbed by them. In her various tellings, she both knows and doesn't know: the conscious mind is unable or unwilling to retrieve some of the detail, the unconscious pushes it forward as something important, something to be written about.

STORIES FROM THE STUDY GROUPS

The children in the study groups were invited, towards the end of their meetings with Chas, to write their own stories. They had already told autobiographical stories in relation to their photographs, read traditional and feminist stories and learned to deconstruct them, and discussed at length their own experience of being gendered and the relation of the process of gendering to storyline and to power and powerlessness. Having struggled with the task of writing their own group stories, with Chas pointing out to them some of the ways in which they were falling into tellings which re-constituted a sexist world, some of the children, at Chas's invitation, set out to write a story of their own.[1]

A story written by Anna from Karobran Public is the story of a scientist doing an experiment that goes wrong.

THE SPIDER ATTACK

In 2100 a scientist Mr S. N. Winson was in his laboratory experimenting with one of his formulas. It was made from metal filings, 1 rotten egg, 3 packets of bubble gum. The experiment had o be done with ants.

A terrible accident happened while he was in the middle of his experiment .

Mr Winson turned around to pick up the jar of ants, he accidentally knocked over the jar of ants, the ants scattered all over the floor. In his rush to collect the ants he knocked over the formula and it spilled all over the ants. Immediately the ants grew to be twenty centimetres by five centimetres big black hairy spiders.

Mr Winson sat back in his chair speechless he was so terrified. The spiders were crawling all around the laboratory. Mr Winson quickly tried to make a formula that would make the spiders shrink back to be little black ants again.

The formula was not successful and it just blew up in his face. The noise made the big black hairy spiders angry and they climbed up onto the bench and started attacking Mr Winson and his equipment. He was screaming for help but because he was alone with no-one else around, nobody could hear him.

The spiders were getting more aggravated because of the screaming. They had big sharp metallic teeth and were gnawing away at the equipment and Mr Winson's legs and trousers. The spiders were getting smaller and smaller as they were using their energy chewing everything.

Mr Winson stopped screaming for a moment and realised that the more the spiders ate the more the more they shrunk.

He said I've got it, I will let them chew on and while they're in the process of doing that I'll get my jar and collect the middle size black hairy spiders.

After he collected the spiders in the jar they started to try to eat through the glass but their metallic teeth wouldn't chew through the glass. After a while the black spiders shrank back into little black ants again.

---

[1]The children wrote their stories at home sometimes on home computers and sometimes in handwriting. We do not know how much editing help was provided by friends or family. Many of the stories are highly polished and have few spelling or grammatical errors. In reproducing them here I have added in occasional full stops and commas and amended spelling errors as part of the normal editing process adults would expect on their work prior to publication. It could be argued that this interferes with the data and that I should reproduce it exactly as the children produced it. I have decided against this since I do not like my own technical errors to be included in my published work particularly if they distract the reader from what I want to say. On the other hand I have not changed Aboriginal grammar to Standard English nor have I changed unusual word usage since either of these would interfere with the voice of the writer.

Following Mr Winson's experience with the ants he decided never to mess with formulas or ants ever again and he set off into the bush to set free his collection of little black ants.

This seemed, at first sight, a strange story to hand in to a study group that has been working on gender, power and text. Unless, of course, it is actually about just that. The details that make this seem to me a possible story about gender and power and about sexual abuse in particular, are located in the interaction between the scientist and the spiders. The scientist is 'Mr Winson'. Anna wanted to be a boy, a *son* for her father, *win*ning at sport, making her father very proud. *Win-son* is also a child, since he plays with bubble gum and rotten eggs. The distance between the characters of Anna and Mr Winson is readily bridged (*'between an adult and a child, between an author and a character what an unfathomable distance, from one heart to another what secret proximity'*. Cixous, 1988, p. 35). Through some accident on the part of our central character, (s)he is confronted by rapidly swelling, black hairy objects, twenty centimetres by five centimetres. (S)he is speechless with fear. ('Mr Winson sat back in his chair speechless he was so terrified'.) (S)he is attacked and screams, which only makes things worse, as the attackers become angry at the screaming. And anyway (s)he is alone and no one hears. (S)he discovers that the action of attacking, of *eating*, actually reduces the size of the spiders (the penis?) thus bringing them back under control.

As Woolf had done, it may be that Anna has gone back and within her body to a set of intensely felt sensations of fear at a grotesque and unpredicted assault over which she felt completely powerless. The story of the spider attack may be a recognisable and acceptable cultural form through which she can tell of those intense sensations.

The interpretation I have made is a chilling one and one that Anna would not necessarily assent to. Shortly after writing this story she refused to participate any longer in the study group, not willing, in particular, to tell stories about the photographs she had taken of her family. It was not until well after the study groups had finished their work, and when writing this book, that the possible significance of the story struck me. It made sense within the context of Anna's aggressive refusal of femininity, her certainty that female protagonists are necessarily vulnerable and incompetent and her refusal to wear dresses without shorts. Like Woolf, in her earlier tellings of molestation, it is highly possible that Anna is not conscious of anything other than the feeling of pain and vulnerability that her story tells.

Counterbalancing the horror that I feel in relation to Anna's story is the fact that it has a strong ending. The protagonist figures out what led to the transformation and decides that (s)he knows how to avoid having it happen again. Although it is a fearful story, it is also a story in which the protagonist remains, for most of the story, in control of the flow of events. (S)he remains, after all, Mr *Win-son*. It is thus a story that achieves a movement beyond fear and vulnerability through gaining a sense of control over the events that gave rise to it. But like Woolf, Anna may make many different tellings of this story before she achieves a final telling.[2]

The story that Mal wrote is his own retelling of the group story that he so persistently undermined in Chapter 4, importing rape in order to turn the girl in the story into the 'real victim'. This was in keeping with his constant verbal sexual attacks on the girls in the study group and yet deeply at odds with his apparent respect for women in his Aboriginal community and for individuals who could successfully cross gender boundaries. Mal's story reveals the way in which any analysis of gender issues cannot be separated from other forms of oppression—in Mal's case the marginality that goes with Aboriginality. Mal's major innovation in his story is to focus attention on the murderer, to undo his marginality, or rather to make that marginality central to the story rather than peripheral to it.

THE CAUGHT MURDERER

One day a car went past with two people in it. They were named Peter and Michelle. They are brother and sister. But in a dark room far away from Peter and Michelle there was a man named Joseph Kenny. He is a killer. He has been caught for murder, tip and run, rapes and other things like that ten times but has escaped. Now a 27 year old lady named Karen Wilks who is a police officer and a 32 year old man who is a detective are out to find him. The detective Brian Haines and police officer Karen Wilks have been teamed up for a long time but have not yet solved a mystery. Can this be their first one? Joseph Kenny was planning another murder. The victims, Peter and Michelle. They were at the movies when suddenly this person said 'what is your order'. 'We don't have an order'. Then Joseph pulled out a gun and shot Peter and then he hopped into the car and drove off with Michelle. He tied her to the seat. He went out into the bush and set the car alight. Michelle was dead within seconds. Joseph ran out into the scrub. But back at the police station a witness is there talking to Police Officer Karen Wilks. She told Karen that a man took off in a car with a girl and also that she seen someone push this man out the door. It was Peter. They sent out a search party and found Joseph Kenny. Now he has been to court and has been charged for murder. Now he is in jail for seven years. The seven years are over. He done it again. Two days after that seven years.

---

[2]Woolf comments in her memoirs that she was obsessed by vivid memories of her mother until she wrote *To the Lighthouse*. In achieving that particular telling she lost the vivid memories of her mother and almost could no longer remember her the novel for the moment having taken their place.

The name of the caught murderer is a combination of a biblical name, and the name of two well-known Australian sporting heroes, Grant Kenny, who was Iron Man, and Brett Kenny, an exceptional footballer. With his interest in sport and football in particular, Mal would have been well aware of these two heroes. His choice of name asks for a reading of his story, not with the detective and the police officer as the only protagonists, but with Joseph Kenny equally central to the story. In this reading, Mal is writing two parallel stories, one about gender and one about race. In the gender story we have pretty much the same as the story the study group wrote with a male and female victim instead of the usual female victim, both being killed, the female experiencing more extensive and detailed victimisation than the man. We have a male and female hero who solve their first mystery (and are thus not all that heroic). We have a female bystander who provides the critical information. In the story running parallel with the gender story is the story about a marginal person named Joseph Kenny, located in a 'dark room far away'. He is an intransigent trouble maker, a rapist, a murderer, on the run. A further clue that Mal positions himself with Joseph Kenny, in addition to naming him after a football hero and an iron man, is the elision between hit and run traffic accidents and tip football. In the list of Joseph Kenny's crimes is 'tip and run'. He murders his two victims and then 'runs out into the scrub'. He is caught and jailed for seven years, but immediately he is released he does it again.

Although Mal does not say Kenny is Aboriginal, he places his (anti)hero in 'the dark', he gives him powers of evading the (white) law, running off into 'the scrub' after his crime, the place Aboriginal people belonged to before white invasion. He refuses to be controlled by (white) law, despite his seven years in the wilderness of jail.[3] Seen from the perspective of Joseph Kenny, the extra savagery meted out to the female victim is not just sexism, but an attack on the oppressive white law *in its own sexist terms*. Mal's story can thus be read as a story of resistance, as his version of what the study group has been learning. He has translated discourses of resistance to resistance against racism. It is a passive/violent resistance that struggles to place the (anti)hero into the picture, as someone who can be written about, whose story can be heard, not as incidental to the 'real' story, but as the story itself.

Hite analyses Jean Rhys's novels as the same kind of struggle in relation to gender, in which Rhys's characters struggle to be read as both victim and protagonist without being judged and rejected. She dwells in particular on the difficulty of having one's words heard as anything

---

[3]Seven is a powerful number in Christianity, the major religion currently practised among urban Aboriginal groups. It is often associated with hard times famines often lasting for seven years for example and in Judges I v 6 the people of Israel spend seven years in the wilderness.

other than gibberish if one tries to speak with anything other than (white) male words, or to position oneself as other than marginal to (white) male action. She points out that marginal characters (women and blacks) are usually flat characters without the complex tensions and motivations that drive the central (white male) protagonists. In contrast:

> Rhys's protagonists are victims who are fully aware of their victimization. Their awareness does not make them any less victimized; it serves only to make them self-conscious in their roles and thus alienated from the society that wants to identify them completely with these roles. Worst of all, because their situation as both marginalized and wholly conscious is impossible in the terms proposed by the dominant culture, the statements in which they express their awareness cannot have any acknowledged context. If they do not speak 'in character', which is to say, in the wholly predictable ways that their role obliges, their utterances are received as senseless. To be outside the machine is to be without a language, condemned to emit sounds that inside interlocuters will interpret as evidence of duplicity, infantalism, hypocrisy—or simply madness.
>
> To women writers—indeed, to women generally in Western tradition—the imputation of madness is a continual and potent threat, for madness is the possibility that haunts their cultural identity as Other. Because the masculinist point of view is by definition the rational and intelligible one, anybody occupying the cultural position of 'woman' is at risk, required simultaneously to be a spokesman for their masculinist viewpoint and to embody its inverse or outside, the possibility of being irrational, unintelligible. To express another point of view—to speak as 'woman' in this culture—is to utter truths by convention so unimaginable that they are likely to be dismissed as gibberish, mere symptoms of hysteria. (Hite, 1989, p. 28)

Mal finds textual, symbolic ways, such as naming, to pull the marginal character of the murderer out of his marginal place. But he can find no way to break the pattern of dominance and intransigence except perhaps to excel at some features of the dominant group's negativity and oppressiveness, not towards himself, but towards women.[4]

Charlotte also avoids the problem of making a radical shift within the everyday, in which a marginal character can be heard as central, by placing her story in another time and another culture. Her story takes up oppressive elements of present day culture—the obligation of each person to become identifiably male or female, and parental authority to insist on this. Cleverly she weaves a tale in which the female child resists this imposition first by listening to her parents

---

[4]How often do marginal groups choose some aspect of the dominant culture to emulate just at the time when the dominant group is calling that practice in question and moving beyond it?

and attempting to do what they ask. Only when she finds this beyond her does she find a way to escape the problem by transforming herself. She does so using both recognisable threads of traditional femininity, along with the name her parents have given her.

MALU KUNGKA

A long time ago in the Dreamtime there was a young girl called Malu Kungka, 'malu' meaning 'kangaroo' and 'kungka' meaning 'girl'. She was from an Aboriginal tribe called 'Walungi' and she was a very strong and independent girl. Sometimes her father would even take her hunting. She didn't resemble a girl at all or even a child for that matter. She was always wandering off into the scrub looking for an adventure while all the other children would play in the tribal ground where they had set up camp and would play all day with each other.

Many years passed and Malu Kungka was still carrying on her tradition of wandering off and exploring new places and things.

One night Malu Kungka's parents were talking about Malu Kungka, they decided that her father would not take her hunting with him any more because she was growing up and she must be like the other children and learn how to be a woman, for it was not long before she would be an adolescent and she still hadn't a care in the world except for the animals and trees and all those sorts of things. The next day Malu Kungka's parents told her what they thought, though they regretted it because now she was sad and puzzled.

That day she did not eat as she usually did, she sat down in the red dust and drew pictures of things whilst pondering over what her parents had said. She was confused, 'What do I have to do to prove I am a woman, I am a woman aren't I?' she thought. Now she was more confused than ever, she did not know much of these things for she never thought of them as important, therefore she never thought of them at all.

The next day she set about finding a way of proving that she was a woman. The first thing she did was to watch all the other Kungkas practising what they had learnt from their parents. She observed that they would sit in groups and weave baskets, sing songs and make carriers out of bits of hollowed out trees and big pieces of bark. She tried doing all these things, unfortunately in vain for she could not do any of these things. Still she practiced each of these things every day, for she was determined to get it right.

The initiation would be held at the next full moon and the moon was already three quarters full, she had only one week in which to become a woman. Finally she realized she could not become a woman that way and she would have to find a spiritual way of becoming a woman and the only way of doing that would be to ask for the help of Malu Biamee because the kangaroo was her symbol and 'Malu Biamee' meant 'Kangaroo God'. Now she would have to hold a special ceremony. So the night of the initiation when the moon was high she gathered ten of the wisest and oldest women of the tribe and pleaded with them to help, finally they agreed.

They collected the things essential for a ceremony of this type and set off following Malu Kungka to a special place that she had often seen the kangaroos meet at. The moon was shining as bright as day when they began to paint, they used special ground rocks and the melted fat of a kangaroo, they painted various kangaroo symbols all over their bodies. Then they put a hollowed out kangaroo's body on the back of Malu Kungka and then they started dancing a special dance with songs to go with it. When that was over they all placed different offerings in the centre of the circle.

The next day Malu Kungka's parents did not find their daughter in her usual place for Malu Biamee had taken pity on her and given her to her one love . . . . . . Nature, where she would be happy for the rest of her life. Malu Biamee had turned her into her true self . . . . . . a Malu!!!

The story begins with a direct challenge to a number of binaries. Malu Kungka's name is part animal and she does not look as if she is either a child or female. She spends time hunting with her father or adventuring in the scrub on her own, in marked contrast to other children. Her parents decide she must become like the others. She ponders and questions this decision, then makes every attempt to do what her parents want. But she cannot. She decides to find a 'spiritual way of becoming a woman'. With the aid of the spiritual power of the older women she is transformed, as in any traditional romance story, into her 'true self' and 'given to her one love'. Further, in becoming a kangaroo, she simply takes up the name her parents gave her. It is a radical solution, precisely because it is woven out of threads that her parents cannot legitimately object to, yet at the same time refusing the path they have pushed her towards. The alternative path is one that disrupts the boundary between nature and culture, one of the significant metaphors that holds the male–female binary in place. Malu Kungka shifts to the female side in order to escape the restrictions of the binary itself—a version of Cixous's 'writing the feminine'.[5]

But disruptions to traditional cultural patterns are not always heard as such, as Anna forcefully reveals in the following conversation. Chas read Charlotte's story to the Karobran study group when she was talking to them about the possibility of writing their own stories. Anna perceives Malu Kungka as weak, a 'sook'. Real power lies, for Anna, in what she herself has already achieved, that is in persuading her father to let her continue being non-feminine. Predictably Mal (and probably Ken) are intent on sexualising Malu Kungka and so reducing her power. Predictably, too, they link that reduced person to the female members of the study group. Natalie and Chas insist that Malu Kungka is powerful. While Anna finally concedes that Malu Kungka reveals some power in her ability to persuade the old women to transform her, she refuses to speak of these women in respectful terms. And, further, she cannot see

---

[5]Some of Angela Carter's stories in *The Bloody Chamber* and stories such as Paul Goble's *The Girl Who Loved Horses* also disrupt the human–animal binary as Charlotte's story does.

removal to another world as any kind of solution. She is, for now, locked into the binary gender order which is in turn located in an intractably real world. In this model, only her own individual heroic efforts will enable her to transcend gender boundaries:

CHAS: Can anyone think of any other ways that this resists the dominant discourses?/

ANNA: Hey

CHAS: Well she's very strong and she's independent that's sort of not like the dominant discourse about the way girls are

ANNA: How could she be strong and independent if all she does is go wandering off into the bush in another world?

MAL: Well you wouldn't go around in the bush, like there might be tigers and that/

NATALIE: Not tigers

MAL: Not tiger/

NATALIE: Not in the bush

MAL: wolves and that, foxes in the bush

KEN: Yeah but foxes don't hurt you

CHAS: Well what sort of a girl is this Malu Kungka?

ANNA: Queer

CHAS: You think she's queer Anna?

KEN: She likes going on adventures

MAL: Well Anna you think she's queer, you must be queer

ANNA: No, I'm not Malu Kungka

CHAS: Anna why do you think she's queer?

ANNA: Because she . . . she got upset because her parents said something to her and she got all depressed and wouldn't eat anything/

CHAS: Yeah

NATALIE: I reckon that/

ANNA: Like if your mum said you can't go hunting with your dad 'cause it's dark and all spooky and/

NATALIE: Spooky, all spooky

ANNA: spooky and um, 'cause it was too dangerous, would you not eat anything?

CHAS: Well sometimes when I get upset I don't eat anything

ANNA: Do you sit and sook?

. . .

CHAS: She is very resourceful because when she realises that she can't make the baskets and be a woman in the traditional sort of a way she's resourceful enough to try and think of another way of achieving her goals isn't she? What do you think the/

NATALIE: Chas she's powerful/

CHAS: She's powerful yep/

NATALIE: in her own way

ANNA: In one way she's not too powerful in another way she is

CHAS: Well tell me the way she is and she isn't

MAL: That way she's powerful I can tell you now ((laughter))

ANNA: She's powerful because she can get those chickies, those old chickies, to um go out in that thing with her

CHAS: The old women?

KEN: (   )

ANNA: She went and/

ROSIE: I beg your pardon Ken?

BRIAN: So would you be if you weren't allowed to go home

ANNA: and why she's not powerful because um she couldn't force her parents to make, let her go with her dad hunting

Aleisha, so quiet through the study group discussions, chose an entirely different strategy for disrupting gender relations. Like Mal, she is very subtle in the way she creates her characters as Aboriginal, the name Cinderfella being the only direct indication of the protagonist's race (his 'blackfella' status). Her main strategy is laughter and she achieves this by taking a traditional story and reversing the roles, thus showing how familiar and yet how ridiculous they are. She thus picks up the threads of the conversations in the study group around the text of *Snow White* and makes a traditional story into a feminist text.

The rather absurd male protagonist is a football hero and the central female hero is, without any negative judgment, 'the tart of the town' who finds her pimply hero and settles down with him. Although, as Walkerdine (1984) points out, stories based on role reversals are inadequate to the extent that they do not catch girls' imaginations, nor provide any alternative to the patterns of desire generated out of the traditional romance narrative, when used with laughter as they are here, they mock and disrupt the traditional narrative enough to show a strong need for an alternative.

CINDERFELLA

There once was a prince named Cinderfella George. He played football and girls were only allowed to come and watch. He was top footballer. He was the ugliest guy in town but he had some love potion. That's how come he was so sexy when he played football. The love potion only lasted for one hour and football went for one hour. That's how come Cinderfella jumped in his car as soon as he finished playing. But half way home he would change into the boring old George. After he finished football he always lost one footie boot because he was Cinderfella and he was slowly changing into George and the boots were slowly getting too big. And that's how come they always fell off and all of the girls would run for his boot but Melissa Cook always got it. She was the tart of the town. She was a fast runner and that's how come she got the football boot. She went around to all of the houses in town to see whose foot fitted in the boot. This was the big moment. Melissa was at the last house in town. 'Could this be Cinderfella's house?' she asked herself. She knocked on the door and this boy named George answered the door. He was so ugly because he had freckles on his legs and warts on his fingers and pimples on his face. Anyway she was just about to put the footie boot on him when his feet grew a little bigger. And the shoes that he was wearing even grew big holes in them. At last she put the boot on him. When it fitted, she was so happy she even kissed him on the lips where he had no pimples. From then on she started going out with him and whenever he went out of the house he drank some love potion. Of course they only went out for one hour and everyone lived happily ever after.

According to du Plessis:

> If one sees inside one's gender, class, race, sexuality, nationality, and these from and engaged with one's time, then culture is a process of rereading and rewriting, a practice . . . [T]he feminist cultural project is [n]o less than the reseeing of every text, every author, every canonical work, every thing written, every world view, every discourse, every image, everything unwritten, from a gender perspective.
>
> This is a major cultural project, intimately linked to the practice of questioning powers of all sorts, to the uses of culture in all arenas, to the nature, or definition of culture. And this is a central project of our generation (of women), this feminist cultural practice. (1990, p. 165)

It is a major cultural project of our generation of women. Yes. But it must also be a major cultural project of our generation of men. It makes no sense to exclude members of our culture from such a profoundly important cultural process just because of the genitals they happen to have, or because of the power our culture has given some of the people with those genitals. My three sons continually remind me of that.

TWO EDGES

Barthes (1989) refers to texts which rupture the known, familiar cultural forms as involving both a (re)creation of the familiar, pleasurable cultural forms that we know so well and at the same time opening up a possibility of the death of language as we know it. In such writing, he says, 'the language is redistributed':

> Now *such redistribution is always achieved by cutting*. Two edges are created: an obedient, conformist, plagiarizing edge (the language is to be copied in its canonical state, as it has been established by schooling, good usage, literature, culture), and *another edge*, mobile, blank (ready to assume any contours), which is never anything but the site of its effect: the place where the death of language is glimpsed. These two edges, the compromise they bring about, are necessary. Neither culture nor its destruction is erotic; it is the seam between them, the fault, the flaw, which becomes so. (Barthes, 1989, p. 6)

Barthes refers to the cultural edge as the 'pleasure' edge and the other disruptive edge as 'bliss'.[6] All feminist stories we write necessarily contain the familiar, known, pleasure edge, just as do so many feminist interactions in the everyday world. One cannot live entirely on the other disruptive edge. The children of the study groups, like anyone else, took pleasure in the known familiar cultural patterns in terms of which they could be competent members of their social groups. Their knowledge of other possibilities, or even of the flaws in the familiar cultural patterns, did not erase that pleasure. At the same time the creation of the cutting edge, of the other possibility, has the potential to disrupt and to erase some aspects of the familiar cultural patterns. It has that power, though, only to the extent that we can see it and know it: it *is never anything but the site of its effect*.

The following story was written for me by my youngest son, Daniel. At the time the study groups were meeting I was pondering all of the elements of story telling that may unwittingly reconstitute the gender order that any feminist story is attempting to undo, worrying about how to be aware enough to remove them all, and beginning to realise that that is actually impossible. As Barthes makes clear, any story has to incorporate what we know already if it is to be comprehensible, if it is to be pleasurable enough to capture the reader's imagination. It must do both of these if it is to move us on to a new possibility different from the ones we know already. Daniel and I had discussed different ways of beginning stories, talking about the ways in which we anticipate whole storylines just out of what we are told in the first few lines. We tried out his response to possible beginnings of a story I was thinking of writing— seeing how the idea of who the character might be was suggested through the very act of drawing attention to her appearance (and thus constituting her as an object of the male gaze), or by placing her in an interior rather than an exterior setting. I said I was unable to write a feminist story because I had become paralysed with knowing too much about the way each phrase could wind back into existence the world I was trying to undo. Daniel said he did not think it was so difficult and went off to write his own story about a woman he called Vuthsanya.

Like Daniel, Vuthsanya is the third child and, like Daniel, Vuthsanya had a hard father whom she hardly knew.

---

[6]Barthe's use of sexual metaphors to analyse the processes of reading/writing is a fascinating and productive one. Many of his examples though are violent and destructive. I continually find myself having to distance myself from these in order to enjoy the insights that his ideas produce.

VUTHSANYA

Now it so happened that a third child was born to King Rian, and was not a male. This angered the King greatly, for it had been foretold that his third child was to be gifted with great powers of knowledge and skill, especially in battle.

The King himself was a mighty ruler and man of renown. He was so angered by the birth of his third daughter, that he refused to speak to her or even to see her. Her name was Vuthsanya and she only ever looked upon her father's face once. She had eyes of the blackest of black and secrets the darkest of dark.

On her twelfth birthday she left the castle and the Kingdom carrying only the clothes on her back. The King soon learned of her departure, yet he sent no search party and shed no tear. Many others did, for Vuthsanya was well liked by the people although none could claim to know her well.

The next ten years were the coldest and hardest years the Kingdom had ever known. Crops failed, sickness plagued the land, the sun seldom shone, and the King was growing old. It was then that a terrible creature came to the land. He was Teg-Mushrak, one of the ancient tormentors, who took delight in death and destruction. In looks he was something like a giant ogre, yet much more repulsive. Mushrak terrorised the Kingdom for months without rest. Rian had sent many brave knights out to finish him, but none came back.

In frustration and dismay the King sent forth a demand for Mushrak to meet him on the field of battle. This challenge was accepted gleefully by the blood hungry Tormentor. So it was set. In one week, on Mid-Winter's Eve, the two shall meet in battle on the Felion Plains below the cliffs of Aspirion.

The day quickly came and the King went to meet his doom. The people were frightened and would not come out of their houses. Children wept and the men felt shamed for there was nothing they could do but hope.

Rian reached the plains and there was Mushrak, picking his teeth with the splintered thigh bone of a victim. He laughed and spat at Rian who was clad in bright armour, riding a white steed and carrying a long shining lance. 'Prepare to meet your end!' yelled King Rian, as he charged towards the foul creature with blood in his eyes. But Rian was not the young warrior he once had been and Mushrak leapt aside with surprising speed and knocked Rian from his horse with a tremendous blow. The King fell to the ground and was dazed. He unsheathed his sword but Mushrak leaped in the air and dealt his head a mighty kick which rendered him unconscious, and at the ogre's mercy, of which there was none.

Mushrak was preparing to sink his teeth into his prize when he heard the beating of huge wings above him, he wheeled around and was dealt a sickening blow across the side of the head. Mushrak stumbled with blood pouring out of his face, saliva dribbling down his chin and gave a thunderous bellow of anger. He turned to face his foe, and his anger, as great as it was, gave way to a chuckle, and then a laugh. 'A woman dares to attack Mushrak, the most powerful and wonderful creature in the land' he snorted, 'I will teach you the folly of your ways!'

Vuthsanya was sitting astride a black Pegasus with her long sword drawn and no light shone from her eyes. She leapt from her mount with agility and stood to face Mushrak. She said nothing.

The giant ogre lunged towards Vuthsanya, but she nimbly ducked aside and slashed his side so that blood poured out like water. This angered Mushrak beyond belief and he spun around, madly trying to claw at this arrogant pest. But he was no match for Vuthsanya. With two more blows, Mushrak was begging for mercy. The next blow split Teg-Mushrak's skull in two. He was dead and Vuthsanya stood tall and proud over her fallen foe.

Now King Rian awoke from his slumber and saw what had taken place and looked for the mighty warrior who had done this amazing deed, for he would most certainly be the King's new champion. But all he could see was a mighty black Pegasus flying off into the distance with a woman's figure astride. It seemed then to Rian that he knew who this was, though he could not say, or perhaps would not.

Rian rode home and the people rejoiced to see their King return. To this day people still tell the story of Rian's battle with Teg Mushrak and how he split the monster's head in two and so saved the land. Only two people know what really happened that day, and so do you.

Of course we can read this story conservatively, *with* the grain of the traditional gender relations. In such a reading there are many features that appear to confirm familiar cultural patterns:

- fathers do not welcome or value daughters, particularly when their heart is set on a son capable of heroism;
- good daughters cope with such rejection with silence and with absence, since there is nothing they can say to undo such rejection;
- mothers are also silent and do nothing to question or reverse the plight of their daughters;
- even where the daughter is the exception to the rule and is capable of heroism, the father will not acknowledge such heroism, nor will the daughter ask him to do so.

But there is also much about the story that makes a different reading possible, a reading that runs against the grain of discourses that constitute women inside the male–female binary. That alternative reading blissfully disrupts the familiar patterns of gender relations and provides the reader with an alternative storyline.

First, the father's belief in the inferiority of women is shown to be wrong. There is a wisdom greater than the King's which foretells that girls *can* have powerful knowledge and be great warriors. ('[I]t had been foretold that his third child was to be gifted with great powers of knowledge and skill, especially in battle'.) Her knowledge and her strength are not only greater than his, but perhaps more importantly cannot be attributed to him. As well the powerful and all rejecting father is shown to be dishonest, claiming her accomplishments as his own. His law rests on a shaky foundation that not only invites criticism but is recognisable as falsely depending on the unacknowledged support of women.

Second, the daughter reveals that his judgment is of no consequence to her. She can walk away from it and set up an alternative life in which she is clearly extraordinarily powerful. It is within her gift to save her father and his kingdom from a destructive evil, which she does, but his recognition of this fact is of no consequence to her. This can be read as a profound negation of the word/the law/the power of the father. She thus has far greater moral stature than he since she does not hold grudges or seek revenge even where this would seem to be an entirely reasonable response.

There are some additional features of the story that involve the reader in reading against the conservative grain of the story. One of these is the ending where the author invites the reader to position her/himself as one who knows the truth, and thus as one who shares Vuthsanya's knowledge. The reader then stands with Vuthsanya against the power of the father.

The story is told from the moral position of Vuthsanya but in an interestingly 'unfeminine' way. The kinds of details that are normally revealed in the telling of women's lives are left completely untold. She is a genuine protagonist mixing some features of the male heroic position with some features of the heroine. As heroine she is, at the beginning, vulnerable in the way that heroines usually are. She is at risk of being rejected by a central male figure, in this case, the father. She has no safe domestic scene and is cast adrift, presumably with the task of finding a new one. But she turns this around. Her story becomes one that is more typical of the male hero. She is powerful, competent and strong. Neither her home base nor her appearance is described (except for the blackness of her eyes whose most prominent quality is what they hide). She is not the object of another's gaze, and nor does she need anyone else to make her safe.

Since the story begins with the familiar scene of rejection, it has the power to 'hook' a female reader who can connect with the subjectivity of Vuthsanya and know her vulnerability. It maintains this connection in a number of ways. Vuthsanya remains caring in that she saves her father when he needs it and she does not confront or demand in an 'unfeminine' way. Her warrior-like skills are the most significant point of departure in her character from current accepted forms of femaleness/femininity, though if understood in mythical/symbolic terms as bringing an end to an evil which destroys the land, they stand

well within radical feminist and eco-feminist versions of female-
ness/femininity. Vuthsanya is thus not a character who asks us to
negate our femininity, but who says that along with feminine qualities
and even when positioned as inferior/female, women can be heroic and
can thus exist outside and independent of the male–female binary. She
can exist not as *woman* but as a multiple being who incorporates and
reconstitutes that which was previously understood as essential to either
masculinity or femininity.

Daniel and I talked a lot about feminism and stories after he had
written *Vuthsanya,* and, of course, I encouraged him to write more. The
second story he wrote for me is called *Bazbarel.* Like Vuthsanya,
Bazbarel leaves her family and community to make her own life. The
horror that she faces is not rejection by the father, but rape by the men of
her village. Instead of absence, we have powerful presence in this story
and the female hero chooses a very different path from the one chosen
by Vuthsanya. Where the alternative life that Vuthsanya had created for
herself, and out of which she could be so powerful, is left invisible,
Bazbarel's life apart from her people begins to be told. The almost
unimaginable creating of a life outside the oppressive gender order is
struggled after. The issue of sexual assault is made central in the battle
that Bazbarel fights. The story contains a desperate and bloody assertion
that the old gender order *will no longer exist.*

BAZBAREL

Bazbarel lived in the winter lands of the Ice God Segan. The men from her
village were fierce warriors and relied on what they could take from others
rather than provide for themselves. Once a week a raiding party would go out to
plunder and slaughter neighbouring villages and travelling caravans. The loss of
lives was often high but they knew no other way to live.

Only the men were trained to become warriors and for this reason a
male child was prized beyond all else. It was a woman's place to run the village
in all but warfare and council decisions. Their day was full and they had no time
to complain, for all the good it would do.

Bazbarel had never liked her life here, but she felt that she had little
choice. She saw herself as a Magician and she had a taste for battle, but Sorcery was
forbidden in the Winter Lands and was punishable by death. And a woman
warrior was unheard of. So it was that in the winter of her sixteenth year, Bazbarel
left her home and her people and headed into the snow covered forest. She knew
not what lay ahead, nor did she care, anything was better than nothing.

The first years were hard ones with little comfort or rest, but Bazbarel
was not one to give up. Her hands, soft as snow at first, soon became as hard
and rough as the bark on the trees. She taught herself to hunt, and she learned
which nuts and berries were good to eat, at the cost of a fever and constant
vomiting for seven days and nights. A small cave was her home, and this she

had made warm and comfortable and safe from the icy storms that raged in the cold months.

Bazbarel loved her new life, and although she was kept busy from dawn to dusk she still found time for her favourite thing, sorcery. Long into the night she practiced and experimented always finding something new and exciting. Over the years she had acquired books, potions and powders, scrolls, amulets and many other strange and mystical devices which she could lose herself in for hours. By the time Bazbarel reached her 25th winter, she was an accomplished sorcerer and could communicate with the animals and trees through the power of her mind. She could summon a storm and she could create a rainbow with a few words.

Bazbarel had almost forgotten her old life. One day, when she was out in the woods, she chanced upon a raiding party from her old village. They were resting their horses by a small stream that ran through the forest. Bazbarel hid in the bushes. She was not scared, but she did not wish to have anything to do with her past.

Unknown to her, though, she was being watched, and as she turned to leave, she was struck with something heavy. Barely conscious she was dragged towards the group of warriors. She was not recognised, for the years had shaped and hardened her into a woman unlike those in the village. She remembered the pain and anger as one after the other raped her, then left her bleeding in the snow. She vaguely remembered their laughter as they rode away from her broken body.

It could have been days or weeks that she lay there, not wanting to move for fear of living. Somehow, though, she found her way back to her warm cave, and there she sat and thought. Slowly and painfully she remembered her pride and who she was. She wanted and needed revenge.

The child was born in early spring, a beautiful baby boy, full of health and spirit. She waited until he was twelve moons old, and then, according to the spell she had chosen to exact her revenge with, she sacrificed him with a golden dagger under the light of a half moon. She felt no regret or loss. The child was not hers, it was forced upon her, she had no choice, she could not love it.

She drained the blood and began to weave her spell. Long hours it took. The many complex incantations and rituals drained Bazbarel to the point of exhaustion. After two days she passed out, there was no more she could do.

Bazbarel awoke to the howling of the wind outside her cave. She did not recognise her surroundings at first, but slowly her head cleared and she remembered what she had done.

As she had a thousand times before, she let her mind go blank as her inner eye drifted out through the cave and up over the forest. Along the snow covered hills she went to the place of her birth. All around the village were crying women and children, the men lay in the bloodied snow, torn apart by some incredible force. They had looks of terror and agony on their faces. Bazbarel had a smile on hers. She went outside to walk in the snow, she knew not where she was going, nor did she care.

The loud careless laughter of men who exploit women, their bodies and the land will echo through the land no more. There will be no future life through such plundering and exploitation. Bazbarel, buzzing and clanging with rage will bend her mind, summon all her power and all her wisdom to bring it to an end. She will stretch her mind beyond the bounds of the limited rationalist knowledges of men and say *no more*.

But when I first read this story I was unable to accept that Bazbarel did not love her 'beautiful baby boy, full of health and spirit', even if I accepted that his life could not be. I could hardly bear to keep reading. What of female *jouissance*, the boundless gift of oneself, of love? I had been reading with Bazbarel, experiencing her story as if I were her. But the mirrors in which I saw myself through her experience were too deeply troubled by this failure to love. I shared her sharp clear anger. I knew the need for it and the power of it, but . . .

I suggested another version of the killing of the son, one that allowed me to travel to the end with her, to see the men in the snow, fearful and torn, and to walk away not caring:

. . . It could have been days or weeks that she lay there, not wanting to move for fear of living. Somehow, though, she found her way back to her warm cave, and there she sat and thought. It was not enough to escape and protect herself from these men. Their degradation knew no bounds and must cease.

The child was born in early spring, a beautiful baby boy, full of health and spirit. She wanted not to love him, but could not resist him. The spell she had begun to weave over the men of her village required his blood and tears. When twelve moons had passed she killed her baby with a silver dagger in the light of a half moon and the tears of her grief washed them both, and mingled with his blood.

With blood and tears she wove her spell. Long hours it took. The many complex incantations and rituals drained Bazbarel to the point of exhaustion. After two days she passed out. There was no more she could do. Bazbarel woke to the howling of the wind outside her cave. She did not recognise her surroundings at first, but slowly her head cleared and she remembered what she had done.

As she had a thousand times before she let her mind go blank as her inner eye drifted out through the cave and up over the forest. Along the snow covered hills she went to the place of her birth. All around the village were crying women and children, the men lay in the bloodied snow, torn apart by some incredible force. They had looks of terror and agony on their faces. Bazbarel went outside to walk in the snow. She knew not where she was going nor did she care.

For me, now, in this different ending, I share Bazbarel's unequivocal stand against the men's sexualisation of her body, their reduction of her to object, their achievement of themselves as men through her violation. She refuses the old order, her anger is sharp and clear and she knows what needs to be done. But she does not compromise her *jouissance.*

Yet in this other ending I place a limit on women's anger, a boundary outside which it cannot go. Woman's power is only allowable if she is identifiably a woman. Daniel is quite clear he wants the first ending. He can position himself as Bazbarel, and as himself at the same time. Male *and* female. The anger he feels at the degradation women experience at the hands of men makes him feel deep shame at being a man. There is, in his ending, no compromise in moving beyond the male–female binary. We cannot nostalgically cling to the symbolic forms of masculinity or femininity if that means the continuation of forms of gender relations which he finds intolerable.

Perhaps both endings are necessary, in the same way that Allende provides two endings for her story of *Eva Luna.* During the entire novel her two major characters lead separate lives. Then at the end they meet and:

> Once we were close, I was able unobtrusively to drink in the smell of the man, recognizing, at long last, the scent of the other half of my being. I understood then why from the first I thought I had known him before. Quite simply, it all came down to the elemental fact that I had found my mate, after so many weary years searching for him. (Allende, 1987, p. 306)

And then:

> That night, and many following nights, we made love with such ardor that all the wood in the house glowed like polished gold. Later, for a judicious period of time we loved each other more modestly until that love wore thin and nothing was left but shreds.
>
> Or maybe that isn't how it happened. Perhaps we had the good fortune to stumble into an exceptional love, a love that I did not have to invent, only clothe in all its glory . . . (Allende, 1987, p. 307)

Until we have invented new storylines, new discourses, we are still enmeshed in the old. And even when we invent the new, the old can still claim us, draw us in with their familiarity and the hooks of our old and current unsatisfied desires. Double endings are one way of disrupting the certainties of the old, or even the certainties attaching to storyline itself. They disrupt the sense of inevitable endings to a given sets of events. In the place of inevitability we have possible endings and even multiple endings.

WHAT IS AND WHAT MIGHT BE

So what is the story of this book? It is a book that asks you as reader to look differently and to share with children that different looking— listening—writing—telling—of new stories. It is a book about confronting the dilemmas of gender—seeing that those dilemmas have different meanings depending on the subject position that they are viewed from, the patterns of power and powerlessness, the analytic tools at one's disposal. It is about confronting the dilemmas of oppositional and hierarchical gender relations head on with clear sharp anger, by disrupting old and creating new patterns, by seeing the dilemmas, not as cultural recipes/judgments/requirements, but as shifting cultural patterns that can be, that are being and that will be changed.

Any attempts to disrupt old cultural patterns and to invent new ones must deal simultaneously and in a multi-faceted way with individual psyches, with social structures and patterns and with the discursive practices with which those psyches and those structures are constituted. A poststructuralist analysis does not invent a new structure to replace the old, but provides insights into the discursive mechanisms which hold existing structures in place. Those insights allow a different relationship to structure, a recognition of it as something which is not absolute, which can be acted upon by individuals and by collectivities. While its constitutive power must be recognised, the possibility that it can also be laughed out of existence, played with, disrupted, or used to manufacture new possibilities, can also be recognised.

The children in the study groups revealed the destructive ways in which boys return repeatedly to practices which sexualise and oppress girls. They showed how this was a taking up of hegemonic forms of power in the face of other forms of powerlessness—the powerlessness of being Aboriginal, or being a child. These patterns of power and powerlessness must be addressed, must be made part of any group's understanding as it attempts to move beyond oppressive forms of gender relations. Adults who maintain their authoritative relations with children and at the same time attempt to empower the girls in gender terms will achieve little. The girls already want many of the forms of power previously only possible for boys. The boys already believe that they should not be dominating and controlling girls, but this knowledge is in tension with their need to achieve their masculinity in recognisable, hegemonic terms.

But gender has not been taught to them explicitly. It is implicit in acts of learning to talk, learning to read, learning to be a 'good child' or a competent person. Because of its embeddedness in approved dominant discourses its creation and maintenance are invisible and also intractable. Poststructuralist theory opens up the possibility of making it visible. But making it visible to the children in the study groups was accompanied by repeated (re)turnings to the dominant discourses through which they knew themselves, through which they achieved the (pleasurable) sense of themselves as competent members of the social world.

Children have a boundless, exploratory energy and a passion for understanding—not necessarily of the contents of any lesson, but of life itself. They want to talk about their experience of the social world and their embeddedness in it, their emotional bodily relations to it, and their pleasurable experience of competencies in relation to it. Their endless energy in talking about and exploring their experiences and their desire for agency are central to the opening up of a different kind of agency—one in which they are able to see and articulate the very fabric in which they are embedded.

Positions of power and powerlessness are achieved through talk, through social practices and through social and architectural structures. Power lies in the (pleasurable) knowledgeable constitution of oneself within these practices and structures and in access to powerful positionings within known discourses and storylines. Agency, as it is usually understood, is a combination of individual choices, of power and correct subjection. Such a combination is unavailable to many, most noticeably to those who are not adult, male, heterosexual, middle class and white. A different definition of agency is offered here and that is to do with a combination of:

- the ability to recognise the constitutive power of discourse;
- the ability to catch discourse/structure/practice in the act of shaping desire, perception, knowledge; and
- engagement in a collective process of re-naming, re-writing, re-positioning oneself in relation to coercive structures.

This can be compared to a movement from pleasure to bliss or to a movement from sanity to 'madness' (or a knowledge of how to break the rules in creative and exciting ways). It is an engagement in a redistribution of language, a movement beyond the endless stultifying repetitions of the culture. Barthes comments:

> The stereotype is the word repeated without any magic, any enthusiasm, as though it were natural, as though by some miracle this recurring word were adequate on each occasion for different reasons, as though to imitate could no longer be sensed as an imitation: an unconstrained word that claims consistency and is unaware of its own insistence. Neitzsche has observed that 'truth' is only the solidification of old metaphors. (1989, p. 42)

The familiar patterns of schooling to which we have all been exposed are most often the learning of stereotypes, and very rarely about the learning of the new that comes about from the disruption of those stereotypes, the creation of the cutting edge. Deconstructive reading and writing open up a movement into an (inconclusive) future, through running against the grain of *what is*, at the same time as making *what is* more visible.

Each of us, including the children, needs to make existing relations of power more visible, not just in terms of gender, but also in terms of race, and class and age relations. We are each caught up in relations of power and powerlessness that act on us shaping and forming us in particular ways. We cannot resist those relations, since they form the very conditions which make our existence possible. We are in that sense living our lives in a knotted web of discourses and passions, a web that is of our own making, and out of the substance of which we are each continually being made-up. We are each both the weaver and the web, the ones who tie the knots, and who are tied. In this book I have tried to show how it is possible to make some of the knots in the web visible, and with what discursive thread they might be tied differently.

For some readers, the apparently relentless tying back up of the knotted fabric of gender, which is visible in the children's talk, might seem very negative. Their celebration of *what is* and their resistance to critique may appear intractable. But the existing relations of power through which the conditions of our possibility are forged are not so easily thrown off, precisely because we are both the weaver and the web. As Hillevi Lenz-Taguchi wrote in response to my writing about this dilemma:

> Feelings of transgression give me a temporary feeling of freedom, which fades away. In the very process of persistent weaving, I am always in a state of resistance, where knots untied will stick up their grinning faces again and again, and where I as a weaving subject will always struggle with being meshed within the fabric—wanting it badly and hating it! But simultaneously—with joy, fear and pain—I spin those delicate threads that necessarily 'go against the grain,' making the fabric uneven or leaving it with mysterious holes of uncertainties, doubts, desires and excitements. (Lenz-Taguchi, cited in Davies, 2000b, p. 169)

In this book I have sought to make the fabric of gender relations, with its grinning knots and gaps and passions, visible. I have shown how they are embedded in the ongoing minute detail through which identities are made. I have also sought to show that movement is possible, not through the imposition of a new discourse which attempts to obliterate the old, but as a set of unfolding practices that we might each develop as we begin to imagine, to speak, to write, new possibilities.

While there is much that is revealed here, in this writing, that is painful, this deconstructive, poststructuralist approach to research and to writing also involves an acute awareness of life. Poststructuralist practices invite an openness to the unexpected. They turn a critical gaze towards oppressive patterns of power and powerlessness, and they engage a strong will to action. As Derrida (1992, p. 83) says, deconstructive work may appear to be negative to some, but its impulse is towards life: "For me it always accompanies an affirmative exigency, I would say that it never proceeds without love. . .".

Bibliography

Adan, Jane, 1991, *The Children in our Lives*, State University of New York Press, Albany

Allende, I., 1987, *Eva Luna*, Bantam Books, New York

Althusser, L., 1971, *Lenin and philosophy and other essays*, New Left Books, London

____, 1984, *Essays on Ideology*, Verso, London

Andersen, H.C., 1987, *Hans Andersen Fairy Tales*, Tiger Books International, London

Aries, P., 1962, *Centuries of Childhood*, Penguin, Harmondsworth

Baker, C. & Davies, B., 1989, 'A lesson on sex roles', *Gender and Education*, vol. 1, no. 1, pp. 59-76

____, 1992, 'Literacy and gender in early childhood', *Discourse,* vol. 12, no. 2, pp. 55-67

Baker, C. & Freebody, P., 1989, *Children's first school books*, Basil Blackwell, Oxford

Barrett, M., 1980, *Women's Oppression Today: Problems in Marxist Feminist Analysis*, Verso, London

Barthes, R., 1984, *Camera Lucida. Reflections on Photography*, Flamingo, London

____, 1989, *The Pleasure of the Text*, Noonday Press, New York

Benhabib, S., 1987, 'The generalized and the concrete other: The Kohlberg-Gilligan controversy and feminist theory', *Women and Moral Theory*, eds E. F. Kittay & D. T. Meyers, Rowman and Littlefield, New Jersey

Bird, L., 1992, 'Girls taking positions of authority at primary school', *Women and Education in Aotearoa*, vol. 2, eds S. Middleton & A. Jones, Bridget Williams Books, Wellington

Bleier, R., 1984, *Science and Gender. A Critique of Biology and its Theories on Women*, Pergamon Press, New York

Brooks, P., 1984, *Reading for the Plot: Design and Intention in Narrative*, Random House, New York

Carter, A., 1987, *The Bloody Chamber and other stories*, Penguin, Harmondsworth

Chappell, A., 1984, 'Family fortunes: a practical photography project', *Gender and Generation*, eds A. McRobbie & M. Nava, Macmillan, London, pp. 112-29

Cixous, H., 1974, *Prenoms de Personne*, du Seuil, Collection Poetique, Paris

____, 1981, 'The laugh of the Medusa', *New French Feminisms. An Anthology*, eds E. Marks & I. De Courtivron, The Harvester Press, Brighton, pp. 245-64

____, 1986, 'Sorties: Out and out: Attacks/Ways Out Forays', *The Newly Born Woman*, eds H. Cixous & C. Clement, Manchester University Press, Manchester, pp. 63-132

____, 1988, 'Extreme fidelity', *Writing Differences. Readings from the Seminar of Hélène Cixous*, ed S. Sellers, Open University Press, Milton Keynes, pp. 9-36

____, 1990, 'Difficult joys', *The Body and the Text*, eds H. Wilcox *et al.*, Harvester Wheatsheaf, New York

Cocks, J., 1991, 'Augustine, Nietzsche, and contemporary body politics', *Differences*, vol. 3, no.1, pp. 144-58

Cole, B., 1986, *Princess Smartypants*, Hamish Hamilton, London

Conley, V. A., 1991, *Hélène Cixous. Writing the Feminine*, University of Nebraska Press, Lincoln

Connell, R.W., 1987, *Gender and Power*, Allen and Unwin, Sydney

Corbalis, J. and Craig, H., 1987, *The Wrestling Princess and Other Stories*, Knight Books, London

Crawford, J. et al., 1992, *Emotion and Gender. Constructing Meaning from Memory*, Sage, London

Davies, B., 1982, *Life in the Classroom and Playground. The Accounts of Primary School Children*, Routledge and Kegan Paul, London

____, 1983, 'The role pupils play in the social construction of classroom order', *British Journal of Sociology of Education*, vol. 4, pp. 55-69

____,1988, *Gender, Equity and Early Childhood*, Curriculum Development Centre, Schools Commission, Canberra

____, 1989a, *Frogs and Snails and Feminist Tales. Preschool Children and Gender*, Allen and Unwin, Sydney

____, 1989b, 'Education for sexism: a theoretical analysis of the sex/gender bias in education', *Educational Philosophy and Theory*, vol. 21, no. 1, pp. 1-19

____, 1990a, 'Lived and imaginary narratives and their place in taking oneself up as a gendered being', *Australian Psychologist*, vol. 25, pp. 76-90

____, 1990b, 'The problem of desire', *Social Problems*, vol. 37, pp. 801-16

____, 1990c, 'Agency as a form of discursive practice. A classroom scene observed', *British Journal of Sociology of Education*, vol. 11, no. 3, pp. 341-61

____1991, 'The concept of agency. A feminist poststructuralist analysis', *Social Analysis. Special Issue on Postmodern Critical Theorising*, vol. 30, pp. 42-53

____, 1992a, *Guidelines for the elimination of gender stereotyping from primary school textbooks*, Commonwealth Secretariat, London

____, 1992b, 'Women's subjectivity and feminist stories', *Research on Subjectivity: Windows on Lived Experience*, eds C. Ellis & M. Flaherty, Sage, Newbury Park CA

____, 1992c, 'A feminist poststructuralist analysis of discursive practices in the classroom and playground', *Discourse,* vol. 13, no. 1, pp. 49-66

____, 1993, *Poststructuralist Theory and Classroom Practice*, Deakin University Press, Geelong

____, 2000, *(In)scribing Body Landscape Relations*, Alta Mira Press, Walnut Creek

Davies, B. & Banks, C., 1991a, 'The gender trap. A feminist poststructuralist analysis of primary school children's talk about gender', *Journal of Curriculum Studies*, vol. 24, no. 1, pp. 1-25

____, 1991b, 'Becoming male: the acquisition of masculinities: a childhood perspective', *Conference on Masculinity*, Macquarie University, Sydney

Davies, B. & Harre, R., 1990, 'Positioning: the discursive production of selves', *Journal for the Theory of Social Behaviour*, vol. 20, pp. 43-63

____, 1991/1992, 'Contradiction in lived and told narratives', *Research on Language and Social Interaction*, vol. 25, pp. 1-36

Davies, B., & Hunt, R. (2000). 'Classroom competencies and marginal positionings,' *A Body of Writing*, B. Davies, Alta Mira Press, Walnut Creek, pp. 107-131.

Davies, B. and Munro, K., 1987, 'The perception of order in apparent disorder: a classroom scene observed', *Journal of Education for Teaching*, vol. 13, pp. 117-131

de Paola, T., 1981, *Oliver Button is a Sissy*, Methuen, London

de Salvo, L., 1991, *Virginia Woolf. The Impact of Childhood Sexual Abuse on her Life and Work*, The Women's Press, London

Deutscher, P., 1992, 'The evanescence of masculinity: deferral in St Augustine's Confessions and some thoughts on its bearing on the sex/gender debate', *Australian Feminist Studies*, no. 15, pp. 41-56

du Plessis, R.B., 1990, *The Pink Guitar. Writing as Feminist Practice*, Routledge, New York

Foucault, M., 1977, 'What is an author?', *Language, Counter-memory, Practice*, ed D. Bouchard, Cornell University Press, Ithaca, New York

———, 1980, *The History of Sexuality vol 1*, Vintage, New York

Gilligan, C., 1982, *In a Different Voice. Psychological Theory and Women's Development*, Harvard University Press, Cambridge

Goble, P., 1986, *The Girl Who Loved Horses*, Aladdin Books, Macmillan Publishing Co., New York

Graham, B., 1987, *Crusher is Coming*, Lothian Publishing Co. Pty Ltd, Melbourne

Greer, G., 1986, *The Madwoman's Underclothes. Essays and Occasional Writings 1968-85*, Picador, London

Haraway, D., 1988, 'Situated knowledges: The science question in feminism and the privilege of partial perspective', *Feminist Studies*, vol. 14, pp. 575-99

Harre, R., 1989, 'Language games and texts of identity', *Texts of Identity*, eds J. Shotter & K. J. Gergen, Sage, London

Harre, R. and Secord, P., 1972, *The Explanation of Social Behaviour*, Blackwell, Oxford

Haug, F. et al., 1987, *Female Sexualisation*, Verso, London

Heilbrun, C.G., 1988, *Writing a Woman's Life*, The Women's Press, London

Henriques, J. et al., 1984, *Changing the Subject: Psychology, Social Regulation and Subjectivity*, Methuen, London

Hite, M., 1989, *The Other Side of the Story: Structures and Strategies of Contemporary Feminist Narrative*, Cornell University Press, Ithaca, New York

Hutcheon, L., 1989, *The Politics of Postmodernism*, Routledge, London

Irigaray, L., 1985, *This Sex Which is not One*, Cornell University Press, Ithaca, New York

Jackson, D., 1990, *Unmasking Masculinity. A Critical Autobiography*, Unwin Hyman, London

Jones, K.B., 1991, 'The trouble with authority', *Differences*, vol . 3, no. 1, pp. 104-27

Kantor, R., 1988, 'Creating school meaning in preschool curriculum', *Theory into Practice*, vol. 27, no. 1, pp. 25-35

Kenway, J. and Willis, S. (eds), 1990, *Hearts and Minds. Self Esteem and the Schooling of Girls*, Falmer Press, London

Kimmel, M., 1990, 'After fifteen years: the impact of the sociology of masculinity on the masculinity of sociology', *Men, Masculinities and Social Theory*, eds J. Hearn & D. Morgan, Unwin Hyman, London

Lacan, J., 1966, *Ecrits*, Tavistock, London

___, 1975, *Encore, Le Seminaire de Jacques Lacan, Livre XV*, du Seuil, Paris

Laqueur, T., 1990, *Making Sex. Body and Gender from the Greeks to Freud*, Harvard University Press, Cambridge

Leahey, T., 1991, *Negotiating Stigma: Approaches to Intergenerational Sex*, Ph.D Thesis, University of New South Wales, Sydney

Levine, M., 1991, 'Translator's Introduction', *Return to Freud. Jacques Lacan's Dislocation of Psychoanalysis*, ed S. Weber, Cambridge University Press, Cambridge

Luke, A., 1991, 'Stories of social regulation: the micropolitics of classroom narrative', *The Insistence of the Letter: Literacy and Curriculum Theorizing*, ed. B. Green, Falmer Press, London

Marx, K., 1976, *Das Capital, Vol. 1*, Penguin, Harmondsworth

McClary, S., 1991, *Feminine Endings. Music, Gender and Sexuality*, University of Minnesota Press, Minnesota

Morrison, T., 1983, 'Interview with Claudia Tate', *Black Women Writers at Work.*, ed. C. Tate, Continuum, New York

Munsch, R. and Marchenko, M., 1980, *The Paper Bag Princess*, Annick Press, Toronto

Myerhoff, B. and Metzger, D., 1980, 'The journal as activity and genre: Or listening to the silent laughter of Mozart', *Semiotica*, vol. 30, no. 1/2, pp. 97-114

O'Harris, P., 1984, *The Fairy Who Wouldn't Fly*, Angus and Robertson, Sydney

Patterson, A., 1992, '"Personal response" and English teaching', *Child, Citizen and Culture: Genealogies of Australian Education*, eds D. Meredyth & D. Tyler, Griffith University, Brisbane

Pavarotti, L. with Wright, W., 1981, *My Own Story*, Sidgwick and Jackson, London

Phelan, S., 1991, 'Specificity: beyond equality and difference', *Differences*, vol. 3, no. 1, pp. 128-43

Porter, E., 1991, *Women and Moral Identity*, Allen and Unwin, Sydney

Richardson, L., 1990, 'Narrative and sociology', *Journal of Contemporary Ethnography*, vol. 19, no. 1, pp. 116-35

Sarup, M., 1988, *An Introductory Guide to Post structuralism and Postmodernism*, Harvester Wheatsheaf, New York

Saussure, F. de., 1974, *A Course in General Linguistics*, Fontana, London

Sayers, J., 1986, *Sexual Contradictions: Psychology, Psychoanalysis and Feminism*, Tavistock, London

Schaffer, K., 1988, *Women and the Bush*, Cambridge Press, Melbourne

Scott, J., 1991, 'The evidence of experience', *Critical Inquiry*, Summer, pp. 773-97

Sellers, S. ed., 1988, *Writing Differences. Readings from the Seminar of Hélène Cixous*, Open University Press, Milton Keynes

Walkerdine, V., 1981, 'Sex, power and pedagogy', *Screen Education*, vol. 38, pp. 14-24

____, 1984, 'Some day my prince will come', *Gender and Generation*, eds A. McRobbie & M. Nava, Macmillan, London, pp. 162-84

Walkerdine, V. and Lucey, H., 1989, *Democracy in the Kitchen. Regulating Mothers and Socialising Daughters*, Virago, London

Weber, S., 1991, *Return to Freud. Jacques Lacan's Dislocation of Psychoanalysis*, Cambridge University Press, Cambridge (trans. Michael Levine)

Weedon, C., 1987, *Feminist Practice and Poststructionalist Theory*, Blackwell, Oxford

Wex, M., 1979, *'Let's take back our space'. 'Female' and 'male' body language as a result of patriarchal structures*, Frauenliteraturverlag Hermine Fees, Berlin

White, P., 1981, *Flaws in the Glass. A Self-portrait*, Penguin, Harmondsworth

Williams, J., 1978, *The Practical Princess and Other Liberating Fairy Tales*, The Bodley Head, London

Wilshire, D., 1989, 'The uses of myth, image, and the female body in re-visioning knowledge', *Gender/body/knowledge. Feminist Reconstructions of Being and Knowing*, eds A. M. Jagger & S. R. Borno, Rutgers University Press, New Brunswick, pp. 92-114

Woolf, V., 1976, *Moments of Being*, Triad/Granada, London

Yeats, W.B., 1962, *W.B. Yeats Selected Poetry*, Pan Books, London

Zipes, J., 1986, *Don't Bet on the Prince. Contemporary Feminist Fairy Tales in North America and England*, Gower, Aldershot

Index